The Psychology and
Physiology of Stress

Contributors

WILLIAM S. ALLERTON
FRANK H. AUSTIN, JR.
PETER G. BOURNE
ALBERT J. GLASS
ROBERT J. T. JOY

ROBERT M. ROSE
NGUYEN DUY SAN
ROBERT E. STRANGE
GARY L. TISCHLER
VINCENT WALLEN

The Psychology

and Physiology of Stress

With Reference to Special Studies of the Viet Nam War

Edited by

Peter G. Bourne

Department of Psychiatry
Stanford University Medical Center
Palo Alto, California

ACADEMIC PRESS   New York and London 1969

ACADEMIC PRESS, INC.
111 Fifth Avenue, New York, New York 10003

United Kingdom Edition published by
ACADEMIC PRESS, INC. (LONDON) LTD.
Berkeley Square House, London W1X 6BA

LIBRARY OF CONGRESS CATALOG CARD NUMBER: 78-91416

PRINTED IN THE UNITED STATES OF AMERICA

List of Contributors

WILLIAM S. ALLERTON[1] (1), *Office of the Surgeon General, Department of the Army, Washington, D. C.*

FRANK H. AUSTIN, JR.[2] (197), *Bureau of Medicine and Surgery, Department of the Navy, Washington, D. C.*

PETER G. BOURNE[3] (95, 219), *Neuropsychiatry Section, United States Army Medical Research Team, Viet Nam*

ALBERT J. GLASS[4] (xiii), *Psychiatric Consultant to the Surgeon Far East Command*

ROBERT J. T. JOY[5] (149), *United States Army Medical Research Team, Viet Nam*

ROBERT M. ROSE (117), *Department of Psychiatry, Division of Neuropsychiatry, Walter Reed Army Institute of Research, Washington, D. C.*

NGUYEN DUY SAN[6] (45), *Army of the Republic of Viet Nam, Cong Hoa General Hospital, Saigon, South Viet Nam*

ROBERT E. STRANGE[7] (75), *Neuropsychiatry Branch, U. S. S. Repose (AH-16)*

[1]*Present address: Northern Virginia Mental Health Institute, Falls Church, Virginia.*

[2]*Present address: Life Science Department, Naval Safety Center, Naval Air Station, Norfolk, Virginia.*

[3]*Present address: Department of Psychiatry, Stanford University Medical Center, Palo Alto, California.*

[4]*Present address: Department of Mental Health, State Capitol, Oklahoma City, Oklahoma.*

[5]*Present address: Biological and Medical Sciences Division, Office of the Director of Defense Research and Engineering, Office of the Secretary of Defense, Washington, D. C.*

[6]*Present address: Department of Psychiatry, University Hospital, Ann Arbor, Michigan.*

[7]*Present address: Neuropsychiatry Services, United States Naval Hospital, Philadelphia, Pennsylvania.*

GARY L. TISCHLER[8] (19), *Psychiatry Section, 67th Evacuation Hospital, Qui Nhon, Republic of Viet Nam*

VINCENT WALLEN[9] (167), *Clinical Psychology Services, United States Air Force Hospital, Tachikawa, Japan*

[8]*Present address: Department of Psychiatry, Yale University School of Medicine, New Haven, Connecticut.*

[9]*Present address: Psychology Services, The Veterans' Administration Center (Kecoughton), Hampton, Virginia.*

Preface

This volume is a compilation of information concerning man's response to the stresses of combat in Viet Nam. With contributions by representatives of the three armed services as well as the Army of the Republic of Viet Nam, I have attempted to present a comprehensive account of advances both in the clinical and research spheres that have evolved from this conflict. In earlier years, works on combat stress focused largely on those who became casualties rather than on those who made a successful adaptation to combat, and also, for obvious reasons, emphasized the psychological rather than the physiological response. In Viet Nam a significant number of individuals have been present in the war zone for the express purpose of studying the effects of combat on the American fighting man, and improved logistics have made possible meaningful study of altered physiology in response to combat. This has offered the opportunity to broaden our conceptual framework and consider a more balanced approach, blending our understanding of the successful soldier with that of the psychiatric casualty and an appreciation of altered physiology with our knowledge of man's psychological adaptation to combat stress.

As an extreme human experience combat offers a unique opportunity to study man's response to stress. By virtue of its life endangering potential it serves to magnify the adaptational maneuvers which are equally relevant but less apparent in noncombat circumstances. Historically, the lessons of combat psychiatry have contributed significantly to our overall knowledge of psychiatric illness. It is hoped, therefore, that while this volume deals specifically with the combat situation it may contribute both to a greater understanding of man's response to stress in general and to the treatment of the mentally ill in all situations.

PETER G. BOURNE

Palo Alto, California
August, 1969

Contents

Introduction

Albert J. Glass

1. Army Psychiatry in Viet Nam

William S. Allerton

2. Patterns of Psychiatric Attrition and of Behavior in a
   Combat Zone

   Gary L. Tischler

3. Psychiatry in the Army of The Republic of Viet Nam

   Nguyen Duy San

4. Effects of Combat Stress on Hospital Ship Psychiatric Evacuees

   Robert E. Strange

5. Urinary 17-OHCS Levels in Two Combat Situations

   Peter G. Bourne

6. Androgen Excretion in Stress
Robert M. Rose

7. Heat Stress in Army Pilots in Viet Nam
Robert J. T. Joy

8. Background Characteristics, Attitudes, and Self-Concepts of Air Force Psychiatric Casualties from Southeast Asia
Vincent Wallen

9. A Review of Stress and Fatigue Monitoring of Naval Aviators during Aircraft Carrier Combat Operations: Blood and Urine Biochemical Studies

Frank H. Austin, Jr.

10. Military Psychiatry and the Viet Nam War in Perspective

Peter G. Bourne

Introduction

Albert J. Glass

A new generation of the US Armed Forces is now engaged in another interminable overseas combat campaign with all of the frustrations, privations, and hazards. Only fragmentary reports of the psychiatric experiences of this war in Viet Nam have thus far appeared. However, all accounts, which include semi-official reports (Office of the Surgeon General, 1968), agree that the rate of psychiatric breakdown in US combat personnel is considerably lower than that of WW II and the Korean War, and even WW I. The overall incidence of psychiatric disorders from the US Army in Viet Nam is stated to be no higher than from troops stationed in the United States. Moreover, relatively few instances of so-called combat fatigue, common in WW II and Korea, have been observed among the psychiatric disorders of the present conflict. It would seem that combat psychiatric casualties, which were a numerous and vexing problem in previous US wars of this century, either have been markedly diminished by preventive measures, such as the one-year rotation policy for combat personnel, or perhaps are not produced in large numbers by the brief, episodic nature of the fighting in Viet Nam.

This volume, the first extensive publication of psychiatric experiences in Viet Nam, provides information bearing upon the above stated issues. It includes (1) descriptive chapters on the organization and development of US Army psychiatry in Viet Nam, psychiatry in the Army of the Republic of Viet Nam (South Viet Nam Forces), and psychiatric disorders of Marine and Naval personnel who have been evacuated to an off-shore based hospital ship; (2) an analysis of psychiatric attrition in the combat zone; and (3) studies of steroid and other biochemical responses to combat stress which involve measurements of 17-hydroxycorticosteroids, androgens, and various phospholipid fractions.

To provide for an adequate introduction to the contributions of this book, a brief historical review of combat psychiatric disorders is presented to serve as a background so as to appreciate changes in their frequency, terminology, and manifestations.

I. World War I

Combat psychiatry is of relatively recent origin. It has been only since the early days of WW I (1914–1918) that the failures of military personnel to cope with the extraordinary demands of combat have become recognized as legitimate casualties of war. Similar failures of adaptation in previous wars were regarded as cowardice, desertion, or misbehavior before the enemy, or other expressions of moral condemnation, to be punished as violation of military discipline. This attitudinal change has come about gradually with increased understanding of the psychological and sociological determinants of behavior. However, overt refusal by words or acts to participate in combat continue to be regarded as evidence of willful disobedience and are dealt with by punitive measures. In effect, failure in the combat role must be manifested by symptoms or behavior which is acceptable to the mores and standards of the group as indicating an inability rather than an unwillingness to function.

Because of the importance of acceptability, manifestations of combat psychiatric casualties and, usually, their terminology, have generally indicated a direct causal relationship with various traumatic conditions of the battle environment. For example, the psychiatric casualties of WW I seemed to be a direct result of enemy shelling. The individuals involved appeared dazed, and tremulous with or without confused or dissociated behavior or major conversion symptoms, all of which were apparently the immediate consequence of nearby shell explosion; hence, the terminology "shell shock." For a time, "shell shock" was considered to be caused by temporary or more persistent brain damage from the airblast of high explosives. Thus, initially at least, psychiatric conditions were accepted on the basis of organic injury much like brain concussion. After a relatively brief period, certainly by 1915–1916, it became clearly evident to the Allied Medical Services that "shell shock" was entirely a psychological disorder (Salmon *et al.*, 1929). However, by this time the syndrome had achieved the status of a "disease" and, therefore, an inability to function.

Members of the combat reference group, including commanders

and medical officers, could readily understand and accept "shell shock" as a direct consequence of unavoidable events of battle which might happen to anyone. In contrast, the German High Command and its medical services in WW I, and later in WW II, never accepted "shell shock" or the concept of psychologically induced casualties. This issue was debated and settled in the negative by outstanding German neurologists and psychiatrists at a special medical conference in 1916. Obviously, the rate of psychiatric casualties in the German armies of WW I and WW II was nil; so much for the comparison of psychiatric rates.

II. Between WW I and WW II

Between WW I and WW II psychiatric casualties or, more particularly, the chronic residual syndromes thereof, including many neurotic-type cases later adjudged to be the result of combat experiences, became established as the "war neuroses" or "traumatic neuroses." These cases represented a large proportion of veterans receiving disability compensation. Although these persistent disorders were considered to have been precipitated by the psychological trauma of battle, considerable clinical experience with these problems produced a widespread impression that psychiatric casualties originated mainly from individuals who were vulnerable to battle or other situational stress by reason of predisposing character or personality defects (Glass, 1966). Conceptually, the limited or inadequate capability of individuals to deal with stressful situations was considered the result of faulty personality development and conformed to the prevailing psychoanalytic model, particularly of the psychoneuroses and character neuroses. Thus, the war neuroses came to be regarded as a category of psychoneurosis and were so generally designated.

III. World War II

For the above and other reasons of need and expediency, immediately prior to WW II it was almost unanimously held by prominent civil and military medical authorities that the war neuroses and other military psychiatric problems could be largely prevented by exclusion, through screening examination at induction, of persons of "substandard mentality and physique" (Glass, 1968). It was considered axiomatic that modern war required only those personnel with "superior mental and physical stamina" (Glass, 1968). Particularly emphasized was the "careful detection and elimination of unstable persons and mental misfits" (Glass, 1968). The subsequent failure of the screening program in WW II has been well documented. In 1943, the incidence of psychiatric disorders was three times that of WW I, despite a psychiatric rejection rate of three to four times that of WW I (*Bull. US Army Med. Dept.*, 1943). At least partly as a result of reliance upon screening, there was little preparation prior to WW II for the management of psychiatric disorders, combat or otherwise. Indeed, the organization of psychiatric services in combat divisions which was established in WW I was abandoned at the onset of WW II.

When psychiatric casualties appeared in large numbers following the North African invasion during the Tunisia fighting, the first large scale land combat of the US Army in WW II, the terminology utilized was mainly "psychoneurosis"-anxiety, mixed or conversion types. With such labeling and its connotation of personality defect, psychiatric disorders were not accepted by the combat group as being the result of battle conditions but rather were considered a consequence of failure in screening. Moreover, for psychiatric casualties and other combat participants, the unfamiliar and unwieldy term "psychoneurosis" could only be interpreted as "psycho." Thus, perhaps it was more than a coincidence that many psychiatric casualties from the Tunisia fighting were described as manifesting dramatic and bizarre reactions with dissociative or regressive behavior which seemed to portray the fearful plight of the individual unable to cope with battle conditions. There were terror states with gross tremors; marked startle reactions, in which the person responded to even slight noise as if battle were upon him, tearing at the ground with his hands to obtain cover; frozen states with mutism, in which persons permitted themselves to be led about like small children; and catatonic-like syndromes of retardation or excitement. All of these reactions were observed hundreds of miles from the combat area in safe rear hospitals (Grinker and Spiegel, 1943).

Later in the Tunisia Campaign, exploratory efforts were made to reestablish the WW I forward treatment for acute psychiatric breakdown. Psychiatric casualties were held in a field medical facility near the fighting for several days of treatment which consisted of sedation to insure rest and sleep, adequate food, and opportunities to bathe, shave, and discuss their experiences. Again it was found that a large proportion of cases could be returned to combat duty. Shortly thereafter, a new terminology for psychiatric casualties, i.e., "exhaustion," was officially established. By directive from the senior US Army Commander in Tunisia, all psychiatric disorders in the combat zone were ordered to be diagnosed as "exhaustion" regardless of manifestations. Other and more definitive terminology was permitted in rear medical facilities. "Exhaustion" was selected because it best described the appearance of most psychiatric casualties and indeed the other combat participants at this phase of the continuous Tunisian fighting. As described by Hanson (1949),

> Their faces were expressionless, their eyes blank and unseeing and they tended to sleep wherever they were. The sick, injured, lightly wounded, and psychiatric cases were usually indistinguishable on the basis of their appearance. Even casual observation made it evident that these men were fatigued to the point of exhaustion. Most important of the factors that produced this marked fatigue was lack of sleep.

Another account was provided by the sensitive observer-reporter Ernie Pyle (1943):

> For four nights and days, they have fought hard, eaten little, washed none and slept hardly at all. Their nights have been violent with attack, fright, butchery and their days sleepless and miserable with the crash of artillery. The men are walking—their walk is slow for they are dead weary as you can tell even when looking at them from behind. Every line and sag of their bodies speaks their inhuman exhaustion. On their shoulders and backs they carry heavy steel tripods, machine gun barrels, leaden boxes of ammunition. Their feet seem to sink into the ground from the overload they are bearing.

During the Tunisian fighting and many other campaigns of WW II, exhaustion was perhaps the most commonly encountered experience and outward impression of personnel in combat. WW I was characterized by static type trench warfare with limited movement to and from nearby tactical objectives during which troops were subjected to artillery fire, as well as between battle episodes. Receiving shellfire was therefore the most common and constant experience—thus, "shell shock" was an apt description. By contrast, WW II was a war of movement, with distant objectives to be attained in successive combat phases by troops mainly on foot who fought up and down valleys and mountains carrying on their persons much of the needed weapons, ammunition, and other supplies. In this type warfare, which includes physical fatigue and the emotional strain of continued battle, "exhaustion" serves as a most appropriate terminology to indicate a direct causative relationship between psychiatric casualties and the situational stress of combat. Indeed, Hanson (1949), the psychiatric consultant in the Mediterranean Theatre who initiated forward treatment in Tunisia, and others firmly believed that physical fatigue played an important precipitating role in the etiology of combat psychiatric breakdown. "Exhaustion" was readily accepted by both psychiatric casualties and the combat reference group. Again, combat psychiatric casualties became a rational consequence of battle conditions. Almost all combat personnel could appreciate that anyone could become exhausted by the stress and strain of continued battle. Moreover, the introduction of forward treatment, consisting of a brief respite from combat with sleep and food, was appropriate to the new terminology. Soon there appeared the simplistic generalization, almost universally accepted, that "every man had his breaking point."

With the establishment of "exhaustion," manifestations of psychiatric casualties became less dramatic. Combat personnel did not need to portray "psycho" to communicate inability to function in battle. During the Sicily Campaign, which followed soon after the Tunisia fighting, the majority of psychiatric casualties mainly displayed evidences of tension with tremor, irritability, noise sensitivity, and verbalized their problem as "I can't take it any more," and "I can't stand the shells," or "shelling," with or without manifestations of physical fatigue, depending on the length of time in continuous combat. There were relatively few instances of dissociative type behavior or major hysteria. "Shell shock" died hard, surviving mainly as "blast concussion" which, except for rupture or damage of eardrums, had a similar symptomatology and clinical course to "exhaustion."

As the war proceeded, psychiatric services were expanded to combat units including the assignment of division psychiatrists. Further experiences produced new insights relative to psychiatric casualties.

(1) *Causation.* As with "shell shock" of WW I, it became increasingly apparent that "exhaustion" was mainly, if not entirely, a psychologically induced disorder. Psychiatric casualties were

nonexistent from troops who had advanced for days against little enemy opposition, despite the presence of severe physical fatigue, including lack of sleep, rest, and food. Conversely, many psychiatric casualties occurred just prior to, or in the early phases of, combat when there was little opportunity to develop physical fatigue. Obviously, in such individuals the "breaking point" had been reached early. Clearly, immediate and continued threat from battle danger was the essential element in the etiology of combat psychiatric breakdown (Drayer and Glass, 1969).

In time "exhaustion," regardless of manifestations, came to be regarded as a diagnostic and geographic entity to designate a temporary inability to cope with the uncertain but ever present threat of danger inherent in combat situations. It became evident that the impairment of physiological capacity, by means of physical fatigue or intercurrent illness, reduced the ability of the individual to maintain adaptation under combat conditions. However, the influence of other members of the combat unit, variously termed group cohesiveness, group identification, the buddy system, and leadership, served to sustain individuals in battle situations. Repeated observations indicated that the absence or inadequacy of such sustaining influences or their disruption during combat were mainly responsible for psychiatric breakdown in battle. These group or relationship phenomena made it possible to explain marked differences in the psychiatric casualty rates of various units who were exposed to a similar intensity of battle stress. Awareness of such sociological determinants facilitated the utilization of preventive measures to enhance group identification, improve leadership, and, in general, raise the level of group morale. This conceptual viewpoint also made understandable the success of the brief treatment regimen which had been empirically developed in WW I. The short respite from battle not only alleviated physiological deficits but coupled with prompt return to the reconstituted unit, which had been disrupted in combat, made it possible for the individual to resume sustaining relationships with others of the battle group.

(2) *Frequency.* During WW II, it was repeatedly demonstrated that the psychiatric casualty rate varied directly with the frequency of battle casualties, i.e., rising and falling with the incidence of wounding. For this reason, psychiatric breakdown was most numerous from troops locked in prolonged heavy combat in either offense or defense. Once battle contact with the enemy was

broken with subsequent advance or retreat, psychiatric casualties declined precipitiously, as did the battle casualty rate (Drayer and Glass, 1969).

Further observations indicated that psychiatric casualties were most frequent and their manifestations most severe in situations when a unit, new to battle, was committed to its first prolonged major combat action. Thereafter, both the incidence and severity of psychiatric breakdown were diminished despite repeated exposure to intense battle with many replacements new to combat. Apparently the initial severe battle period seemed to facilitate the removal of less effective junior and senior combat leaders, promoted necessary interrelationships for group identification and provided the experience to improve technical competence in the use of weapons and in techniques of individual survival. It would appear that a majority of individuals are capable of adaptation under combat conditions, although it was rare to find anyone who admitted becoming "used to it" or immune from its terrorizing effects. Further, combat participants who were unable to cope with battle conditions learned that this inability could be communicated to the group on a rational, conscious basis without resorting to bizarre or "psycho" type manifestations.

Many observers noted that psychiatric casualties were derived mainly from the "new" and "old" members of a combat unit. A larger incidence always occurred from the "new" men due to numerous replacements from the marked attrition from battle and nonbattle losses which resulted inevitably in a high proportion of "new men" in combat units. The smaller incidence from the "old men" who had previous good or even superior combat records displayed characteristic phobic avoidance manifestations relative to battle stimuli. These cases became known as the "old Sergeant Syndrome" with little or no acute symptoms in noncombat areas, but rather self-blame and loss of self-esteem for inability to control behavior in combat (Drayer and Glass, 1969). It was evident that rotation from combat would have prevented the "old Sergeant Syndrome." Such a policy was strongly urged in WW II but rarely implemented.

(3) *Manifestations.* In WW II, characteristic problems arose relative to the identification of psychiatric casualties which created difficulties in obtaining valid and, therefore, comparable "NP" rates of various combat units. Reasons for such problems could be traced to the following influences: (1) Somatic complaints of mili-

tary personnel with mainly psychological disorders had become well established early in WW II and was of widespread prevalence in the United States and other noncombat areas. Extension of this phenomenon to combat was inevitable. (2) The stigma of mental illness persisted for the individual, despite increased understanding and acceptance of psychiatric casualties; and (3) onus for combat psychiatric breakdown was partly shifted to command as high NP rates of combat troops became regarded as evidences of low unit morale and/or faulty leadership. Thus, there were individual and group needs to avoid the NP label and utilize organic diagnoses as a more acceptable designation for relief from combat.

As a consequence, numerous combat personnel were medically evacuated with mild or ill defined organic diagnoses, based mainly upon somatic symptomatology. There occurred persistent syndromes of headache, low back pain, digestive upset, painful feet, increased sweating with palpitation, and weakness with giddiness. Most of these symptoms could be equated with the physical discomforts endured by combat participants, but could be readily believed as indicating the presence of an illness. Even more frequent were residual type disorders from old and recent injuries, disease and surgery such as painful scars from wounds and surgical procedures, upper abdominal discomfort following infectious hepatitis, and fatigability after recovery from malaria (Glass, 1968).

The experienced combat psychiatrist in WW II soon recognized that the formal NP rate did not always include all psychiatric casualties. He learned that unusual increases in various categories of nonbattle losses could represent undiagnosed psychiatric disorders, especially when a low NP rate was associated with a high incidence of battle casualties. Particularly suspect in this regard was the LIA (lightly injured in action) rate, composed mainly of bruises, sprains, and contusions. Repeated observation indicated most of these cases represented obvious psychiatric casualties. Other psychologically induced battle losses included self-inflicted wounds (SIW) and AWOL from battle. Both of these categories rarely occurred during battle but were usually initiated prior to combat from rear locations.

In practice, most division psychiatrists and their treatment facilities were stationed at divisional clearing stations so as to receive medical evacuees from all divisional elements. In these locations, all psychiatric casualties, as well as evacuees with questionable organic diagnoses, could be readily referred for consultation. In addition, the biweekly Divisional Psychiatric Report regularly recorded for each battalion the incidence of battle casualties, NP casualties, disease, and other categories of nonbattle losses.

Another factor which influenced the NP rate was the location of treatment. As the organization of divisional psychiatric services became more sophisticated, the less severe "exhaustion" cases were held at battalion and regimental aid stations, kitchen areas, and other nearby rear combat installations for brief periods of sleep, rest, and food with prompt return to duty. Rarely were these milder "exhaustion" cases recorded in the NP rate.

In summary, the manifestations of psychiatric casualties were of such a protean nature that their identification at times was difficult to establish. One learned to be skeptical of low NP rates in combat unless the circumstances under which psychiatric casualties were diagnosed and evacuated were known (Glass, 1957).

IV. The Korean War

During the Korean War, the psychiatric experiences and lessons learned in WW II were not forgotten. Within months after its abrupt onset in late June 1950, the three-echeloned system of psychiatric services of WW II was established and as the conflict proceeded, elaborated and expanded. Forward treatment at the division level was extended to include a greater number of battalion aid stations than in WW II, so as to better implement the cardinal principles of combat psychiatric treatment, i.e., proximity, immediacy, and expectancy (Rioch, 1968).

The unsuccessful psychiatric screening program of WW II was abandoned. Emphasis was placed upon the situational and social determinants of combat adjustment. "Exhaustion" was changed to "combat exhaustion" to avoid confusion with physical exhaustion and its implication for the causation of psychiatric breakdown. Later, "combat fatigue" was adopted for Navy and Marine personnel, a term which has survived to become of general usage.

After the first year of the Korean Campaign, a war of movement changed to a more static type warfare, with intermittent episodes of intense combat. Consequently, the physical exhaustion aspects

of combat were markedly diminished and "genuine" combat exhaustion became uncommon. More and more "combat exhaustion"
or "combat fatigue" came to designate a temporary or more persistent failure to cope with the circumstances of the combat
situation, including its intensity and duration, and the adequacy
of sustaining influences rather than individual vulnerability
from personality attributes. As a result, the terminology "psychoneurosis" was little used in the combat zone.

Perhaps because of expanded psychiatric services, the frequency
of psychiatric casualties during the initial and more intensive
combat phases of the Korean War did not reach even one-half of
the high rates of WW II. After the first year, a rotation policy of
nine months in combat was instituted which practically eliminated
psychiatric casualties from the "old" men. Rotation also seemed to
favorably influence the other combat personnel which, together
with change to intermittent warfare, was probably responsible for
decreasing psychiatric casualties in the latter phases of the
Korean War, which reached levels not much above NP rates in
noncombat areas (Glass, 1957).

V. Viet Nam

In light of psychiatric experiences in previous wars, the following comments are offered relative to the events of military
psychiatry in Viet Nam as reported in various chapters of this
volume.

The intervening years since World War II and Korea have apparently elaborated a belief that so-called combat fatigue is a
specific diagnostic category in which more or less "normal"
persons, with previously satisfactory military performance, have
been exposed to severe and prolonged traumatic combat experience
usually associated with marked fatigue, sleep deprivation, and
inadequate diet. With this definition of combat fatigue, it is not
surprising that few cases have been reported from Viet Nam. Indeed, in the writer's experience, few instances of this version of
combat fatigue occurred in World War II or Korea except, perhaps,
in some cases of the "Old Sergeant Syndrome."

Conceptually, the causation of combat psychiatric casualties
seems to have come around full circle over the past several decades.
Initially, in World War II the major cause of combat psychiatric

breakdown was considered a neurotic disorder or personality defect which rendered the individual vulnerable to battle stress. During this period, psychiatrists were preoccupied with what appeared to be an excessive prevalence of neurotic predisposition in young military personnel, as most psychiatric casualties readily gave considerable history of past and current symptoms and behavioral difficulties in a seeming effort to convince themselves and others of an inability to tolerate combat. Most of these data were obtained in rear hospitals where psychiatrists had little knowledge of the circumstances of combat and only the patient's history to explain psychiatric breakdown. Understandably, at this time few psychiatric casualties could be returned to combat duty.

Under these defeatist conditions, "exhaustion," the precursor of combat fatigue, was created to place emphasis upon the situational causes of psychiatric breakdown, and to avoid "psychoneurosis" with its implication of innate vulnerability to battle stress. As psychiatrists moved forward to function in the combat zone, realistic explanations for psychiatric breakdown were found in the environmental and situational circumstances of combat itself. The frequency of psychiatric casualties seemed to be more related to the characteristics of the group than the character traits of the individual. Reports appeared during and after World War II citing the successful combat adjustment of individuals with previous well-defined neurotic and personality disorders (Glass, 1968). Moreover, prospective studies failed to reveal any significant correlation between past and current neurotic or behavioral deviations and later military effectiveness or combat performance (Glass, 1949; Glass *et al.*, 1956).

Perhaps the relatively scant consideration given to underlying personality defects of psychiatric casualties in the later phases of World War II and in the Korean War may have unwittingly fostered later impressions that combat fatigue only occurred in normal individuals, a belief which was even incorporated in official diagnostic manuals. Currently it would seem that the clock has been turned back. Psychiatrists reporting from rear medical installations are again finding psychiatric casualties to be mainly composed of psychoneurotic and personality disorders. It would appear that personality configuration has again become dominant as the major determinant of behavior in combat. "Exhaustion," which formerly included almost all psychiatric disorders in the combat zone, has become "classical" combat fatigue; this category is restricted to relatively few individuals who possess a theoretically healthy psychic apparatus but are temporarily overwhelmed by extraordinary circumstances of trauma and deprivation. Thus, the old mechanistic stress predisposition formula has returned, and psychiatric casualties have been recaptured for personality theory by permitting a mild exception to the rule of internal direction of behavior. But, are these traditional concepts tenable in view of the mounting evidence over many decades that behavior and adaptation are the complex resultant of many forces, not the least of which are interpersonal relationships, group membership, and cultural values?

Perhaps the marked decreased evacuation of psychiatric casualties from forward areas in Viet Nam may be, in part, responsible for the apparent present preoccupation with individual vulnerability. As reported by Allerton, few psychiatric casualties are evacuated to rear medical facilities. Such evacuees generally include the more severe or refractory disorders in which psychopathology is readily apparent. A similar phenomenon was noted in World War II when psychiatrists receiving evacuees in rear hospitals had the impression that psychiatric casualties represented more severe clinical states than their colleagues who functioned in forward assignments.

Reasons for the low rate of psychiatric disorders in Viet Nam have been thoroughly discussed by Allerton. In effect, a generation of career military psychiatrists have focused attention of officers including senior commanders upon their responsibilities relative to the situational and social determinants of combat adjustment. For many years, this theme has been repetitively stressed at the various military schools, such as West Point, the Infantry School, Command and Staff College, and the Medical Field Service School. Such an emphasis has had a favorable impact upon training, leadership, and the conditions under which soldiers live, work, and fight.

However, there may be additional explanations for the remarkably small incidence of psychiatric disorders in Viet Nam which involve the criteria for the recording of psychiatric casualties as associated with the unique nature of combat operations. As reported from Viet Nam, troops not only fight intermittently, but after battle episodes usually have an opportunity to recuperate and regroup, often under relatively secure conditions. Such cir-

cumstances would seem to be present in search and destroy
missions and in enemy perimeter attacks upon US bases or fixed
positions. If this assumption is correct, the nature of most combat
in Viet Nam would fulfill the major requirements of forward
psychiatric treatment, i.e., immediacy, proximity, and expectancy,
which could prevent psychiatric breakdown in potential cases, as
well as provide prompt treatment for incipient psychiatric casualties. In addition, as described by Allerton, overt psychiatric
syndromes are managed successfully by general medical officers of
the combat units, mainly on an outpatient status and are likely
not to have been included in the formal psychiatric rate because
such cases would not be considered lost to duty for a full day.
Under these conditions, it is probable that only the more severe
or refractory disorders would be placed on a full patient status
or be referred to division psychiatric personnel and become recorded as psychiatric casualties. Some confirmation of this
hypothesis is suggested in the chapter by Allerton where it is
noted that over a 12-month period (1967–1968), each division
evacuated an average of four psychiatric patients per month.
This is an extraordinarily low rate of evacuation from a usual
divisional strength from 15,000 to 18,000 personnel, and less than
the rate of psychiatric hospitalization for divisions based in
noncombat areas.

If the above stated conditions are even partially corroborated,
the much lower NP rate in Viet Nam as compared to that of
previous wars is understandable. In World War II, and to a lesser
extent, in the Korean War, the majority of mild as well as almost
all moderate and severe psychiatric casualties were evacuated to
divisional clearing stations and included in the NP rate.

An excellent and comprehensive chapter on patterns of psychiatric attrition in combat is contributed by Tischler who has
thoroughly reviewed the recorded past experiences on this subject. The chapter includes detailed studies which demonstrate
that psychiatric casualties have their highest frequency from personnel new to combat. These results are consistent with repeated
observations made by psychiatrists in World War II. Findings of
the study also confirm experiences of the Korean War in that with
the establishment of a rotation policy, psychiatric breakdown
was least prevalent from the "old" combat participants despite
the increasing tension and other manifestations of the "short
timer's" syndrome as these men neared the end of their 12-month

term of duty. However, a statistical bias exists in the case studies of this chapter which exaggerates the findings of increased psychiatric casualties from new arrivals to Viet Nam. This error stems from the usual large attrition in combat due to battle and non-battle losses which make mandatory a high input of replacements to maintain unit strength. For this reason, it is common for combat units to have a higher proportion of more recent members than could be accounted for on the basis of replacements for losses by normal rotation. This situation is illustrated by the case history of Henry as cited in Tischler's chapter, who had completed only seven months of his 12-month term; but upon return to his unit after a brief recreational leave (R&R), he found himself to be the only "old timer" in his squad.

With such a high proportion of "new" men in the military population at risk, it is inevitable that any sample of psychiatric disorders in this or similar studies will contain a large number of subjects who are in the first three months of the 12-month combat tour. If the reverse were the result, one would have a significant and unusual finding of apparent invulnerability of persons new to combat. Conversely, the small number of "old" men remaining in the population at risk must bias accordingly the frequency of psychiatric casualties from individuals in the last three months of the required tour of duty.

VI. Biochemical Responses in Combat

This volume includes several studies of steroid and other bio-chemical responses to combat stress which represents important and unique contributions to military psychiatry. Relevance of these studies to the problems of adaptation under combat conditions should be apparent. Throughout the recorded history of warfare, most participants in combat have been known to experience various types of mild to severe bodily and emotional discomfort which were generally ascribed to the influence of fear. In World War II, much of the stated inability to cope with combat conditions was attributed to such somatic and/or psychological reactions which came to be regarded as manifestations of illness; first, as "psychoneurosis" and later as "exhaustion." However, most personnel were able to function adequately in combat, although with few exceptions they readily admitted awareness of varying degrees of tension and somatic discomfort. Initially, it appeared that most individuals, by virtue of endowment and personality, were better able to contain the noxious effects of combat fear than the more vulnerable minority of "weaker" persons. However, "everyone had his breaking point." As previously stated, the frequency of crippling physiological and psychological disorders was found to be more related to other circumstances of the combat situation than the intensity of battle-induced fear.

For almost 20 years, attention has been focused upon various aspects of adaptation to stress situations by the Neuropsychiatry Division of the Walter Reed Institute of Research, directed by Dr. David McK. Rioch. Investigation of the biochemical components of the problem has been carried out by Mason and his associates assisted by Brady and his group in the collaborative use of operant conditioning techniques, also developed in the laboratories of the Walter Reed Army Institute of Research (WRAIR).

Initially, elevations in adrenal cortical secretions of animals and man were utilized to quantitate responses to different stimuli of threat or challenge. Later, measurements of other neuroendocrine secretions were added to create a profile of endocrinological reaction to various environmental and psychological conditions of change and threat. The insights obtained by this continued research activity have opened up a new dimension of knowledge relative to the threat–defense system of adaptation. Results have confirmed clinical impressions that an event is only stressful for the individual when he perceives it as such, and that "ego" defenses or the characteristic manner in which an individual deals with uncertain threat, such as by denial, suppression, reliance upon others, religious faith, and compulsive activities, depending upon their effectiveness, correspondingly control the endocrinological response to stressful situations.

Two of the biochemical studies reported in this volume by Bourne and Rose are an extension of the WRAIR program to the realistic stress laboratory of combat in Viet Nam. Bourne, as a member of the Neuropsychiatry Division of WRAIR, coordinated the studies in Viet Nam with the laboratory support of Rose, Mason, and his associates. The data of these research efforts have confirmed previous results obtained in noncombat settings; new information about endocrinological responses to danger being significantly influenced by social factors of group consensus and support, and about the leadership role and its obligations being reflected in the levels of steroid secretion has been derived from these data. In effect, as stated by Bourne, "in man's response to stress, attention must be paid to the threat itself, the psychological style of the individual in coping with the environment, and the social context in which he exists."

Biochemical responses to aviator stress in Viet Nam combat are reported in this volume by Austin; this represents another valuable contribution to military psychiatry. Studies include determinations of blood plasma phospholipid fractions in Navy attack carrier pilots flying combat missions over North Viet Nam. Promising results were obtained in that one of the fractions, phosphatidyl glycerol, was more responsive to this type of combat stress than the other fractions. These findings point to the definite possibility of obtaining a much needed objective quantitative index to be used with clinical evaluation and other measures in the identification of impending or incipient breakdown in combat performance.

VII. Summary

This volume is a most timely presentation of military psychiatry in Viet Nam. Some of its writings indicate considerable differences in concepts of causation, frequency, and manifestations of psychiatric casualties in Viet Nam as compared to WW II and the Korean War. Curiously, participation in war, and perhaps also in love, provides such an intense and unique personal experience that the individuals so involved seem impelled to place emphasis upon differences rather than similarities with like events of the past or even the future. For this reason, the writer, a veteran of psychiatry in WW II and Korea, felt an obligation to utilize this introductory chapter as a means of integrating the past and present experiences of combat psychiatry. With this approach, it is hoped that the reader can better appreciate the contributions of this volume in the context of the evolution of military psychiatry over a continuum of time and changing circumstances. It may well be that, even though a generation apart, marked similarity of wartime experiences will be revealed rather than differences.

REFERENCES

Bull. U.S. Army Med. Dept. (October 1943). Neuropsychiatric disease: Causes and prevention. 1, 9-13.

Drayer, C. S., and Glass, A. J. (1969). Neuropsychiatry in World War II. *In* "Mediterranean Theatre," Vol. II. Medical Department U.S. Army (in preparation).

Glass, A. J. (1949). An attempt to predict probable combat effectiveness by brief psychiatric examination. *Am. J. Psychiat.* 106, 81.

Glass, A. J. (1957). Paper presented at Symposium on Prevention and Social Psychiatry, April 15-17, 1957. Walter Reed Army Inst. of Res., Walter Reed Army Med. Center, U.S. Govt. Printing Office, Washington, D.C. Pp. 185-197.

Glass, A. J. (1966). "U.S. Army Medical Department: Neuropsychiatry in World War II." Vol. I, Chapter 1. Office of the Surgeon General, Department of the Army, Washington, D.C. Pp. 7, 10.

Glass, A. J. (1968). "U.S. Army Medical Department: Internal Medicine in World War II." Vol. III, Chapter XXI. Office of the Surgeon General, Department of the Army, Washington, D.C. Pp. 678, 685, 707-709.

Glass, A. J., Ryan, F. J., Lubin, A., Ramana, C. V., and Tueker, A. C. (1956). Psychiatric prediction and military effectiveness. *U.S. Armed Forces Med. J.* 7, 1427, 1575.

Glass, A. J., Ryan, F. J., Lubin, A., Ramana, C. V., and Tueker, A. C. (1957). Psychiatric prediction and military effectiveness. *U.S. Armed Forces Med. J.* 8, 346.

Grinker, R. R., and Spiegel, J. P. (1943). "War Neuroses in North Africa." Josiah Macy Jr. Foundation, New York.

Hanson, F. R. (1949). The factor of fatique in the neuroses of combat. *Army Med. Bull.,* Suppl. 9, Nov. 1949, pp. 147-150.

Office of the Surgeon General, Department of the Army (1968). "The Mental Health of U.S. Army Troops in Viet Nam Remains Outstanding." Washington, D.C. March 12, 1968.

Pyle, E. T. (1943). "Here Is Your War." Henry Holt & Co., New York. Pp. 247-248.

Rioch, D. McK. (1968). Prevention, the major task of military psychiatry. *Psychother. Psychosom.* 16, 55-63.

Salmon, T., *et al.* (1929). "The Medical Department of the United States Army in the World War: Neuropsychiatry." Vol. X, pp. 507-512. U.S. Govt. Printing Office, Washington, D.C.

1// Army Psychiatry in Viet Nam

William S. Allerton

I. Introduction

Army psychiatry is writing a most interesting chapter in its participation in the present conflict in Viet Nam. The growth and maturation of preventive psychiatric concepts, particularly in the last 25 years would seem to be reaping significant rewards. The ratio of mental health personnel to combat troops is higher than in any previous conflict in which the United States has been involved. Incidence rates of psychiatric illness in the combat area are lower than those recorded in any previous military operation. Despite the controversial nature of the conflict and the questionable support, at times, by the citizenry of our country, the morale of troops present in Viet Nam appears to be of high order and possibly significantly better than troop morale in both World War II and Korea. In order to appropriately evaluate the causes and importance of these aforementioned trends, this chapter will set forth a brief historical background, a discussion of army psychiatric organization in the United States and overseas prior to the Viet Nam conflict, programs in Viet Nam prior to August 1965, and psychiatric organization in Viet Nam from 1965 to the present. Treatment methods currently used in Viet Nam will be discussed, statistical trends will be elaborated, and evaluation of such statistical trends will be attempted.

II. Historical Background

A. Combat Psychiatric Experience in Previous Conflicts

1. *Civil War*

During the Civil War, both the Union and Confederate Armies attempted to utilize hospital ships to evacuate their wounded situated in areas near the Atlantic coastline. It has been reported that both armies were forced to abandon the use of such ships because a large number of individuals suffering from what was then called "nostalgia" practically clogged the gangplanks. This precluded such ships' properly caring for the physically sick and the wounded.

2. *World War I*

In World War I, the importance of early treatment of psychiatric problems was recognized, and cantonment psychiatrists were established in a successful attempt to preclude hospitalization for psychiatric reasons of all save those with serious psychiatric disturbances (Bowen, 1928).

3. World War II

Lessons learned during the Civil War and World War I were lost, unfortunately, and it took considerable time during World War II to properly implement preventive psychiatric concepts. This became an absolute necessity when, in a given month in 1943, General George Marshall observed that there were more individuals being discharged from the army for psychiatric reasons than the number of individuals being inducted into the army. This obviously most disturbing situation led to a series of efforts designed to reduce the number of individuals being hospitalized and evacuated for psychiatric reasons. Perhaps paramount in the immediate attempts to rectify this problem was the placing of psychiatric personnel in the table of organization of the division (Glass, 1949), thereby placing psychiatric personnel as close to the immediate area of conflict as seemed feasible. Such personnel could then train general medical officers at the battalion level and could themselves implement preventive concepts in the combat situation.

Mental hygiene consultation services were developed in the continental United States, placing mental health personnel out of the hospitals and as near to the troops being evaluated and treated as was possible (Perkins, 1955). Hospital treatment techniques were instituted to preclude unnecessary length of hospitalization and inappropriate evaluation. As a result of all of these experiences, cardinal principles of preventive psychiatry in the military evolved. They were: (1) Early detection of psychiatric difficulties in individuals and in groups; (2) early treatment of individuals requiring treatment in the area closest to their training or to their combat participation; (3) avoidance of a hospital atmosphere; (4) early return to full duty of the majority of individuals psychiatrically treated.

4. Korean Conflict

Although army psychiatry continued to grow in its training programs, at the time of the advent of the Korean conflict certain of these important preventive concepts had fallen to disuse. By

1950, there were only two operating mental hygiene consultation services in the continental United States (Allerton and Peterson, 1957). Further, the position of the psychiatrist at division level was in serious jeopardy. Within a short period of time after the advent of hostilities in Korea, however, army psychiatry again reorganized into a more preventive posture implementing the lessons learned during World War II combat. Insuring the continued status of a division psychiatrist, developing neuropsychiatric (NP) treatment teams for utilization in the combat area, and the re-emergence of mental hygiene consultation services at all major posts in the continental United States eventually led to even better preventive psychiatric programs and results than was the case in World War II.

B. Organization of Army Psychiatry in the United States and Overseas Prior to the Viet Nam Conflict

In the years following the Korean War, predominant reliance on the mental hygiene program in the continental United States and outpatient treatment in overseas areas became the bulwark of the army's psychiatric program. In excess of 50% of all mental hygiene personnel were assigned in such positions. Less than 50% of the army's mental hygiene personnel were assigned to hospital situations (Tiffany and Allerton, 1967). The status of division psychiatry was maintained in the training situation both to buttress mental hygiene consultation services on fixed posts and to prepare for immediate utilization in the event of conflict. Hospital treatment practices were more clearly related to tertiary prevention than had been the case in the past (Glass *et al.*, 1961). Primary prevention in the form of increased consultation to command level by mental hygiene personnel was maximized, and secondary preventive techniques in the form of early detection, early treatment, and early return to duty were implemented regularly. Overseas, the importance of preventive work in division organization was vigorously maintained for the first time in a period of relative peace. Hospital treatment practices in overseas areas were aimed at a reduction of evacuation for psychiatric reasons. As a result of all of these programs, the admission rate for psychiatric reasons in the army was reduced from 24 per 1000 troops per year in the early 1950's to 5 per 1000 troops per year in the mid 1960's. At the same time, outpatient or mental hygiene consultation service treatment rates rose from 107 to 1000 troops per year in early 1951 to more than 304 per 1000 troops per year in 1965 (Tiffany and Allerton, 1967).

III. Psychiatric Programs in the Republic of Viet Nam Prior to August 1965

A. Early Assignment and Utilization of Psychiatrists and Mental Hygiene Personnel

As the number of military personnel assigned to advisory functions in Viet Nam grew, the necessity of providing some mental hygiene personnel in this overseas area became apparent. The first psychiatrist was assigned in 1962 in the Eighth Field Hospital, and from that time until the development of major military operations in Viet Nam, there were psychiatric personnel assigned in this area. The operation of military psychiatry in Viet Nam was somewhat encumbered during these early years because of lack of mobility and difficulty in implementing preventive concepts throughout the country. Nonetheless, military psychiatry was present early and had definite impact.

B. Walter Reed Army Institute of Research (WRAIR) Participation in Research Programs Prior to the Military Buildup

As early as 1963, the Walter Reed Institute of Research under the direction of Dr. David McK. Rioch, Chief of the Department of Neuropsychiatry, began mental hygiene research programs directed, in part, toward a study of the advisors' function. From 1963 through 1964, various teams of psychiatrists, social workers, and psychologists, with the help of an anthropologist who had been working in the country made important contacts with the military command in evaluating the advisory function of US personnel. Group process conferences were held with key military personnel of the United States at all echelons (Hausman and Kolmer, 1965). Important contacts were established with South Viet Nam psychiatric personnel, both within and without their military organization. Crosscultural problems were explored, as were the difficulties in the parallel chains of command of the United States and Vietnamese military organizations. Military psychiatry enjoyed a relatively unprecedented type of support from General Westmoreland down to the battalion commander. It is perhaps of some significance that the United States Ambassador to Viet Nam took the time to visit the WRAIR team in Saigon. Although predominantly engaged in research, the teams provided by the Walter Reed Institute made their presence felt in an operational sense. Consultation was available to Special Forces as well as to the more conventional military units. The concept that military psychiatry was concerned with prevention and not just with treating "crazy people" seemed to be apparent to military command to a much greater degree than perhaps was ever before the case. Thus, prior to the large military buildup, a preventive milieu was present on the ground in this geographical area.

IV. Psychiatric Organization in Viet Nam, 1965-1968

A. Psychiatric Consultant USARVN

The importance of having a psychiatric consultant in an area of operations had long been emphasized (Peterson and Chambers, 1952). Shortly after the beginning of the major troop buildup in August 1965, the first psychiatric consultant was assigned to Viet Nam. This was a senior, American Board of Psychiatry and Neurology certified, army psychiatrist whose mission was to establish and implement a sound psychiatric program in Viet Nam (Johnson *et al.*, 1967). He was assigned with equal status to the medical and surgical consultants in that country and was provided with necessary transportation for visiting major medical installations throughout the country. In consonance with the 12-month rotation policy, the initial consultant, as of this writing, has been succeeded by yearly replacements, and four such individuals have served in that capacity to date. They all have performed their mission of coordination of psychiatric facilities and program planning in a superior fashion.

B. Deployment of KO Teams

Almost simultaneously with the assignment of a consultant to Viet Nam, the first KO team (neuropsychiatric treatment center team) was assigned to Viet Nam. A second team was assigned less than 12 months later. Since May 1966, there have been assigned two NP treatment centers based on these teams (Jones, 1968).

These centers provide backup to the division psychiatric programs, conduct the major inpatient treatment facilities in country,
and handle outpatient referrals from local geographic areas. A KO
team consists of three psychiatrists (one of whom is the commander of the team), one neurologist, one clinical psychologist,
two social workers, and 12 enlisted mental hygiene personnel.
When they are attached to an existing medical unit with logistic
support, they function with both inpatient and outpatient facilities. In Viet Nam, these two KO teams have had final evacuation
authority for all army psychiatric patients coming to the attention
of army medical facilities. These teams have played a paramount
role in providing early treatment and early return to duty, and
have further resulted in the lowest evacuation rate for psychiatric
reasons in the history of the Army Medical Service. A great debt of
gratitude is owed to those psychiatrists who, as a result of World
War II and Korean experience, recognized the necessity for organizations such as these.

C. Division Psychiatry

As each division was assigned to Viet Nam, a division psychiatrist with his team of one social worker and eight enlisted mental
hygiene specialists was assigned with a division. The time of their
deployment varied with the specific division. In some instances
these personnel went with the advance party, but more frequently
they were not assigned until the majority of the combat elements
(three brigades) were already deployed. In many instances, the
division psychiatric personnel had already been working with the
specific division prior to its deployment to Viet Nam, had famil-
iarity with the structure of command, and had already served in
consultative and evaluative programs. The importance of having
mental hygiene personnel at division level has long been recognized and the ability to assign such individuals early has served a
very essential preventive function. Present army brigade organization has led to certain problems in proper preventive psychiatric
coverage for the division (Jones, 1967). Division headquarters and
the three brigade headquarters are frequently at some considerable geographic distance. Most division psychiatric coverage has
required the assignment of two of the enlisted personnel to each
brigade with the remaining two staying at division headquarters,

often with the psychiatrist and the social worker. This arrangement has required considerable mobility on the part of the division psychiatrist and the division social worker. Such mobility has not always been optimal. Most of the division psychiatrists so assigned, however, have been able to make frequent visits to all the medical units in the division. In recent years, the average young general medical officer assigned to the army has had considerable exposure to psychiatry, and, in most instances, reasonable exposure to army preventive psychiatric concepts during his initial military orientation at Fort Sam Houston. The division psychiatrist's role as consultant to other medical officers is somewhat simplified as compared with what it might have been several decades ago, since considerable groundwork has already been laid. The majority of psychiatric problems in the divisions in Viet Nam are handled at the very local level by general medical officers. Referrals to division level for the most part include diagnostic problems, military members with overt psychotic reactions, occasional cases of neurotic difficulties, and individuals with character disorders. Since the advent of major hostilities in Viet Nam, the appearance of the syndrome termed "combat exhaustion" has been surprisingly low (Johnson *et al.*, 1967). The excellent training of the individual soldier, the 12-month rotation policy, and the nature of the fighting in the Viet Nam conflict probably all have contributed to this low incidence. It is likely, however, that the maintenance of the preventive posture on the part of army psychiatry and acceptance of this by the entire Army Medical Service, as well as major elements of command, have played a vital part in this low incidence. The role of the division psychiatrist and his team remains an important, if not the most important bulwark, of the army's combat psychiatric program.

D. Psychiatry in Field and Evacuation Hospitals

In addition to those psychiatrists and psychiatric personnel assigned at division and KO team level, psychiatric personnel have been assigned to various field and evacuation hospitals to provide appropriate geographical coverage. They receive both outpatients and inpatients from their local geographic areas, frequently working in close association with neighboring division psychiatric elements. They have provided short-term inpatient care by referring on to one of the NP treatment centers (KO teams) any patient they feel required evacuation.

As of this writing, there are 23 psychiatrists assigned to all army medical facilities in Viet Nam. Together with their allied mental hygiene personnel, they provide the highest ratio of psychiatric personnel to troop strength than has ever been assigned by the army to a combat theater.

E. Evacuation Policies

Only those psychiatric patients who are felt to require more than 30 days of hospitalization are evacuated out of country. In actual practice, most psychiatric patients who may require such relatively prolonged hospitalization are evacuated within a week or two after admission; few are kept in Vietnam for a longer portion of the 30 day "evacuation policy" period. The majority of patients evacuated are suffering from psychoses; the evacuation rate is low, and approximates the incidence rate of psychotic disorders in the army world wide. This means that the command has been educated to handle administrative problems themselves and that all psychiatric problems, save the severe psychotic disturbances, are ordinarily appropriately treated and returned to full duty. For the past 2 years, the vast majority of all army psychiatric patients evacuated from Viet Nam have first gone to Japan. There, a certain percentage are returned to noncombat duty in that area, a very few are returned to Viet Nam, and the remainder are evacuated to the United States.

V. Problems in Psychological Adjustment in Viet Nam

Most of the advisors to the Republic of Viet Nam's Army consensually validated similar experiences in their overall psychological adjustment during their 12-month period of assignment to Viet Nam. They described an initial feeling of enthusiasm and stimulating interest in developing techniques to work with their Vietnamese counterparts. Many of them ascribed this kind of feeling to what they believed to be an American cultural trend to be bursting with enthusiasm and to have high expectations for accomplishment. Several months after their arrival, they found their jobs often so frustrating and difficult that many of them felt quite depressed. Crosscultural problems, difficulties in the chain of command, and hostility toward certain culturally different practices engaged in by the Vietnamese led to frustration and to a feeling of hopelessness. This was in marked contrast to their initial enthusiastic approach.

With longer tenure, however, these advisors began to feel that they could see opportunities for steady improvement. Their goals then seemed to be realistically oriented. Unfortunately, as the period of their assignment drew to a close, they felt that they had not had sufficient time to accomplish their mission as advisors. Following the military buildup, when actual military operations became paramount and when the advisory functions at times seemed to take a less prominent role, Dowling (1967) interestingly noted somewhat similar periods of adjustment in combat troops, as well as in medical personnel assigned. He described the first phase of assignment in Viet Nam as that of "apprehensive enthusiasm." The second period, he described as "resignation." The last period seemed to differ somewhat from that experienced by the advisors and may have been related to concern about leaving the country alive and uninjured. He described the last period in Viet Nam as a period of "anxious apprehension."

Although adequate statistical information is not yet available and may be difficult to obtain, many of the conventional indices of morale would seem to indicate that psychological adjustment problems in Viet Nam have been somewhat minimal. AWOL, desertion, and court martial rates have not been particularly high in the country. In fact, in many instances they have been lower than those experienced in stateside assignments. Problems with alcoholism, though present, do not seem to be in any way out of proportion to the problems observed elsewhere in the Armed Forces. Although much has been written about the use of drugs by our troops in Viet Nam, there does not appear to be any significant statistical information which would lead one to believe that problems with marijuana, the opium alkaloids, or hallucinogens have any higher incidence among troops in Viet Nam than might be the case for the same age group in metropolitan centers in this country.

VI. Treatment Methods

A. Preventive Approach

Induction and enlistment standards have varied greatly during the history of the United States Armed Forces. In general, intellectual standards for enlistment and induction are perhaps higher at this time than they were at times in the past, for example, during World War II. It should be observed, however, that psychological maladjustments during previous conflicts were not particularly related to intelligence level and that groups of individuals with borderline intelligence did not constitute a particularly large percentage of those individuals coming to psychiatric attention. The military has long since learned that preinduction screening to try to preclude psychological maladjustment is costly, impractical, and unrewarding. Although, in general, it has been possible to eliminate from induction people who are overtly psychotic or who are markedly deviant in their social behavior, no valid method has been found to screen out individuals who might become neurotic, psychotic, or emotionally disturbed. The test of performance appears to be the only valid measure of adjustment to military service. During basic and advanced training, the mental hygiene services in the continental United States do all within their power to provide their commands with important consultation services that will insure proper utilization of manpower. Most individuals who are likely to show serious psychological maladjustment within the military will do so during their early period of training. Approximately 50% of all psychotic disorders occur during the first year of military service. It seems likely to this writer that this may often be more a function of case finding than the result of a new external stress. Most psychotics having an early "break" demonstrate by history a marginal, if not psychotic, adjustment prior to military service. One might therefore say that screening by the test of performance, in general, has been accomplished prior to the time the troops are sent overseas into a combat area.

The constant maintenance of sound preventive psychiatric principles on the part of the military service and not just psychiatry alone has been the mainstay of preventive combat psychiatric practice. The cardinal preventive principles remain: (1) Early detection and evaluation of problems (this includes consultants to command, troop unit contacts, and evaluation of group problems, as well as the evaluation of the individual soldier who might be referred). (2) Early treatment (including rehabilitation, reassurance, occasional sedation, and sometimes tranquilization). (3) The maintenance of a nonhospital atmosphere. Treatment occurs as near as possible to the area in which the individual or the group is assigned. Evacuation to hospital facilities is avoided whenever possible, and all hospital facilities in the combat area established for psychiatric treatment are designed to give a military troop unit appearance rather than a hospital appearance. (4) The expectation for early return to full duty is maintained whenever possible for the vast majority of psychiatric patients referred.

B. The Role of the General Medical Officer

The medical officers at battalion level have the responsibility for much of the primary prevention occurring in combat psychiatric practice. Division psychiatrists serve as consultants to them, but they evaluate and treat most of the group and individual problems occurring in the local unit. Fortunately, most young medical officers today have had increasingly rich training in psychiatry during their medical school training and advanced specialty training. Most curricula today include some orientation to social psychiatric frames of reference. All medical officers coming on duty in the United States Army receive orientation about army psychiatry during their course of instruction in basic military medicine at Fort Sam Houston. Fewer general medical officers today are prone to evacuate to psychiatric installations individuals with mild to moderate emotional problems than was the case in previous conflicts. This, I think, may be ascribed to their better training and to the increased availability of good psychiatric consultants at division, field, KO, and theater level.

C. Treatment at the Division Level

Most division psychiatry teams today spend a considerable amount of their time in consultation, not only with other medical officers but also with units of command. Some divisions in Viet Nam have evaluated and treated several hundred patients per month, but some have evaluated or treated as few as 30 patients during any given month. Since the division strength is somewhere between 15,000 and 18,000 men, this is an extremely low individual figure. Accurate records of outpatient contacts are hard to come by, but figures of incidence of hospitalization or excused from duty status do provide a valid frame of reference for the incidence of psychological maladjustment. Such figures will be presented later in this chapter.

D. Treatment at the Field and Evacuation Hospital Level

This includes some inpatient as well as outpatient work. The number of psychiatric inpatients in field and evacuation hospitals in Viet Nam has been surprisingly low. However, much of the work of the field or evacuation hospital psychiatrist has been concerned with consultation to command (often support rather than combat units) and the evaluation of referred patients on an outpatient basis.

E. Treatment at the KO Team Level (Psychiatric Treatment Center)

The two neuropsychiatric treatment centers in Viet Nam, both consisting of the KO teams previously described, receive all army patients referred through army channels who have been considered to require further hospitalization by the lower echelons. Only these KO teams evacuate psychiatric patients out of the country. Parrish (1968) reports that, during the past 12 months (1967–1968), each division has referred an average of four patients per month to the KO teams (Neuropsychiatric Treatment Centers). In addition to the KO teams' inpatient work and their preparing patients for evacuation, they also function as military community mental health centers with a capacity for crisis intervention and for extensive outpatient treatment facilities. It is of some moment to note that there are no "closed ward" facilities in the army psychiatric establishment in Viet Nam. In fact, there are no "closed" psychiatric facilities operated by the army in the entire Pacific area, including Japan, Okinawa, Hawaii, and Korea, as well as Viet Nam. A patient being evacuated from Saigon first finds himself in a closed psychiatric facility when he arrives at one of the treatment centers operated by the army in the United States. Since the author is an advocate of open-ward facilities, it is not inappropriate to suggest that army psychiatry could again learn something from its own combat psychiatric experiences. We have too long suffered, I feel, from the false belief that residents in training would not feel comfortable if their psychotic patients were not in a secure locked environment.

F. Utilization of Pharmacological Treatment Methods

With the advent of the utilization of tranquilizers, particularly the phenothiazines, the utilization of pharmacological treatment methods has been altered in Viet Nam as compared with experiences in Korea and World War II. Less sedation in the form of barbiturates has been utilized, and phenothiazines have often been used where the barbiturates previously might have been the drugs of choice. (It has been observed that fewer drugs of any type are being used by psychiatrists in their combat psychiatric experiences in Viet Nam.) The amount of phenothiazine and other tranquilizers used in the combat area by all medical officers is probably less than for a similar population in the continental United States. Evidence tends to show that temporary removal from a stressful situation coupled with the fostering of an expectation of early return to duty is a much more meaningful part of the therapeutic regime than any of the drugs (barbiturates or tranquilizers) that have been or are being used.

VII. Statistical Trends

A. Incidence Rates

The rate for the period from January 1965 through December 1966 for psychiatric patients in Viet Nam hospitalized or otherwise excused from duty was 12 individuals per 1000 troops per year. The rate for calendar year 1967 decreased to approximately 10 per 1000 troops per year. In the first 6 months of calendar year 1968, including the period of intense "Tet Offensive" combat, the rate was, again, 12 per 1000 troops per year. These rates do not include individuals seen as outpatients but, in effect, do reflect those individuals who are unable to function on full duty status because of psychiatric problems. These rates compare favorably with the rates experienced in other overseas areas and in many US Army posts in the continental United States. They compare even more favorably with past combat psychiatric experience. Similar rates in Korea for the period of intense combat from July 1950 to December 1952 were 37 per 1000 troops per year. The lowest such incidence rate in World War II for a combat theater was 28 per 1000 troops per year, and the highest reported for the First Army in Europe was 101 per 1000 troops per year (Office of the Surgeon General, 1968). Thus, Viet Nam incidence rates were one-tenth of the highest rate ever reported in World War II and less than one-third of the rates reported during stressful periods in the Korean conflict.

B. Evacuation Rates

The evacuation rate for psychiatric reasons from Viet Nam has remained relatively static since early 1965. This rate is 2 individuals per 1000 troops per year. This rate, incidentally, is approximately the same as the incidence rate of hospitalization for psychotic disorders army-wide for the past five decades. It is likely that, for all intents and purposes, only psychotic individuals are being evacuated medically for psychiatric reasons from Viet Nam, and that the incidence of such disorders is approximately the same under the stress of combat as it is in training or garrison status. During World War II, 23% of all medical evacuations from combat theaters were for psychiatric reasons. This dropped to 6% during the Korean War, 5% for the years 1965–1966 in Viet Nam, and to an all-time low of between 2 and 3% for fiscal year 1967–1968 (Office of the Surgeon General, 1968).

VIII. Evaluation of Statistical Trends

A. Factors Involved in Low Incidence

There is little doubt that various command policies and programs have contributed importantly to the low incidence of psychiatric difficulty previously documented. The fact that a 12-month rotation period has been instituted and maintained for Viet Nam has, without question, ameliorated many of the problems that existed during the Korean War and World War II. Since a definite time period is set in the mind of the individual, he does not have to concern himself as much with the imponderables relative to just when he might return home. The excellent training which soldiers now receive in their basic and advanced training undoubtedly contributes to their sense of wellbeing and to their positive expectancy. This is a crucial factor in morale and in decreased psychiatric problems. The combat situation itself, which has remained so fluid during this conflict, has resulted in relatively brief periods of fighting. Unlike experiences during more conventional wars, soldiers do not have to spend lengthy periods of time in trenches or foxholes and are rarely subjected to continuous artillery bombardment or aerial bombing. Thus, relatively few cases of what previously has been referred to as "combat fatigue" have occurred in Viet Nam. What the psychiatrist more often sees is the more conventional characterologic, neurotic, or psychotic difficulties that are not particularly related to external stresses.

Another factor which may be involved in the low incidence is that, although certain areas in Viet Nam are potentially very dangerous, there is no area within the country which is without danger. There is little merit in developing secondary gain type symptoms which might consciously or unconsciously be utilized to extricate oneself from a dangerous situation. Many soldiers believe, and perhaps correctly so, that it is more dangerous in a bar in Saigon than out in the field in some type of search and destroy mission. All of the aforementioned factors have made significant contributions to the low incidence of psychiatric difficulty presently experienced. However, were it not for the well-planned preventive psychiatric programs currently implemented in Viet Nam, and those which have enjoyed long and productive tenure in the army establishment as a whole, rates undoubtedly would be higher. I, for one, feel quite strongly that in the last analysis the preventive psychiatric program may be the most important factor contributing to low incidence. It should be mentioned in passing that army psychiatry itself has contributed to some of the command policies, i.e., the 12-month rotation period, improved training, etc., which play their individual roles.

B. Factors Involving Incidence of Evacuation

The 30-day command policy for evacuation is not of particular significance in the evacuation rates for psychiatric problems. If the policy time were set higher, the number of evacuations would probably remain the same. In the unlikely possibility that it were set lower, evacuation rates probably still would not alter perceptively. Most patients who would require more than a week of in-patient hospitalization for psychiatric reasons are probably too sick to be returned to combat duty in any event. This fact, however, is a function of the operational policy of avoiding lengthy hospitalization in all save severe depressions or psychotic disorders. The operational policy adopted by army psychiatry and the treatment methods employed in the combat area are obviously the crucial variables in the excellent posture of the Army Medical Service in avoiding unnecessary evacuations for psychiatric reasons.

IX. Summary

Army psychiatry was prepared as never before to handle its responsibilities in a combat situation when the Vietnamese conflict developed. Appropriate psychiatric personnel and facilities were assigned early and in relatively optimal organizations and locations. Incidence rates for psychiatric disability and for evacuation from the theater are appreciably lower than in any conflict in which United States forces have participated. A significant contribution to these excellent results is considered directly related to the army's preventive psychiatric program.

REFERENCES

Allerton, W. S., and Peterson, D. B. (1957). Preventive psychiatry — the army's Mental Hygiene Consultation Service (MHCS) program with statistical evaluation. *Am. J. Psychiat.* 113, 788.

Bowen, A. S. (1928). "The Medical Department of the United States Army in the World War," (Frank W. Weed, ed.), Vol. X, Chapt. IV, p. 75, U.S. Govt. Printing Office, Washington, D.C.

Dowling, J. (1967). Psychological aspects of the year in Viet Nam. *USARV Med. Bull.* 2, 45.

Glass, A. J. (1949). *Bull. U.S. Army Med. Dept.* 9, Suppl., 45.

Glass, A. J., Artiss, K. L., Gibbs, J. J., and Sweeney, V. C. (1961). The current status of army psychiatry. *Am. J. Psychiat.* 117, 676.

Hausman, W., and Kolmer, H. S. (1965). Operational psychiatric research in the field in Viet Nam. *Proc. 11th Ann. Human Factors Res. Develop. Conf., Fort Benning, Georgia.*

Johnson, A. W., Jr., Bowman, J. A., Byrdy, H. S., and Blank, A. J. (1967). "Army Psychiatry in Viet Nam," Social and Preventive Psychiatry Course, January 23–27. Walter Reed Army Inst. of Res., Walter Reed Army Med. Center, Washington, D.C.

Jones, F. D. (1967). Experiences of a division psychiatrist in Viet Nam. *Military Med.* 132, 1003.

Jones, F. D. (1968). "Army Psychiatry in Viet Nam," presentation to the Fourth Global Medicine Course, April 19, 1968. Walter Reed Army Inst. of Res., Walter Reed Army Med. Center, Washington, D.C.

Office of the Surgeon General, Department of the Army (1968). "The Mental Health of U.S. Army Troops in Viet Nam Remains Outstanding." Washington, D.C.

Parrish, M. (1968). Personal communication.

Perkins, M. E. (1955). "U.S. Army Medical Department — Preventive Medicine in World War II," (John Boyd Coates, Jr., ed.), Vol. III, Chapt. VI, p. 215. Office of the Surgeon General, Dept. of the Army, Washington, D. C.

Peterson, D. B., and Chambers, R. E. (1952). Restatement of combat psychiatry. *Am. J. Psychiat.* 10, 249.

Tiffany, W. J., Jr., and Allerton, W. S. (1967). Army psychiatry in the mid '60s. *Am. J. Psychiat.* 123, 811.

2 // Patterns of Psychiatric Attrition and of Behavior in a Combat Zone

Gary L. Tischler

I. Introduction

It has been repeatedly demonstrated that, under the conditions of modern warfare, a significant loss of effective manpower will result from the failure of individuals to come to terms with demands inherent in the situation at hand. This failure is reflected in the high admission rates for neuropsychiatric casualties recorded in World War I, in World War II, and in the Korean War. During the Second World War between January 1943 and December 1945, there were 409,887 neuropsychiatric patients admitted to army hospitals in the overseas theaters alone. Of these patients, 127,660 were evacuated to the United States. In other words, approximately one out of every three hospitalized neuropsychiatric casualties was evacuated and hence lost from overseas duty. The figures do not reflect the incidence of self-inflicted wounds, "accidental" injuries, hospitalization for somatic complaints without evidence of "organic" pathology, refusal to obey orders, or desertion. These phenomena, which also account for a loss in effective manpower, are regarded by Glass (1958) as disguised psychiatric disorders. They occur with increased frequency among combat troops when there is a decrease in the number of overt psychiatric casualties. Realization of the magnitude of attrition resulting from psychologically induced symptoms and behavioral abnormalities spurred efforts to delineate the correlates of attrition.

A. Correlates of Attrition

Field observation, epidemiological research, and clinical studies showed psychiatric attrition to be a corollary of a number of factors. Foremost was combat. Admission rates among troops engaged in actual combat were from five to ten times greater than those recorded elsewhere in the army. For example: The overall admission rate to overseas hospitals for neuropsychiatric conditions in 1944 was 47.0 per 1000 mean troop strength. Appel (1966), citing a period from June through November of that year, reported an annual admission rate for combat divisions serving in the European Theater of approximately 250 per 1000 mean troop strength. In infantry batallions, where a much higher proportion of men were directly exposed to combat, he states that for short periods of time the rates went as high as 1600–2000 per 1000 troops per year. Tompkins (1959) demonstrated a significant relationship between danger and the incidence of neurosis among combat fliers. As the actual danger involved in flying duty increased from training — to coastal reconnaissance — to night fighting — to day fighting — to night bombing, the relative incidence of neurosis also increased. It has also been shown that psychiatric attrition is a corollary of the intensity of combat (Glass, 1958; Appel, 1966). They utilized the number of wounded in action as a measure of the intensity of combat. Their data indicated that an increase in the number of battle injuries was invariably paralleled by an increase in the number of psychiatric casualties. Indeed, a ratio of one psychiatric casualty for every four battle casualties has prevailed with some consistency in combat situations since World War I.

Combat was not the sole correlate of attrition. For instance: In 1944, the admission rate for battle injuries for the Mediterranean Theater was 131 per 1000 mean troop strength as opposed to a rate of 34 per 1000 in the Southwest Pacific Area; nevertheless, the neuropsychiatric admission ratio was higher in the Southwest Pacific Area. Nonbattle factors, such as isolation, monotony, inadequate diet, lack of physical comfort, excessive physical demands, and illness, were indicted as causal agents contributing to the high incidence of emotional breakdown in privation rather than hazard situations (Menninger, 1948; Craighill, 1966). The impact of privation situations was shown to increase with time (Appel, 1966). Men who had been in the service for more than 18 months lost more man-days as a result of illness than those in the service for less than that amount of time.

Time emerges as an important variable in hazard as well as privation situations. Tompkin's (1959) data indicate an inverse relationship between the objective danger associated with a flying job and the relative flying hours per casualty spent on that job. The greater the harm-producing potency of the duty, the fewer flying hours an individual is likely to log before being labeled a casualty. Glass (1958) and Appel (1966) cite a number of reports and studies which relate the aggregate number of days of combat exposure to psychological breakdown. The concensus is that an average soldier can sustain between 80 and 100 aggregate days of combat before being "worn out." After that point, he is likely either to develop a frankly incapacitating neurosis or to become so hypersensitive to shellfire, overly cautious, and jittery that he is rendered ineffective. Data like this lent credence to the phrase "every man has his breaking point."

The phrase itself raises a question about the relationship between predisposition and the "breaking point." The answer to that question has proved evasive. One study of psychiatric casualties revealed that the majority had strong neurotic predispositions (Henderson and Moore, 1944) another showed that fliers who failed under minimal stress exhibited no neurotic predisposition (Hastings *et al.*, 1944). Still a third, cited by Grinker and Spiegel (1945), noted that of 150 men who successfully completed their tours, one-half had a previous life pattern of emotional instability. The consensus of investigators is, however, that men with histories of either severe emotional deprivation and frustration during childhood or of prior maladjustment in family, school, work, or the community are less likely to render effective military service and more likely to be vulnerable to hazard and privation conditions. Brill and Beebe (1955) found that men with preexisting overt neuroses had seven to eight times the chance of developing manifest psychiatric disorders while in the service than previously well-integrated men. The authors pointed out, however, that in all probability only one third of the men serving in the army who could have been disqualified on neuropsychiatric grounds at the time of induction, had their predisposition been known, became psychiatric casualties while in the service. Thus, the studies suggest that, while predisposition may render an individual vulnerable to circumstances in the combat situation, the circumstances per se trigger psychological breakdown. The proper quantity of a specific stimulus to which an individual is sensitized in a particular way determines whether or not that individual will become a psychiatric casualty.

Support for the above position comes from observations that both combat effectiveness and the frequency of psychiatric attrition vary considerably among units exposed to the same environmental hazards and privations. The variation is most generally attributed to differences in morale between the units. The term morale refers to the collective state of motivation existing within a group. It is a state that results from the interaction of a number of factors, including effective leadership, group cohesiveness, the knowledge that adequate rewards will be forthcoming for individual and group efforts, and a sense of purpose.

Leadership is charged with the production and maintenance of morale within a unit. Torrance (1954) compared the behaviors of leaders who led all or almost all of their group members to safety with that of leaders whose groups suffered unusually high casualty rates. He identified the capacity to exercise power, to maintain communication linkages between group members, to restructure a situation so as to meet changing demands, and to maintain a goal orientation as critical factors differentiating the effective from ineffective leader. Subsequent work by the same author (Torrance, 1958) indicated that expertness, willingness to share danger and discomfort, willingness to take risks, and willingness to make decisions were also qualities relevant to effective leadership. The importance of the bond between leader and led is underlined in an example cited by Appel (1966). He refers to a report from the Pacific Theater which indicated that the number of men evacuated from each company of an infantry division engaged in heavy combat was in direct proportion to the number of unit leaders evacuated.

Where leadership is effective, a strong sense of group cohesiveness develops. Grinker and Spiegel (1945) constantly refer to the cohesiveness developed by combat flying teams as the most potent of the available environmental resources. They point out that where cohesiveness is great, the probability of psychiatric attrition decreases. Observations concerning the performance of elite or special units tend to confirm the position of these authors.*

While numerous factors determine a unit's collective state of motivation, morale is best measured through the attitudes of the men toward the task at hand. Stouffer (1949), evaluating attitudes toward combat while in training and again immediately prior to D Day, found that units previously manifesting good attitudes toward combat suffered 30–60% fewer nonbattle casualties than units whose attitudes toward combat had not been as good. Morale and its corollaries, effective leadership and group cohesiveness, clearly operate as factors mitigating against psychological attrition.

B. The Resultant Paradigm

In the preceding pages, the multiple and varying factors identified by field observation, epidemiological research, and clinical studies as influencing the rate of psychiatric attrition have been reviewed. These factors fall into two major categories: (1) stressors — stimuli that strain an individual's adaptive capacities and (2) resources — supports that strengthen an individual's adaptive capabilities. In general, emotional breakdown was conceptualized as resulting from an imbalance between environmental stressors and resources.

More specifically, the paradigm evolved to explain psychiatric attrition held that each man has particular stressor tolerances and specific resource requirements. The balance between the two is

---

*See, for example, Summary and discussion of papers on ecology and epidemiology of mental illness. *In* "Symposium on Preventive and Social Psychiatry," pp. 199–206. U.S. Govt. Printing Office, Washington, D. C., 1958. Comments of the discussants indicate that Niesei troops serving in the Fifth and Seventh Infantry Divisions exhibited lower incidence rates for neuropsychiatric disorders even though they were frequently called upon to undertake extremely hazardous assignments. The same observation was made concerning an elite unit, the First Special Service Force in Italy.

determined by the personality structure of the individual and reflected in his stressor-stimuli threshold. It is an ideosyncratic balance. As long as the balance is maintained, however, that person will be able to come to terms with the situation at hand. If the balance is disturbed, either through an increase in stressor intensity or a decrease of available resources, than the signs of overt and covert psychiatric illness will begin to emerge. Not only must a given situation be of a given intensity to lead to a breakdown in effective psychic functioning, but it must also be of a given kind for a particular person.

A latency period precedes the "breaking point." During this time, the person appears fully able to cope with the demands confronting him. As time passes and the environment remains ostensibly unchanged, the demands intrude with a greater forcefulness and urgency. Stressor stimuli accumulate and build up in intensity. Ultimately, the individual's stressor-stimuli threshold is reached. At this point, the likelihood of psychological attrition increases materially.

II. The Present Study

Since the effects of stressors are cumulative, it should be possible to reduce attrition from psychological causes by imposing temporal limits upon exposure to stressors. Such limits are currently being imposed in Viet Nam by virtue of both the tactical situation and the 12-month rotation policy. Initial reports indicate that psychiatric disability is less prevalent than in preceding wars (Tiffany and Allerton, 1967; Strange and Arthur, 1967). The authors consider the decreased prevalence as due to: (1) The rigorous application of the principles of combat psychiatry, including early treatment in forward areas, deemphasis of the hospital atmosphere in favor of a military milieu, and the expectation of return to duty; (2) intermittent rather than continuous combat exposure with periods of relative calm interspersed; and (3) a limited, finite tour of duty. It is the aim of the present study to examine patterns of psychiatric attrition during the time-limited tour and to explore how individuals come to grips with a limited finite tour of duty. To accomplish this aim, data has been obtained from 200 enlisted men referred for evaluation and/or treatment to the neuropsychiatric service of an evacuation hospital in Viet Nam.

A. Characteristics of the Population

Table I contains a demographic profile of the 200 men. The majority were between the ages of 17 and 24 years, white, and single. Less than one-half of the group had completed high school. Of those who had, a little over a quarter went on to college. In terms of their army career, most were enlistees, rather than draftees, who had been in the service for less than 3 years. During their time in the service, the majority had achieved a rank of at least E-3, Private First Class. From a clinical standpoint, character and behavior disorders were by far the most common diagnoses. The diagnosis of psychosis or psychoneurosis was made in only 13% of the cases.

B. Time and Attrition

Figure 1 illustrates at what point in the tour the men were referred for evaluation. If one uses the number of referrals per unit of time spent in Viet Nam as a measure of attrition, the first 3 months represent the period of maximal vulnerability. Twenty-three percent of the men were referred during the first month of their tour, 11% during the second month, and 13% during the third. Thus, almost one-half of the men referred for neuropsychiatric evaluation and/or treatment had been in the combat zone for less than 4 months. Attrition falls off markedly after the third month. There is little variation in the number of referrals of men in the fourth through ninth months of their tour. After the ninth month, however, a gradual but progressive decrease can again be observed. Of the men referred, 5.5% were in the tenth month of their tour, 5% were in the eleventh month, and 2% were in the twelfth.

The data indicate that the relationship between time and psychiatric attrition is phasic. Periods of high, decreased, and minimal attrition are observed. The period of maximal attrition includes the first 3 months of the tour; the period of decreased attrition, the fourth through ninth months; and the period of minimal attrition, the final 3 months of the tour. For the 200 men seen, the mean rate of referrals per unit of time spent in Viet Nam was 31.3 during the period of maximal attrition, 13.5 during the period of decreased attrition, and 8.3 during the period of minimal attrition.

TABLE I
Characteristics of the Population

Demographic Features	Number	Percent
Age (years)		
18–20	84	42.0
21–24	75	37.5
25–29	21	10.5
30–39	19	9.0
40+	2	1.0
Marital status		
Single	124	62.0
Married	68	34.0
Divorced–separated	8	4.0
Race		
White	153	76.5
Negro	38	19.0
Other	9	4.5
Years of education		
0–8	24	12.0
9–11	78	39.0
12	73	36.5
13+	25	12.5
Military characteristics:		
Classification		
RA	139	69.5
US	61	30.5
Years in service		
less than 3	141	70.5
3–6	33	16.5
6+	26	13.0
Rank		
E-1	3	1.5
E-2	19	9.5
E-3	110	55.0
E-4	40	20.0
E-5	17	8.5
E-6	6	3.0
E-7	2	1.0
E-8	2	1.0
Clinical Diagnosis		
Psychosis	6	3.0
Psychoneurosis	20	10.0
Character and behavior disorder	117	58.5
Transient situational disorder	36	18.0
Other, including neurological disorders	21	10.5

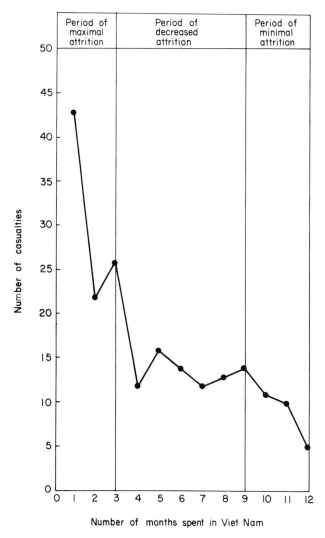

FIG. 1. *The number of casualties referred for psychiatric evaluation as a function of time spent in Viet Nam.*

As Table II indicates, the characteristics of the populations vary from period to period. Significant differences exist in relation to age, marital status, relations with parents, AWOL's, Article Fifteens, and court martials. Trends toward significance are noted for intactness of the nuclear family and military status such as classifi-

TABLE II
Phase-Specific Population Characteristics

	Period of:					
	Maximal attrition		Decreased attrition		Minimal attrition	
	Number	Percent	Number	Percent	Number	Percent
Age						
17–20	44	47	24	30	6	24
21 and over	50	53	63	70	19	76
Race						
White	75	80	63	78	17	68
Other	19	20	18	22	8	32
Marital status[a]						
Married	30	32	24	30	14	56
Other	64	68	57	70	11	44
Educational level						
less than 12	46	49	40	49	16	64
12 or more	48	51	41	51	9	36
Classification[b]						
RA	64	68	53	66	22	88
US	30	32	28	34	3	12
Rank[b]						
E-1 to E-3	63	67	57	70	12	48
E-4 or more	31	33	24	30	13	52
Time in army[b]						
less than 3 years	70	74	59	74	12	48
3 or more years	24	26	22	26	13	52
Family						
Relations with parents[c]:						
Positive	69	73	64	79	12	48
Negative	25	27	17	21	13	52
Nuclear family[b]:						
Intact	63	67	48	59	11	44
Not intact	31	33	33	41	14	56
Military service record						
AWOL[a]						
None	79	84	57	70	16	64
One or more	15	16	24	30	9	36
AR 15[a]						
None	61	65	40	49	10	40
Court martial[a]						
None	81	86	64	79	15	60
One or more	13	14	17	21	10	40

[a] χ^2 value significant at the 5% level.
[b] χ^2 value significant at the 10% level.
[c] χ^2 value significant at the 1% level.

cation, rank, and time in service. Sixty percent of the men between the ages of 17 and 20 presented during the initial 3 months of the tour. The majority came from nuclear families that were intact, neither parents being dead, separated, or divorced. Their relationship with their parents was described as positive. Over half had completed high school. Most were single. From a military standpoint, the greater proportion were enlistees who had been in service for less than 3 years and were of the rank of PFC. The service records of these men were better than those of men referred for evaluation in either of the subsequent periods. Note the increment in the proportion of men with AWOL offenses, Article Fifteens, and court martials between the period of maximal attrition and the period of decreased attrition. Indeed, service record and age are the factors that most differentiate these two groups. Their composition is fairly similar in other parameters. In contrast, the group referred during the period of minimal attrition is quite distinctive. More than three-quarters of the men were 21 years old or over. The majority came from nuclear families no longer intact and described negative relationships with their parents. Only 36% completed high school. The largest proportion of married men, enlistees, men with more than 3 years of military service, and men above the rank of E-3 are found in this group. The incidence of AWOL's, Article Fifteens, and court martials is greater during this period than during the others.

Thus, the data point not only to a phasic variation in psychiatric attrition during a time-limited tour in a combat zone, but also to the existence of a characteristic target population during each phase. In order to understand the relationship between time and psychiatric attrition, it is now necessary to examine each phase in more detail.

C. The Period of Maximal Attrition

Upon arrival in Viet Nam, an individual is plunged into an alien and hostile environment. At the debarkation point, he is bombarded by a host of new sights, smells, and sounds. Soon, because there are no front lines, the hazards of war encroach upon his life space. The newly arrived soldier does not know the harm-producing potential of this new environment. He is unsure of what stimuli represent cues of actual danger. He has not learned the most efficacious measures for avoiding or minimizing harm. The situation is both ambiguous and anomalous. As a result, the surrounding world seems fraught with danger. All new experiences are threatening. An enormous anxiety tempered with a sense of helplessness and hopelessness results from this confrontation with the unknown. The confrontation poses the finite threat of dissolution. While each man copes differently with the threat of dissolution, three basic patterns of action can be discerned. (1) Fusion with the group; (2) a search for authoritativeness; and (3) a flight into work.

Fusion with the group occurs almost immediately. During the initial 3 months of the tour, one rarely sees individuals by themselves. The fusion, however, is most dramatically visible at points of debarkation. Here, men stand and move only in groups. Their faces are dazed and frightened. The faces quickly coalesce. The face of the individual becomes the mask of the collective. This fusion renders the experience of anxiety more tolerable. It allows each man to say: "I am not alone. They are here as well. I am frightened, but they are frightened too." As a result, anxiety need not be thought of as either unique or a sign of individual weakness.

While fusion dilutes the anxiety of the individual, the collective remains threatened by the strange and unfamiliar world in which it finds itself. In response to this threat, the collective initiates a search for authoritativeness. The intent of the search is to find some one figure who possesses sufficient expertise and power to impose a certain degree of order on a frightening external world. This person is endowed with omnipotence and omniscience. His presence creates a feeling of security within the group that further attenuates anxiety. Affiliation, such as that derived from fusion with the group, and reassurance, such as that stemming from a successful search for authoritativeness, have been shown to be effective mechanisms for decreasing hypervigilance and anxiety (Ruesch and Prestwood, 1949; Hudson, 1954; Janis, 1962). They represent attempts to use objects from the immediate environment as counterharm agents. Where successful, these mechanisms sufficiently attenuate anxiety so as to enable both men and groups to address themselves to the task at hand. Previously, every environmental stimulus had been reacted to as though it were a threat — a distraction that made task performance extremely problematic. At this point, one observes a flight into work. The men apply themselves with diligence both to tasks related to the unit's primary mission and to others that give shape to their living areas.

Each man's attention now becomes focused upon a narrower parameter of their immediate life space. As a result, a stimulus barrier is constructed which keeps out extraneous input from the surrounding unknown. This barrier further helps to attenuate anxiety.

The mechanisms of fusion with the group, the search for authoritativeness, and the flight into work do much to contain the free-floating anxiety generated by the men's confrontation with the unknown. There is, however, another form of anxiety noted in the men during the initial months of the tour. It is an anomic anxiety which stems from the realization that many of the transcendent values and basic assumptions previously governing transactions in and with the world are not entirely relevant to present circumstances. Similar experiences of anomie have been described in other transition states, particularly where men have been propelled into extreme situations. These include descriptions of concentration camps (Frankl, 1959; Biderman, 1967), communist prisons (Lifton, 1963), internment camps (Opler, 1967), and disaster situations (Janis, 1962). The experience of anomie and its attendant anxiety evokes in the men a boundless longing for home. To deal with this longing, each soldier attempts to cling tenaciously to all available reminders of the past. These attempts are reflected in the "I was" rather than "I am" focus of conversations, the expectant wait for mail from home, and the painful but repetitive recapitulations of the last days before embarkation. The men are engaged in an escape into the past. The escape is not merely a nostalgic exercise. Neither is it entirely an attempt to deny present realities. Rather, the escape into the past represents a mechanism for bringing into apposition the threads of past and present. Erikson (1950) has demonstrated the potency of temporal discontinuity as a stressor in combat situations. In the case of Sam, the Marine, he pointed out that when one's sense of continuity and sameness becomes disrupted, a crisis of identity ensues. It is as though one's life no longer hung together. This is an experience with which the new arrivee in Viet Nam must contend. His escape into the past makes it possible to forge a symbolic bond linking the temporal dimension of the past to that of the present. This bond reestablishes a sense of continuity and sameness and materially lessens the anomic anxiety which the men are experiencing.

Free-floating anxiety is attenuated through a fusion with the group, a search for authoritativeness, and a flight into work.

Anomic anxiety is dealt with by an escape into the past. The former mechanisms lower individual anxiety levels enough to enable each man to engage in the task at hand and learn new behaviors relevant to his current life situation. The latter, escape into the past, allows the soldier to perform the tasks and learn the requisite new behaviors without the threat of identity discontinuity. Where these mechanisms are operational, the adaptive capabilities of the men are enhanced. Individuals unable to avail themselves of these mechanisms have marked difficulty in coming to terms with life in the combat zone. The following case is illustrative:

Jim, an 18-year-old E-3, had been in Viet Nam for 8 days before being referred to the medical service of the hospital for evaluation of severe abdominal pain and constipation. The pain had been present since his arrival in the combat zone. When no evidence of organic pathology was found, a psychiatric evaluation was requested.

During the initial interview, Jim talked primarily about the 2 weeks preceding his arrival in Viet Nam. Most of that time had been spent on leave at home. He had wanted to say goodbye to his family: "You know! There's always the possibility that you won't see them again. I don't really believe that, but it is something that had to be done." As he began to talk about his father, he became tense, grimaced, and complained about a wave of intense pain: "I remember my dad's last words to me. 'Whatever happens Jimmy, don't ever be afraid. The Man up there will look after you just the way he's always looked after me.'" Jim then remarked, almost as an aside, that his father had lost a leg during the Second World War: "He said that he didn't whimper or nothing—just lay there with all hell going on around him. He's quite a guy!"

Jim began the second session by talking about himself. He was the third son in a family of four. There was one younger sister. The family got along quite well. They did a lot together: "Dad always wanted us to have the best and to be the best. Like football, now he must have started training me when I was 7. Geez! I remember getting up early in the morning and having him put the three of us through his program. Every weekend. Then he'd take us to see games. It was great!" Jim had gone on to high school and made the team. Still, he tended to keep to himself quite a bit, had few friends, and preferred the company of his family. He described his mother as "small, sweet, and soft as mush. She'd always listen to dad." Upon graduating, he had enlisted in the army. Basic training was uneventful, although he neither enjoyed it nor made many friends. Afterwards he went on to train as a radio technician. He received orders to report to Viet Nam as a replacement. The company had been in the country for over 6 months when Jim arrived. He found it "hard to get in with the guys. They sort of called me a crab." When he went to his first sergeant to tell him about his abdominal pain, the sergeant remarked: "Look kid, we all suffer here!" Jim pondered about that remark for a second and then began to talk about his flight to Viet Nam:

> You know I couldn't for the life of me pick out a seat. I didn't want to sit down—like man, if you did then the plane would take off—but if you didn't, well then *it* wouldn't. And then, like the problem of where to sit— you know, what part of the plane was safer, which would float better if we went down over the ocean. Now why in God's name was I worried about that? It's almost like I was sure that I was going to die. Hell! I didn't know what I was getting myself into, but there's one thing for sure— whatever it was, I didn't want it. You know, Captain, it just occurred to me that I was scared shitless!

I remarked that it seemed to me as though he still was, and, until he came to terms about whether or not it was all right for a man to be afraid, he might very well continue to be. Over the next few days, Jim began to visit the surgical wards and talk to the wounded. He listened intently as they told about their experiences and dutifully noted how frightened these men had been. This was a boy who had been unable to fuse with the group, partly because of an inherent aloofness, partly because of being a replacement. His search for authoritativeness had met with rebuff. Anxiety was of such intensity that it effectively prohibited a flight into work. But the root of his dilemma lay in an inability to escape into the past. The route was blocked because of his fear. Fear was totally dissonant to his sense of self. It was a response that had been deemed unacceptable within his family. To be afraid made it impossible to establish a viable symbolic bond between the past and the present. Thus, none of the adaptive mechanisms utilized by the men during their initial months in Viet Nam were available to the patient, and patienthood was the result:

For others, however, the escape into the past could not be handled on just a symbolic level. The longing for home goes unrequited. The present becomes intolerable, and attrition is likely to result:

John was 20 years old when he arrived in Viet Nam. He had been in the army for 9 months before being assigned overseas. Up to this point, he had encountered no difficulties either in basic training or the transportation company to which he was assigned. When I first saw John, his face was a mask of despair. He shuffled into the office, eyes downcast, sat down, put his hands over his eyes, and burst into tears: "I can't do it Doc. Without her I'm nothing—nothing but an empty room."

The patient had been in Viet Nam for only 3 weeks. During that period, he had received no mail from his wife. He had written to her each day, frequently twice, but still there was no answer. He had been married 17 months to a girl whom he had known all of his life.

> When I sit down to write her I see my whole life going on before me—I can see our folks, our home town—everything that means something. It's almost like it's right there to touch, and I want to touch it so bad.

When John first received his orders, he and his wife, Evelyn, sat down, talked about what would happen, and began to think about the plans that had to be made. Evelyn was pregnant. It was decided that she should go to Chicago and live with her parents. John arranged for allotments. He felt that he could get along on $25 a month. The rest would go to his wife. As he went on, it became more and more apparent how interdependent he and his wife were: "Since I've been here, I've never felt so all alone, so cut off." A week after his arrival, he began to think: "What's going on with Ev? Is she settled in? Is she O.K.?" These questions all remained unanswered. Sleep became fitful. His appetite decreased. He became quite restless. During this time, he was working 14–16 hours a day. Then the nature of the questions began to change: "How can I get home?"—that question and its permutations began to plague him. He went to the company commander and was told: "John, I understand the problem. I feel the same way about my wife, and we'll all get home. But first there's a job to be done." John went next to the Chaplain and then to Red Cross. Each time the answer was the same. He began to feel more hopeless and despondent. One night, he bought a bottle of whiskey, found a quiet place in the compound, and began to drink. When the pint was finished, he returned to his tent and slashed his wrists.

During the initial months there were numerous stories like John's. Some of the men had received letters, some had not. The strain that ran through all the stories, however, was an inability to work on a symbolic level — to forge an internal bond between the past and the present that would make separation tolerable.

In the preceding pages, we have explored the impact of a confrontation with the unknown that occurs during the initial 3 months of a time-limited tour in Viet Nam. The confrontation is not only replete with environmental hazards and privations that are potentially finite, but also filled with major psychosocial dilemmas that stem from transition. The impact of both environmental and psychosocial factors is profound. This is apparent in both the nature and the number of referrals for psychiatric evaluation during this time period. As a group, the men have reported positive family relations. Over half had completed high school, one-third going on to college. Their military service records have fewer blemishes than those of the men referred at other times during the tour. The data suggests that we are dealing with a group of men who have been relatively successful in dealing with previous life tasks. That the period of maximal attrition involves a group who had shown a relatively high degree of success in mastering previous role functions indicates that the transition from noncombat to combat duty represents the most serious challenge to the men's adaptive capabilities encountered during the tour.

D. The Period of Decreased Attrition

By the fourth month, each man has acquired a certain degree of mastery over his present environment. Experiences during the initial months now allow for a more accurate differentiation between actual and fantasized hazards. Each man has experimented with numerous behaviors and knows the viability of each as a mode for dealing with particular situations. This, in turn, leads to greater proficiency in judging what situations can or cannot be mastered. There is ample experimental evidence indicating that these factors can materially decrease the degree of threat perceived as existing in the environment. Lazarus (1966) has extensively reviewed the literature on this point. He also indicates that as the inherent ambiguity of a situation decreases as a result of learning and experience, an individual's ability to cope with that environment is enhanced. The increased capability for coping with the environment is coupled with the knowledge of the cost for leaving that environment prematurely. It is calculated in terms of pain and bodily harm. For most, the cost is unacceptable. This cost knowledge plus an increased sense of mastery over an alien world make it possible for the men to come to terms with their present environment. The acceptance is heralded by a retreat from the past. The retreat is evident in the conversations of the men which now focus on their day-by-day activities and in a lessened preoccupation with home and family.

The retreat from the past is not unique to the combat zone. Bettleheim (1943) has described it as a phasic response of inmates in concentration camps. In Viet Nam, the retreat is accompanied by the gradual emergence of an informal social structure, the hedonistic pseudocommunity. The community is an outgrowth of a quest for pleasure and dominant materialism that begins to assert itself during the second quarter of the tour. The hedonism of the men parallels a realization that, while it is not possible to avoid hazards inherent in the combat zone, it is possible to materially influence the state of privation. The quest for pleasure is first noted as the men begin to move out of their compounds into the restaurants, bars, and brothels of town. It reaches its zenith with rest and recreation (R & R), the programmed escape into the exotic. Materialism is in evidence everywhere. One need only walk into a tent in the support area. There will almost invariably be a refrigerator well stocked with soda, beer, and even champagne. Hi-fi and camera magazines abound, and the music coming from the stereo tape recorders competes with the vociferous arguments of the men over which camera, audio, or luxury items one should buy.

The prime mover in the pseudocommunity is the "scrounger." He is a man with special talent in the art of acquisition. Over the months, he has built up an elaborate network of contacts. If you have hamburger, he can get you bread; if you have lues and do not want to go on report, he can see to it that you receive penicillin; if you want an item that is not presently in stock at the PX, he knows the wheres and hows of obtaining it. There is a price. It may be exacted in goods or in service as well as money. The spirit of "Catch-22" abounds.

But the hedonistic pseudocommunity should not merely be regarded as an attempt to restructure reality and make it more palatable. It must be remembered that these men have been in the combat zone for between 3 and 9 months. During that time, each has been forced to come to grips with the demands inherent in the situation. They have had to learn new behaviors. They have been forced to surrender a good deal of autonomous functioning. They have been exposed to death at first hand. All of this occurs in a setting that is essentially hostile — a setting in which they are cut off from those objects that in the past had provided nurturance. The men are literally in a state of psychological bankruptcy. Their resources have been overdrawn. Their egos are depleted. The hedonistic pseudocommunity with its intrinsic narcissism and acquisitiveness allows each man respite and an opportunity to replenish his resources.

The increased mastery over the environment, the knowledge of the cost for leaving the environment prematurely, and the gradual emergence of a structure that tends to nourish the men's depleted psychological resources all account for the decrease in psychiatric attrition noted between the fourth and ninth months of the tour. For some, however, the quest for pleasure and the task of soldiering are incompatible. The incompatibility is evident in the composition of the group referred for psychiatric evaluation during the period of decreased attrition. The majority of the men were over 21, white, and single. They came from nuclear families that were intact and most had enjoyed positive relations with their parents. Over half had completed high school. While most were enlistees who had been in the service for less than 3 years and achieved a rank of E-3, their adaptation to the military had been less than spectacular. The relative incidence of AWOL's, Article Fifteens, and court martials is high. It is a group that has demonstrated some success in role functioning prior to the military. It is also a group that has been in conflict with military hierarchy since entering the system. Indeed, the largest percentage of referrals for evaluation in relation to impending disciplinary action comes from this group.

Conflict between the hedonistic pseudocommunity and the established military hierarchy was not the sole reason for referral during the period of decreased attrition. A number of men were referred after being overwhelmed in an encounter of high hazard potency. Still others were referred not because the quest for pleasure and the task of soldiering were incompatible, but because a flight into hedonism made return to combat intolerable:

Henry was a 21-year-old enlisted man who had been in Viet Nam for some 7 months prior to his referral. He was a member of an airborne unit that had been engaged in fairly heavy combat since its arrival. Four weeks prior to his referral, the company had been surrounded while on a search and destroy operation. A saturation bombing of the area was requested. After the bombing, the enemy withdrew and the company returned to base camp. The cost, however, had been heavy. A number of Henry's close buddies had been killed or wounded. Henry did not remember talking very much about the buddies upon his return to base camp. He was all caught up with the realization that he had emerged unscathed. Besides, he was to leave on R & R the following week. The unit did not engage in combat during that week. Henry had a good deal of time to contemplate what he would be doing when he got to Thailand. His description of R & R was of a complete surrender to pleasure. There were girls and "booze." The days and nights were quiet. He had no thought of killing or being killed. However, R & R lasted only 5 days. As the time came to return to Viet Nam, he noticed that his heart was beating more rapidly, that he was sick to his stomach, and that he was restless and "all tied up in knots." Upon return, he heard that the unit had a new CO who was reputed to be a "bastard" and a "glory-hound, John Wayne type." The actual return to the unit was a lonely affair. There had been another mission in his absence. Casualties had again been high. Of the squad to which he was assigned, he was now the only "old timer." "I felt like a stranger in my own home, and that home didn't look so good either." He began to get suspicious of the new men. He thought that they were talking about him and planning to steal the things that he had brought back from Thailand. The next evening, Henry picked up an M-16. He pointed it at one of the new men, accused the man of wanting to laugh at him, and threatened to shoot. A number of men jumped on him. He was subdued and evacuated shortly thereafter.

E. The Period of Minimal Attrition

As the men enter the last 3 months of the tour, their attention shifts. They become oriented to the future. Previously, the conversations about "the land of the great PX" had been tentative and subdued. Talk would continue for a few minutes and then give way to a consideration of the present. Now there is an aura of excitement and anticipation as they delve back and recollect the images of home, family, friends, and things forgotten. Elaborate plans are made about how the first few hours will be spent—and then the conversation drifts beyond the immediate return and further into the realm of aspiration. Plans for the future are cast in the fading light of the present, and everything is ringed in ebullience and ideality. Still, there is the present to contend with. In combat areas, caution becomes the byword. A feeling of resentment that approaches loathing and hatred occurs when combat missions are called for. Having survived at least 9 months, no man wants to be "zapped" with the end of the tour so palpable. In support areas, fewer people leave the compound. The number who leave decreases each week. The present lingers on, but now tempered with nostalgia, as the men reminisce about the past months spent in Viet Nam. Characteristically, however, the present is talked about in the context of the past. It is almost as though no present should exist. There must only be past and future. The magnetism of the future is so compelling that it blurs the realities of the present and inevitably causes each man to withdraw somewhat from both the environment and the group. The process of disengagement has begun and will continue until the tour is ended.

The group referred for psychiatric evaluation during this period is quite distinctive. It includes the largest proportion of men coming from disrupted nuclear families. Over one-half of the men report negative relations with their parents. Only 36% have completed high school. While the largest proportion of married to unmarried–separated–divorced men are found in this group, more than half (57%) have not received letters from home. The majority are enlistees who have achieved a rank of E-4 or above. Almost half have been in the army for more than 3 years. Despite these indicators of a potential career choice in the military, their service records are extremely poor. Thirty-six percent have at least one AWOL offense on their records; 60% have received one or more Article Fifteens; and, 40% have been court martialed at least once. This is clearly a group of men who have encountered difficulty in mastering a host of role tasks during the course of their lives. They are, in a sense, role failures.

The clinical picture presented by this group supports the notion that a relationship exists between role failure and psychiatric attrition during the last 3 months of the tour. For some, it is a past failure as a son, a husband, a father. The future holds little except more of the same. It is as though life offered no meaningful alternatives. They experience an apathetic disenchantment. For others, however, the threat of present failure in role acts as a catalyst:

Sergeant Graham was referred for psychiatric evaluation following an incident where he had become intoxicated and assaultive. The Sergeant had been in Viet Nam for 11 months. During that time, he had received two letters from his wife: "No sweat Doc, we haven't had anything to say to each other for years." The marriage had been a stormy one. Separations were frequent. They generally resulted from his drinking which was heavy but intermittent.

The Sergeant had been brought up in a foster home. His mother had left his father and him when he was 4 years old. His father, a burly, hard drinking man, could not take care of the boy and had him placed in a home. Several months later, his father disappeared, and Sergeant Graham grew up as a ward of the state. He dropped out of school in the ninth grade: "That book stuff didn't make no sense, and the teachers just wanted to lord it over you." The next few years were spent moving from job to job: "I looked. They looked, and then it was over!" He enlisted in the army, where he had remained for 14 years. Since being in the military, the Sergeant had been reduced in grade three times, always as a result of drunken and disorderly conduct. Each time, he had succeded in earning his grade back. The sergeant was a master mechanic. He had volunteered for Viet Nam to "better myself and get away from my wife." His initial assignment was as a replacement. The bulk of the company to which he had been assigned had left the country some 2 months before. "You see Doc, this new CO—he just doesn't understand me." Sergeant Graham then related a long story about how this "snot right out of college" had questioned his SOP, complained about the slovenliness of his tent, and "just had it in for me in general ever since he got here." His response was characteristic: "If he doesn't like the way I do things, he can go to hell!" At first, though, the sergeant restrained himself: "I wanted that promotion, and I was damned if I would blow the game by exploding in that bastard's face." While the sergeant did not explode, neither did he modify his work habits. The complaints continued. The sergeant concluded that "nothing I do, even if I do something," would make a difference. He was certain that his promotion would not be forthcoming and "the freakin' tour was just another bust." Having reached these conclusions, Sergeant Graham became sullen and began to drink. The drinking had been going on fairly steadily for some 4 weeks and resulted in his being gigged on several occasions. After the last episode, his commanding officer referred him for psychiatric evaluation. Administrative action was pending.

Yet perceived or anticipated role failure were not the only reasons for psychiatric referral during the last months of the tour. For some, the process of disengagement proved inordinately difficult. The months spent in close proximity to a small group of exquisitely interdependent comrades in arms saw the evolution of strong interpersonal bonds. These bonds did not loosen easily, and during this period various depths of depression were experienced. Grinker and Spiegel (1945) have commented on this syndrome as it occurred during the Second World War. For others, particularly combat troops, there was a fear that in the last few weeks of the tour "our luck will run out." Glass (1958) noted such a "short-timer's" syndrome in combat troops during the Korean War. It consisted of disabling tension and phobia occurring in the last weeks or days of a combat tour that made it impossible for the men to function on the line. Strange and Arthur (1967) report similar phenomena in Marines during the tenth and eleventh months of their combat tour in Viet Nam.

Despite the fear of death or injury with rotation so near at hand, the perception or anticipation of role failure, or the pain of disengagement, the last 3 months of the tour represented the period of minimal psychiatric attrition. This is in large part due to the magnetism of the future. From the moment of arrival in the combat zone, existence is titrated to the anticipated date of departure. As the endpoint is reached during the final 3 months of the tour, all else fades into the background. The hopes, wishes, and expectancies render the present in many ways irrelevant and project the men into the future. The idealized future thus acts as an additional support strengthening the internal resources of the men and rendering them less vulnerable to hazards, privations, and adaptive strains during the terminal part of the tour.

III. Concluding Remarks

In studying the relationship between time spent in the combat zone and psychiatric attrition, a periodicity of attrition was noted. During each period, the group of men presenting themselves for psychiatric evaluation exhibited certain distinctive characteristics. These characteristics, when considered as indices of prior psychosocial adaptation, revealed that the soldiers presenting during the initial three months of the tour had been relatively successful in mastering role tasks prior to combat duty, those presenting in the fourth through ninth months of the tour had functioned relatively adequately in their role prior to entering military service, while the group evaluated during the final 3 months of the tour appeared to have experienced considerable difficulty in role functioning both prior to and in the military. To better understand the interrelation of periodicity of attrition and population specificity, behavioral trends typifying each period were examined. These trends or patterns of behavior were shown to be in the service of negotiating some core psychosocial dilemma. The dilemmas were those of transition, depletion, and disengagement. They arose at specific times in the tour. Thus, at a particular time in the tour, each man was confronted by a specific psychosocial dilemma that had to be dealt with. The impact of the confrontation is reflected in both the phase-specific attrition rates and the population characteristics. In other words, the drama of the time-limited combat tour can be said to unfold in three phases. The periodicity of psychiatric attrition and the population specificity result from the inability of particular individuals to negotiate a dominant psychosocial dilemma which becomes ascendant at a sequentially predictable time during the course of the tour. The relationship between dilemma, attrition, specificity, and time is outlined in Table III.

TABLE III

Time-Related Psychosocial Dilemmas, Population Specificity, and Psychiatric Attrition

Time spent in Viet Nam	1–3 months	4–9 months	10–12 months
Psychosocial dilemma	Transition	Depletion	Disengagement
Population specificity	Relatively successful role functioning prior to combat duty	Relatively successful role functioning prior to military service. Conflict within structure of the military	Problematic functioning in various social roles prior to military. Indications of relatively consistent role failure
Psychiatric attrition	Maximal	Decreased	Minimal

All this has not been by way of refuting the validity of the paradigm for psychiatric attrition presented in Section I. In dealing with patterns of behavior and patterns of attrition, in translating population characteristics into indices of role performance, and in looking at the process of "coming to terms" in a psychosocial context, however, our attention has inevitably been drawn to man's symbolic as well as physical universe. The importance of the latter has been consistently demonstrated in the literature. The role of symbolic reality as both stressor and resource has been approached somewhat more tentatively. Perhaps that is because symbolic reality is difficult to measure or quantify. Yet in our consideration of identity discontinuity, we have seen the importance of symbolic reality as a stressor. Conversely, our consideration of the idealization of the future indicated the use of that system as a resource. From the moment that man employs something to stand for or represent another thing, he interposes a symbolic system between receptors and effectors. He learns to use the system to modify and manipulate physical reality and thus acquires a new and unique method for coming to terms with the world around him. Symbolic processes inevitably play a role in human adaptation. This is true in extreme situations as well as the normal course of events.

The present chapter has been devoted to exploring the interplay between symbolic and physical reality. Both confront men as stressors and are drawn upon as resources. We have seen how the finiteness of sequential time, physical reality, and the idealization of time, symbolic reality, can both strain and support an individual's adaptive capabilities. The results suggest that if one is to consider man and how he relates to men, to himself, and to the world around him in a situation that is alien and threatening, but finite, attention must be paid not only to environmental stressors and resources, emotional supports, predispositions, behaviors, psychosocial dilemmas, and psychiatric attrition, but to symbolic processes as well.

REFERENCES

Appel, J. W. (1966). *In* "Neuropsychiatry in World War II" (R. S. Anderson, A. J. Glass, and R. J. Bernucci, eds.), Vol. I, pp. 373-415. U.S. Govt. Printing Office, Washington, D.C.

Bettleheim, B. (1943). Individual and mass behavior in extreme situations. *J. Abnormal Social Psychol.* **38**, 417.

Biderman, A. D. (1967). *In* "Psychological Stress" (M. H. Appley and R. Trumbull, eds.), pp. 242-264. Appleton-Century-Crofts, New York.

Brill, N. Q., and Beebe, B. W. (1955). "A Follow-up Study of War Neuroses." Veterans Admin. Med. Monograph. U.S. Govt. Printing Office, Washington, D.C.

Craighill, M. D. (1966). *In* "Neuropsychiatry in World War II" (R. S. Anderson, A. J. Glass, and R. J. Bernucci, eds.), Vol. I, pp. 417-474. U.S. Govt. Printing Office, Washington, D.C.

Erikson, E. (1950). "Childhood and Society." Norton, New York.

Frankl, V. E. (1959). "From Death Camp to Existentialism." Beacon Press, Boston, Massachusetts.

Glass, A. J. (1958). *In* "Symposium on Preventive and Social Psychiatry," pp. 185–197. U.S. Govt. Printing Office, Washington, D.C.

Grinker, R. R., and Spiegel, J. P. (1945). "Men Under Stress." McGraw-Hill (Blakiston), New York.

Hastings, D. W., Wright, D. G., and Glueck, B. C. (1944). "Psychiatric Experiences of the Eighth Air Force, First Year of Combat (July 4, 1942–July 4, 1943)." Josiah Macy, Jr., Found., New York.

Henderson, J. L., and Moore, M. (1944). The psychoneuroses of war. *New Engl. J. Med.* **230,** 273.

Hudson, B. B. (1954). Anxiety in response to the unfamiliar. *J. Social Issues* **10,** 53.

Janis, I. L. (1962). *In* "Man and Society in Disaster" (G. W. Baker and D. W. Chapman, eds.), pp. 55–92. Basic Books, New York.

Lazarus, R. S. (1966). "Psychological Stress and the Coping Process." McGraw-Hill, New York.

Lifton, R. J. (1963). "Thought Reform and the Psychology of Totalism." Norton, New York.

Menninger, W. C. (1948). "Psychiatry in a Troubled World." Macmillan, New York.

Opler, M. K. (1967). *In* "Psychological Stress" (M. H. Appley and R. Trumbull, eds.), pp. 209–233. Appleton-Century-Crofts, New York.

Ruesch, J., and Prestwood, A. (1949). Anxiety; its initiation, communication and interpersonal management. *A.M.A. Arch. Neurol. Psychiat.* **62,** 527.

Stouffer, S. A. (1949). "The American Soldier," Vols. I and II. Princeton Univ. Press, Princeton, New Jersey.

Strange, R. E., and Arthur, R. J. (1967). Hospital ship psychiatry in a war zone. *Am. J. Psychiat.* **124,** 281.

Tiffany, W. J., Jr., and Allerton, W. S. (1967). Army psychiatry in the mid-60s. *Am. J. Psychiat.* **123,** 810.

Tompkins, V. H. (1959). *In* "The Nature of Stress Disorder" (J. Hambling, ed.), pp. 73–80. Thomas, Springfield, Illinois.

Torrance, E. P. (1954). The behavior of small groups under the stress conditions of survival. *Am. Sociol. Rev.* **19,** 751.

Torrance, E. P., (1958). *In* "Symposium on Preventive and Social Psychiatry," pp. 309–326. U.S. Govt. Printing Office, Washington, D.C.

3 // Psychiatry in the Army of The Republic of Viet Nam

Nguyen Duy San

I. Introduction

Modern psychiatry is relatively new in Viet Nam. The average man has only a vague conception of what psychiatry is or what psychiatrists do. The prevailing understanding, not only of laymen but also of many physicians, is that psychiatry is a specialty of medicine which deals with the care of "insane people." They expect psychiatric patients to be wild and dangerous, even homicidal, and believe that psychiatry is concerned only with severe psychotic reactions for which not much help can be given.

This misconception about psychiatry and the stigma attached to mental illness have delayed the integration of psychiatry into medical education. At the present time, the Saigon Medical School does not have an independent department of psychiatry; the professor of neurology gives the lectures in psychiatry, usually in a perfunctory manner. For the whole of South Viet Nam with a population of 17,000,000 people, there are only three psychiatric facilities with five practicing psychiatrists.

The first facility for the treatment of the mentally ill in Viet Nam was Cho Quan Hospital. Founded in 1862 and primarily specializing in the treatment of communicable diseases, this hospital began to receive psychiatric patients only in 1908. Its psychiatric section is now a 350-bed receiving and acute treatment service, staffed by an internist and a trained psychiatrist who assumes also the administrative responsibility of hospital director.

The Bien Hoa Mental Hospital, situated some 20 miles northeast of Saigon, was established in 1919 and has expanded into a 2000-bed hospital, housing many chronic patients, but also receiving acute cases from the various provinces. Its medical staff consists of two psychiatrists, one internist, and a half-time physician who is employed to take care of tuberculous patients. Except for some 300 patients in the acute treatment service who receive fairly adequate treatment, the remainder of the patients have no treatment program other than custodial care.

In the ancient imperial city of Hue in central Viet Nam, the psychiatric service of the city general hospital has a capacity of 40 beds and is under the supervision of a nonpsychiatric physician.

The Army of the Republic of Viet Nam (ARVN) has its own central psychiatric service in Saigon, which provides care for military neuropsychiatric casualties coming from all parts of the country. The following chapter will give a glimpse into the activities of this service and the management of mental illness in the Vietnamese Army.

First, a brief review of the sociocultural setting and historical background might well offer some clues to the understanding of the average Vietnamese soldier, the vast majority of whom are peasants born and raised in rural areas.

II. Sociocultural Background

A. Cultural Roots

Because of its geographical situation, Viet Nam has been a crossroads for many currents of thought and civilizations. Lying halfway between China and India, Viet Nam early felt the influence of the ancient cultures of these two countries. Buddhism was introduced into the country in the second century A.D., by sea from India and by road from China. Later came Confucianism and Taoism during the Chinese domination. Roman Catholicism was imported in the sixteenth century by Western missionaries, particularly the French. Recently, Protestantism began to spread over the country.

The predominant feature in religious life in Viet Nam is an harmonious blend of Buddhism–Confucianism–Taoism with other elements belonging to native animism and beliefs that existed even before the three great religions were introduced into the country. The Vietnamese are not deeply religious in the Western sense. Religion represents for them a way of life rather than a sacred appeal to a supreme being. When we examine the thoughts of a typical Vietnamese, we can find intermingled with the traditional beliefs the pervasive spirit of Buddhism, the nonaction philosophy of Taoism, and the sense of responsibility drawn from the ethical principles of Confucianism.

During the ten centuries under direct Chinese rule, the Vietnamese absorbed significant elements of China's religious and philosophical doctrines, social system, and methods of administration. While assimilating Chinese culture and using Chinese characters, they managed to retain their language and ethnic identity and finally threw off Chinese rule to establish an independent country. Few people are more acutely conscious of their history than the Vietnamese. The first ancient Viet tribes inhabited a large area in China, south of the Yantze River. Overwhelmed by the strong assimilative pressure from the Chinese in the North, they began a great southward exodus and chose as their new home the delta of the Red River. They continued their expansion to the south, conquered and absorbed the Kingdom of Champa, colonized the lower Mekong delta, and finally, at the first half of the nineteenth century, annexed much of Laos and became suzerain over the rest of Laos and Cambodia (Bain, 1967). Throughout all the vicissitudes of their 4000-year history, the Vietnamese have repelled some 20 invasions from China and foreign forces. Deeply resenting foreign control, the Vietnamese have developed a sense of patriotism which constitutes the strongest driving force capable of mobilizing the whole people to sacrifice their lives and property in order to safeguard their independence and liberty. National heroes and heroines are venerated in shrines and cults. Their exploits are portrayed in historical dramas; they are deified in legends and glorified in epics and folk songs. From childhood, the Vietnamese have listened to the story of their origin which says that the Vietnamese race was the product of the mating of the races of dragons and immortals. They are all aware that their ancestors three times defeated the Mongols (one of the most awesome military forces on earth), and they all know how Emperor Quang-Trung, the Vietnamese Napoleon, annihilated a 200,000-man Chinese army in a lightning battle while the enemies were celebrating their lunar New Year. Such stories among many others have fed a sense of racial superiority and acted as a cement holding together a social structure based on a broad nationalistic spirit.

B. The Family System

The basic building block of the Vietnamese society is the family. Several families form a village which constitutes the economic, social, political, and religious unit of the nation. A man owes allegiance first to his family, then to his village, and finally to the nation. The traditional village is an almost autonomous state, collectively responsible for the behavior and wellbeing of its members. The Vietnamese peasant is as strongly attached to his natal village as he is to his cherished plot of ground. His world is small, and usually his interests do not go far beyond the village sphere. However, he could be aroused to defend his country valiantly in the face of foreign invasions.

Approximately 80% of the Vietnamese population lives in the countryside, and even city dwellers still keep their ties to their village; they often go back to their village to special family gatherings or to visit family tombs.

A Vietnamese family is traditionally patriarchal and includes three generations living under the same roof. It has been compared to a tree, the father being the trunk, living descendants the branches, and the ancestors the roots. A wife is a branch grafted onto the husband's tree. Within the home, the father is administrator, judge, educator, and high priest of the family cult. The mother takes care of the children and is the family business manager (Bain, 1967). A reflection of the Confucian ethic of "Hieu," or filial piety, continues to be the primary virtue of a well-educated person. "Hieu" is manifested in the veneration of ancestors, respect and care for elders, obedience to parents, hard work, and good behavior in order to promote family fame. Children must put the welfare of their elders before their own. The older the parents, the more they are pampered. A dutiful daughter might not marry if there is no son to tend the parents. A son has the sacred obligation to provide male children to perpetuate the ancestor cult and to carry on the patrilineage.

Marriages are generally arranged by the parents or elder relatives of the young persons. The astrologer is first consulted to see that the ages of the couple are compatible and the stars governing their destinies are not antagonistic to each other; then a lucky day is fixed for the celebration of the wedding party. Nowadays, romances and marriages by choice have become more and more frequent. However, in some traditional families, parents' disapproval can still constitute a serious obstacle which might even lead to the suicide of the young couple in some rare instances.

Child-rearing practices vary a great deal from one family to another. In general, infancy is marked by indulgence and constant attention. An infant usually sleeps with its mother and spends most of the time with her. Should it cry, it is always picked up, fed, and comforted. The mother may even hold the child while it naps; she used to recline in a hammock, singing the lullaby, with the child comfortably sleeping in her lap. When the child is more than a year old, it is cared for a great deal of the time by one of its older siblings.

Most of the children receive breast feeding until the age of 2 or 3 years. When a child is hungry, it simply asks for food and in most instances receives it. Weaning is accomplished gradually; however, it might be sudden and irrevocable, usually precipitated by the birth of another child. In such cases, the mother absents herself from the home for a day or two, and on her return, she will dissuade the child by smearing the breast with some peppery or bitter substance. The child's complaints are turned down with teasing and shaming.

Toilet training is casual; small children are permitted to relieve themselves anywhere but in the house.

They begin their peer relationship at a very early stage. They may spend a great deal of the day outside with the older children. They may wander into the neighboring houses or hamlets (or streets) without fear of being punished, and may go home only for meals. This pattern of early peer relationship must have important impact on the development of the child's personality.

As the child grows up, there is an increase in responsibility and demands for obedience. The open expression of anger is strongly discouraged. Older siblings must help the parents in the care of younger ones to whom they serve as examples of good conduct. Every child is expected to learn certain forms of politeness, the foremost of which is respect for the aged, a reflection of the strong value placed on filial piety. It is very important for a child to know how to greet adults, the school teacher, or other respected members of the community. It is a source of great pride to the host when his children enter with arms folded, bow low, and greet the guest. Great deference must be paid the grandparents who are very fond of children and who spend a great deal of their time telling them fairy tales and folk stories. There is a great deal of permissiveness and affection for children among elders.

Boys generally receive more attention and more privileges than girls, because they are the perpetuators of the lineage, and a married girl, with her new duties toward her husband's family, has few obligations to her own family.

With school, the horizons of the child are widened as are the responsibilities and the modes of discipline. He then carries the obligations of a representative of his family in the outer world. He is expected to behave as a grownup and must compete successfully with the peer group. Most children attend school for 5 or 6 years. Girls are expected to assist their mothers in the housework and tend to remain close to the farmstead as they grow older. Boys enjoy more privileges. They are free to wander about the village, having many companions with whom they play marbles or have races, wrestle, and hold cricket or cock fights.

Filial piety indoctrination occupies the most important part in a child's education. The parents are always considered blameless. Hostility as a dimension in the parent–child relationship is something very hard to conceive in the Vietnamese mind. In accord with Confucian values, the father has not only the right but also the duty to correct his children, regardless of their age. Chastisements vary from spanking, whipping, long hours of kneeling, and deprivation of food to humiliation, lowering of status, and even isolation from the family. There are, however, some limitations: Villagers, in general, are very conscious of fondness toward children, and parents are judged by the way they treat them. Brutality to children would disgrace the parents in the eyes of the community.

When anger is expressed by the child toward his parents, it usually takes the form of martyrdom. He might go on a hunger strike or run away from home and stay in some relatives' homes. The mother would respond and cajole him back into eating and take him back home. This kind of dramatic, manipulative device using martyrdom as a form of hostility can be found later among the adult Vietnamese. Thus, the way in which they express their anger toward others is to destroy themselves (e.g., suicide, self-immolation), guilt is used as a manipulative device through the internalizing of the destructive impulse.

The open expression of anger is strongly discouraged not only toward the parents, but also among the peer group, because fighting among children would involve the various parents and become a much broader issue between families. The result is that the usual outlets of children's hostile expression are denied and hostility remains within. Of course, hostility, to one degree or another, exists in every parent–child and peer relationship in every culture. When direct expression is not permitted, it must find some outlet and one can sense the potential for a very explosive situation (Slote, 1966). This partly explains why a normally conciliating, friendly, and self-controlled Vietnamese can become extremely violent and aggressive when circumstances permit him to channel all his monumental amounts of rage. Similarly, such a mechanism may account for fanaticism and heroic deeds of a fighting man whose aggressivity and hostility can be directed toward a common enemy, especially when national cause is at stake. Of course, this aspect of parent–child relationship could be more specifically studied and that should constitute a source of rich data in understanding adult behavior.

On the whole, the world of Vietnamese children is dominated by an absolute, autocratic parental authority and an absolute insistence of good parent image. No wonder that children devote so much of themselves to being the good child and to courting parental approval. The mother is naturally more loved and appreciated as the person who sang their lullabies, who fed them and tended them in health and in sickness, whereas the father represents the figure of authority in the family, to whom children must show respect and admiration. As they grow older, their ego ideal can be transferred to an admired teacher, a tough from the village, and especially to the village chief with his full authority and privileges.

C. Religions and Popular Beliefs

As mentioned above, there is in Viet Nam an amalgamation of Buddhist–Taoist–Confucianist ideology with native animism and popular beliefs and practices.

For most Vietnamese, the cult of ancestors is a religion and the cement binding the family. The dead require devotion just as living elders do. As the result of their veneration of ancestors, Vietnamese are accustomed to dwelling with the spirits of the dead who are considered to be part of the living family. Ancestors' spirits have the power to protect their descendants and must be informed of all family affairs. Brides and new babies are presented to them in solemn ceremony (Bain, 1967). Similarly, great national heroes of the past have the spiritual power to influence present events. Ancestors' tombs also require great care, because it is believed that their damage could bring misfortune to the living.

In addition to the Buddhist pagoda, every village has a "dinh," or communal house, where local heroes or some deities are venerated as the Guardian Spirit of the village. The "dinh" is also the center of communal life and often serves as the administrative building for the village.

Vietnamese believe in reincarnation and individual destiny. A man is born under a particular star. What he has in this present life is the consequence of what he did in his previous lives. Thus, one can improve one's destiny by doing good and avoiding evil.

The world of demons and wicked spirits is very complex. It includes many kinds of demons, phantoms, ghosts, and several deities, such as the Thunder Spirit, the Water Goddess, the Fire Goddess. It is believed that demons and ghosts usually inhabit great trees and abandoned houses or they may wander as errant spirits. They often appear as human shadows, and induce their intended victims to open their mouth or to have sexual intercourse with them, whereupon they draw out the victims' souls and vitality, leaving them insane.

There are three souls and seven vital spirits which collectively sustain the living body of a man (a woman has nine vital spirits). When an individual possesses all the souls and vital spirits, he experiences a sense of wellbeing, but if one or all should depart, sickness, insanity, or death could result. Thus, when a sorcerer first approaches his patient, he usually makes a symbolic gesture with his hands and shouts "Three souls and seven spirits of the named X should return as quickly as possible!" After death, if there is no cult honoring the deceased, their souls become errant spirits, wandering endlessly and doing great harm to the living (Hickey, 1967).

There are also good supernatural beings who devote themselves to the task of helping the sufferers. Among them are immortals, saints, the Spirit of the Hearth, the Buddhist Goddess of Mercy, etc. It is thought that they are capable of passing on special gifts such as literary genius, and some impart medicinal secrets. The souls of Quan Cong, the great Chinese warrior, and of General Tran Hung Dao, the Vietnamese victor of the Mongols, are often summoned by the sorcerers in their exorcism ceremonies.

Although there is now in Viet Nam an increasing awareness of the role played by psychological and environmental factors in the etiology of mental disorders, it still is a common belief, especially in rural areas, that evil spirits cause mental illnesses and only exorcism can help the "possessed" individual. Many sorcerers specialize in curing mental illnesses. Exorcism of the evil spirit is part of the cure and is frequently combined with use of amulets and medicinal herbs. The usual procedure consists in summoning the evil spirit, propitiating it with food offerings and golden votive papers, or, as a last resort, frightening it away by use of the sorcerer's magic powers.

Other patients consult certain Buddhist monks who have the reputation of possessing special skills in the treatment of the mentally ill. Some families send their patients to spend years and years in the pagoda, working for the Buddhist monks in the hope that evil spirits dare not come near Buddha's land.

Some healers claim that their healing powers derive from patron deities without having any contact with evil spirits. Usually, they vacate the village for some time to study healing techniques with the hermits in the Seven Mountains or the Black Lady Mountains, and upon their return, they devote themselves to the mission of "helping mankind." Their prescriptions are amazingly simple: local medicinal herbs and even pure water. They sometimes obtain spectacular results with highly suggestible patients. At the risk of losing their healing powers, they are forbidden to charge fees for their service. However, they may accept tokens of gratitude presented to the patron deities.

Western medicine has not received a wide acceptance in rural areas, especially for the treatment of mental illness. Many villagers continue to be skeptical of it and think that Western medications, which are suitable for people in temperate countries, may be "too hot" for the Vietnamese living in tropical climate. "Hot blood" is also reckoned as a cause of certain mental conditions. Therefore, to cure mental illness, one should cool the blood down instead of warming it up.

Most of the villagers give their preference to traditional Sino-Vietnamese medicine. The practitioners use Chinese drugs and local drugs to make their preparations and resort to traditional healing techniques such as pinching, cupping, bloodletting, or suction with tubes. Some of them practice acupuncture.

D. Attitude of the Society toward Mental Illness

In general, the attitude of the Vietnamese society toward the mentally ill is one of sympathy and compassion mixed with some degree of fear and skepticism. Very often, a mentally ill person is considered as an individual who is born under an unlucky star or who must suffer the consequences of his misdeeds in his previous lives and of those of his parents and ancestors. As long as he remains quiet and harmless, he is left to his own misery or his family care. However, if he becomes violent and dangerous to society's safety, he should be committed to a psychiatric hospital. The theory of demoniacal possession turns out to be favorable for the patient, who himself is guiltless and deserves compassion. Once exorcised, he can regain his place in the society, without stigmatization.

Within the family, the mentally ill receive much affection and indulgence. Here again prevails the Vietnamese concept of the law of compensation: Nothing is perfect; among the children, there must be someone who should suffer so that the others may enjoy good health. Thus, the parents and the other siblings should do their best to care for the unfortunate patient. However, in the eyes of the community, having a member suffering from mental illness constitutes a shame for the whole family. Furthermore, this can create many difficulties for the other siblings when they attain the age of marriage, because many mental conditions are thought to be hereditary and incurable.

Within the army, psychiatric disability is generally well accepted. People in uniform become more aware of the effect of environmental stresses on the personality. They learn that the hardships of military life could wreck an individual's efficiency (Menninger, 1948). Many discover that failure in adjustment is not a disgrace and often could be avoided by appropriate help. Of course, many neurotics and some psychotics are suspected of being unwilling or malingerers, but this can be explained by the lack of understanding of the various manifestations of mental disorders. When they are obviously ill, psychiatric patients are usually treated with sympathy and compassion by those in authority on the same basis as physical illness. The fact that a patient is discharged from the hospital with a psychiatric diagnosis does not constitute a serious stigma for the man as long as he remains effective in his job.

III. Historical Background

During the 80-odd years under French domination, the Vietnamese produced a long series of continuous movements that struggled for national independence. In 1945, the communist-led Viet Minh gained ascendency over the nationalist movement by means of a superior organization and skilled tactics. However, they made many enemies by betraying and murdering noncommunist nationalists who had supported them. The French Indo-Chinese war broke out in 1946. After 3 years of unsuccessful pacification, the French supported the creation of a nationalist government with its own army in an effort to defeat the Communists. Though the independence granted by the French was far from complete and though they distrusted the French, nationalist leaders took the opportunity to achieve their objective.

The first Vietnamese Nationalist Army units were organized in 1950 in batallions using shared support facilities with the French Union Forces.

Viet Nam regained full independence at the time of the Geneva Agreements of 1954, which divided the country along the seventeenth parallel: The north fell to the Communist-controlled government, the south to the Nationalist side. The withdrawal of French troops from South Viet Nam was achieved in 1956 and the Republic of Viet Nam became a truly independent country in its own right, the only hope for those millions of Vietnamese who had no desire to live under Communism.

Cong Hoa General Hospital, the biggest military hospital in the country, was transferred to the Vietnamese Army in April 1956. Its psychiatric service was then directed by a nonpsychiatric physician. Little was known about the management of neuropsychiatric casualties at that time. However, a retrospective examination of medical records may shed some light into the problem.

Army psychiatry then dealt mainly with psychotic patients. The minor personality deviations were not considered medical problems. Neuroses and psychosomatic conditions were treated separately by the Internal Medicine Service. The diagnostic nomenclature confined itself to the description of patients' symptoms: neurovegetative dystonia, neurasthenia, psychasthenia, nervous depression, mental confusion, mania, delirious episodes (bouffées délirantes), state of dementia, idiocy, etc. The psychiatric pharmacopoeia was very limited and included: bromides, barbiturates, amphetamines, and a tonic potion (an alcoholic preparation with cola, calcium, ascorbic acid, and phosphoric acid). There was extensive use of electric convulsive therapy. Hydrotherapy and wet packs were in common use. Highly disturbed patients required restraints, seclusion rooms, and sometimes straitjackets.

The end of 1957 marked a new era in the history of Vietnamese Army psychiatry when our first army psychiatrist returned from his training in the US. Some drastic changes took shape. The diagnostic system was reviewed. The introduction of Largactil (Chlorpromazine) in the treatment of the psychoses helped relieve the tense atmosphere in the wards. The psychiatric approach became more dynamically oriented.

IV. Present Psychiatric Organization in the ARVN

A. The NP Service at Cong Hoa General Hospital

During the past 10 years, the Medical Service of our young army has made great strides in its efforts to conserve fighting strength. However, for a variety of reasons, our achievements have been limited, to a great extent, to the purely organic sphere of disease and injury. Little consideration has been given to the development of army psychiatry. This is reflected by the absence of psychiatric representation in the planning center of the Surgeon General's Office and the existence of only one facility with a small staff to care for neuropsychiatric patients of the whole army (San, 1967).

Only recently, an internist and a health technician were added to the service to cope with its overload. Its medical staff had consisted of one psychiatrist, one nurse, two corpsmen, and two civilian employees acting as guards and orderlies. The assistance of the clinical psychologist and the psychiatric social worker is completely unknown. Paperwork dilutes professional services still further. In addition to his heavy clinical load, the army psychiatrist is burdened with numerous administrative procedures. He is a member of the "disposition board" and the "discharge board." Each one meets once a week. He must evaluate all military prisoners suspected of being mentally ill or awaiting court martial. He is also the psychiatric consultant of the recruitment and induction centers. To complicate life further, he must give psychiatric clearance for a monthly average of 500 servicemen being sent abroad for training.

At the present time, the Psychiatric Service of Cong Hoa General Hospital has a capacity of 80 beds and consists of ten rooms for violent and actively disturbed psychotic patients, and an open ward for less agitated cases. Almost all the neuropsychiatric (NP) casualties in the army from all over the country are referred to this service for treatment and disposition.

The inpatient load varies from 80 to 100 patients, and sometimes more when an overflow of new inductees is sent in for evaluation.

Its outpatient clinic is very active. Ten to 15 outpatients are seen everyday (the dependents of military personnel also have access to psychiatric care, mostly as outpatients).

In order to solve the problem of shortage of beds, quick disposition and a rapid return to active duty is mandatory. The average length of hospitalization for each patient is 4 weeks, with occasional patients remaining up to 6 months.

An ample supply of tranquilizers (mainly chlorpromazine, promazine, thioridazine and meprobamate, chlordiazepoxide, and diazepam) and antidepressants is available. Electric shock treatment is employed regularly, three times a week, for approximately one-tenth of the patients. Brief supportive psychotherapy is given only to a limited number of selected cases, usually in conjunction with drug therapy. Occupational therapy cannot be implemented because of the lack of personnel and the short duration of hospitalization. However, recreational facilities can be considered adequate.

In brief, our Psychiatric Service at Cong Hoa Hospital can be termed as an acute treatment service with a small and very busy staff. Improvements cannot be made unless there is an increase in personnel, including more psychiatrists, a larger nursing staff, and more ancillary services.

B. The Contribution of the Military Medical School

Recently, in order to remedy the lack of psychiatric teaching in the Saigon Medical School, an effort has been made by the director of the Military Medical School, himself a psychiatrist, to give an orientation course on military psychiatry to all the newly drafted doctors and military medical students. Emphasis is placed on the psychological aspects of illness, and especially the basic principles of preventive and combat psychiatry (Glass, 1953). Such courses have stirred great interest among the students and have been proved of considerable help to the future field medical officers (San, 1966).

V. Statistical Data: NP Casualties in the ARVN during 1963–1967

Figure 1 shows an overall picture of neuropsychiatric activities in the ARVN. One can see a steady increase in NP casualties every year during the past 5 years. Two main reasons can account for this: (1) the escalation of the war; (2) the increase in the size of the ARVN.

Since 1964, ARVN medical services began to cover Regional Forces and Self-Defense Corps. From 150,000 men in 1960, the Vietnamese Army has grown continuously into 700,000 men at the end of 1967. It is expected to have 800,000 men serving with the colors by late December 1968. At the present time, the ARVN is composed of these specific elements: (1) The Ground Forces including all infantry divisions, an Airborne division, the Marine Corps and several Ranger battalions; (2) the Vietnamese Air Force;

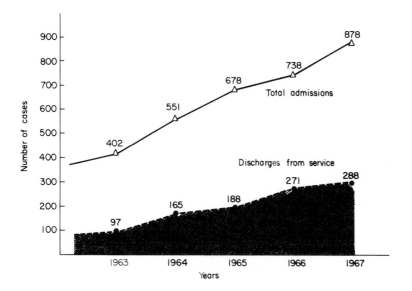

FIG. 1   *Neuropsychiatric activities in the ARVN over 5 years.*

(3) the Vietnamese Navy which includes the Sea Force, the Junk Force, the River Force; (4) the Regional Forces, a voluntary area defense force, in units up to battalion size; (5) the Militia or Self-Defense Corps, a paramilitary force responsible for the defense of hamlets and villages (see Tables I–V).

In addition to the above data shown for 1967, there were a number of miscellaneous patients admitted to the Psychiatry Department for administrative reasons, but they are not included in the psychiatric case total. These consisted of 125 cases of epilepsy, only 12 of whom were felt to have mental deterioration or a secondary emotional disturbance, several patients who had transient febrile delirium, and a variety of medical and neurological problems such as mongolism, hydrocephaly, microcephaly, and postencephalitic syndromes. One should mention also a significant number of 149 new draftees who were referred for observation and evaluation regarding their fitness to duty. These new draftees had exhibited enough evidence of abnormal behavior during their stay at the induction centers to be suspected of being mentally ill. The breakdown of this population by diagnostic categories is shown in Table VI.

TABLE I
ARVN Neuropsychiatric Casualties in 1963

Diagnosis	Number of cases	Percent	Discharges from service	Percent
Psychoses	141	35.0	62	44.0
Neuroses	184	45.7	11	6.0
Combat exhaustion	5	1.2	0	0.0
Character and behavior disorders	45	11.4	9	20.0
Mental retardation	14	3.5	11	78.0
Posttraumatic defect conditions	13	3.2	4	30.0
Totals	402	100.0	97	24.0

TABLE II
ARVN Neuropsychiatric Casualties in 1964

Diagnosis	Number of cases	Percent	Discharges from service	Percent
Psychoses	227	41.3	101	44.5
Neuroses	208	37.8	21	10.0
Combat exhaustion	7	1.2	0	0.0
Character or behavior disorders	63	11.4	18	28.5
Mental retardation	21	3.8	20	95.0
Posttraumatic defect conditions	25	4.5	5	20.0
Totals	551	100.0	165	30.0

TABLE III
ARVN Neuropsychiatric Casualties in 1965

Diagnosis	Number of cases	Percent	Discharges from service	Percent
Psychoses	269	39.6	128	47.5
Neuroses	275	40.5	21	7.6
Combat exhaustion	12	1.8	0	0.0
Character or behavior disorders	92	13.6	22	24.0
Mental retardation	16	2.4	13	81.0
Posttraumatic defect conditions	14	2.1	4	28.0
Totals	678	100.0	188	28.0

TABLE IV

ARVN Neuropsychiatric Casualties in 1966

Diagnosis	Number of cases	Percent	Discharges from service	Percent
Psychoses	352	48.0	188	53.4
Neuroses	246	33.0	31	12.6
Combat exhaustion	7	0.9	0	0.0
Character and behavior disorders	86	11.7	28	32.5
Mental retardation	20	2.7	18	90.0
Posttraumatic defect conditions	13	1.8	6	46.1
NP observation	14	1.9	0	0.0
Totals	738	100.0	271	36.7

TABLE V

ARVN Neuropsychiatric Casualties in 1967

Diagnosis	Number of cases	Percent	Discharges from service	Percent
Psychoses	392	44.7	187	47.5
Neuroses	320	36.5	25	7.8
Combat exhaustion	7	0.9	0	0.0
Personality disorders	113	12.8	45	31.0
Mental retardation	18	2.0	12	66.6
Posttraumatic defect conditions	28	3.1	19	64.0
Totals	878	100.0	288	32.8

TABLE VI

Breakdown of Diagnostic Categories in 149 New Draftees

Diagnosis	Number of cases	Percent
Psychoses	94	63.1
Neuroses	7	4.7
Personality disorders	11	7.4
Mental retardation	3	2.1
Epilepsy with mental deterioration	4	2.7
No disease found	30	20.0
Totals	149	100.0

VI. Comments and Discussion

A. The Low Incidence of NP Casualties

The most striking fact is that the incidence of NP casualties in the ARVN is remarkably low for the number of troops involved. The admission rate for all psychiatric illness remained fairly constant throughout the past 5 years: 1.25 per 1000 average troop strength per year (in the US Army, this rate was 5 in 1965; 7 in 1960; 10 in 1956; and 24 in 1951 during the Korean War) (Tiffany and Allerton, 1967).

We must admit that with only one facility to care for NP casualties and considerable transport problems in getting them to Saigon, only the more serious cases are usually referred to Cong Hoa Hospital. Moreover, there was a sizable number of cases in which psychological etiologies were ignored. Several emotional difficulties considered significant to an American physician might not be so considered by our Vietnamese colleagues. Many neurotic patients were treated as having physical illness. Psychosomatic conditions remained unrecognized as such although the incidence of bronchial asthma, gastritis, colitis, peptic ulcer, migraine and tension headaches, and low back pain is particularly high among ARVN soldiers. Suicide was considered a social problem or a personal affair; usually, after recovering from the critical periods, a suicidal patient was discharged from the hospital without having the chance to see the psychiatrist.

As has been noted elsewhere, even in the civilian population, the incidence of psychiatric illness reported was much lower than would be anticipated. Thus, the low incidence of mental illness in Viet Nam reflects more the limited scope given to psychiatry rather than the reality of things. Furthermore, the lack of facilities to care for psychiatric patients, and the shortage of well-trained psychiatric personnel made it difficult to obtain an accurate estimate of the magnitude of the problem of mental illness in Viet Nam.

B. The Psychoses

1. *Incidence*

Psychoses constituted approximately 45% of the total admissions (Table VI). It can be safely assumed that the figures presented represent all such cases in the army because the symptoms are easily diagnosed and the bizarre behavior is evident: delusions (of persecution, of misidentity, of grandeur), hallucinations (hearing voices or seeing visions), illusions, confusion, and disorientation. Most psychotic patients then require hospitalization. Therefore, hospital admissions become an accurate measure of the incidence of the psychoses in the army. The rate seemed lower for officers than for enlisted men.

2. Types of Reactions

An analysis of the different diagnostic categories of psychotic reactions is given in Table VII.

Schizophrenia was the most common psychotic response, constituting 60% of all psychotic reactions and 25% of all psychiatric admissions.

Paranoid schizophrenics formed the largest proportion of cases. Projection seemed to be the prevalent ego-defense mechanism in Vietnamese culture. The delusional content did not differ much from the description in psychiatric books with some exceptions related to common popular beliefs (delusions of being poisoned or bewitched were the most frequent) and the craving for peace in Viet Nam. In fact, many patients claimed themselves to be the savior of the country, entrusted by God or some omnipotent deities with the mission of preaching love and peace among the people.

TABLE VII
Psychoses in ARVN in 1967

Psychosis	Number of cases	Percent
Paranoid schizophrenia	128	32.6
Simple schizophrenia	21	5.4
Hebephrenic schizophrenia	69	17.6
Catatonic schizophrenia	10	2.5
Undifferentiated schizophrenia	108	27.5
Manic depressive psychosis	41	10.5
Psychotic depression	15	3.8
Totals	392	99.9

The next largest group of psychotic reactions fell into the category of acute undifferentiated schizophrenia. These psychotic episodes were usually of sudden onset and lasted from a few days to 3 or 4 weeks, in which most of the symptoms presented were characteristic of schizophrenia. The response to treatment was rapid.

In the ARVN, no attempt has been made to psychiatrically screen new draftees; even people who have been admitted many times to a psychiatric hospital in civilian life will be drafted. This may explain the relatively high percentage of hebephrenic schizophrenics, a large proportion of whom have been in the service only a very short time before admission to the hospital.

Special mention should be given to the category of manic-depressive psychosis. The majority of the patients had only recurrent episodes of elation without alternation of significant depression. Therefore, the single diagnosis of manic psychosis was often made. The patients tended to present in a highly disturbed and agitated state of rapid onset and equally rapid response to treatment. Maybe the depression was of brief duration and mild in degree and either not noted by the patient's family and associates or not considered significant enough to require hospitalization.

Depressions severe enough to be classified as psychotic reactions were relatively infrequent and constituted only a very small percentage of cases (4% of all psychotic reactions).

3. *Disposition*

The disposition of psychotic patients in the Vietnamese Army was rather variable. Theoretically, once a man developed a psychosis in service, it was expected that he would be discharged from the army. In fact, less than half of these patients was separated from the army, the remaining patients seeming to function quite well after return to duty. It is our impression that if a protected assignment could be provided, there was every reason to believe that these men would be able to give further service, probably both to the advantage of themselves and the army.

In summary, the psychoses in the ARVN constituted 45% of all psychiatric admissions. Many of these patients could have been screened out at induction. Schizophrenic reactions were the most frequent psychotic response to the stresses of military life, especially the paranoid type. Psychotic reactions among the soldiers appeared to have a better prognosis than those seen in civilians, but this may have been due to earlier recognition and relatively more adequate treatment.

C. The Neuroses

1. *Incidence*

It is very difficult to estimate the incidence of psychoneurotic reactions in the ARVN because the vast majority of such cases were not seen by the psychiatrist. However, it can be safely assumed that neurotic reactions constituted the major problem in army psychiatry. Until a recent change in our admission policy, when a concerted effort was made to treat neurotic soldiers as outpatients, the figures consistently exceeded that for the psychoses. In 1963 for example, neuroses took 45% of the total admissions while psychoses had only 35%. Since 1964, an attempt was made to treat all nonpsychotic patients on an outpatient basis whenever possible, the percentage of neurotic reactions was reduced to around 35% of all psychiatric admissions.

2. *Types of Reactions*

An analysis of the different types of neurotic reactions is shown in Table VIII.

TABLE VIII
Neuroses in ARVN in 1967

Neurosis	Number of cases	Percent
Anxiety reaction	193	60.3
Anxiety reaction with related physical trauma	57	17.8
Depressive reaction	46	14.4
Conversion reaction	24	7.5
Totals	320	100.0

Chronic anxiety reactions with a tendency to somatization were most commonly encountered. In about one-third of these cases, some history of physical trauma was related to the onset of symptoms. Many of these cases involved head injuries, but every attempt was made to exclude any case with evidence of brain injury. The patient would tell the story of a car accident or of having been in close proximity to an exploding shell (or mine) which "knocked him out." Furthermore, such reactions were by no means restricted to head injuries, and many patients developed their symptoms after injuries to the extremities or abdomen, especially when some fragments or shell splinters could not be completely removed. All patients, whether they had been injured or not, tended to have a typical symptom pattern of insomnia, headache, palpitation, fatigue, irritability, muscular tension, inability to concentrate, and memory deficits (although psychological testing demonstrated no real memory loss). Other precipitating causes can be: Long sojourn in an isolated outpost under continuous enemy harassment; financial and emotional difficulties; recovery from serious physical illnesses; accidental electrocution; anaphylactic reactions to drugs, especially to penicillin; dissatisfaction due to poor leadership; injustices in the management of rewards (promotions, decorations) and punishments. In most of the patients, symptoms begin gradually progressing to the point of the patient's being unable to function in their units. Although, outright malingering was rare, it is clear that there was a strong manipulative component in many of these cases.

In a comparative study (Bourne and San, 1967) of NP casualties in the US Army and the ARVN, we had suggested that the high percentage of anxiety reactions in the ARVN can be compared to the large number of character and behavior disorders among US Army NP casualties in Viet Nam. In both instances, there was believed to be a significant manipulative component. We suggest that these are equivalent groups of individuals each using the most effective method in his cultural environment to achieve the same secondary gain, namely, escape from an undesirable situation. In the Vietnamese Army, people who appear as disciplinary problems or act in an antisocial manner will almost always be dealt with administratively and will rarely be admitted to the psychiatric service, whereas incapacitating physical ailments guarantee the man's transfer to a medical facility. The soldier may know that discharge from the service is unlikely but that may not be his aim and periodic escape from the environment of his unit may be all that he seeks. Although it can be assumed that such reasoning takes place at a subconscious level and should not be regarded as malingering, occasional patients will express awareness of the manipulative aspects of their symptoms. The fact that so many patients develop anxiety symptoms following hospitalization for physical injury suggests that in these instances it may be a learned process reinforced by their previous experience in the hospital. On the other hand, as advanced medical techniques have been available in Viet Nam for a relatively short time, injuries which might be regarded lightly by an American can still represent a serious threat to life in the minds of many Vietnamese patients, especially when the injury involves the head or the brain, an organ on which the patients set particular value. Thus, a minor physical injury can produce a great deal of anxiety in the patients.

After the anxiety reactions, reactive depressions appeared to be the next most frequent type of neurotic responses. Here, anxiety becomes masked by self-depreciating behavior or depressive affect. In most instances, the onset of such reactions followed shortly after the death of a close family member (sometimes the patient's whole family was killed in the war) or took place subsequent to a defeat or a great difficulty in the social, economic, or personal life. Some of the depressed patients attempted to overcome their guilt and tension by taking alcohol. Others sought dependent support through hypochondriacal complaining.

Conversion reactions were responsible for approximately 10% of all neurotic responses. The symptoms varied from anesthesia, paralysis, and contracture to convulsion, but the most frequent form was aphonia and hysterical mutism. If seen early enough, such cases responded satisfactorily to treatment by suggestion, persuasion, and narcosynthesis. Several spectacular results have been obtained through the use of what we called "the amphetaminic shock" (San, 1963) which was produced by the intravenous injection of from 30 to 100 mg of Maxiton Fort, a French brand name for dextroamphetamine.

A rather special clinical picture of hysterical reaction (one might call it hysterical psychosis) (Hollender and Hirsch, 1964) was presented by some soldiers who wore talismans and amulets (tiger claws, boar teeth, Buddha images, mystical designs). Usually these soldiers should periodically pay tribute to the pagoda or temple or the master sorcerer who had given them the amulets which would make them invulnerable to enemy bullets. They were bound to certain abstentions: not eating onion, garlic, water buffalo or dog meat, not doing evil, and even not having sexual intercourse. If they failed to follow these obligations, the amulet would lose its magical powers and the bearer of the amulet would be punished by the patron deities. Generally, the symptoms began suddenly and dramatically. The patient was brought to the hospital in a highly agitated state suffering from hallucinations, delusions, depersonalization, and self-inflicted smacking. Affectivity was not usually altered; when it was, it was in the direction of volatility and not flatness. The symptoms usually cleared up rapidly with sedation and ventilation of their problems, and seldom lasted longer than 1-2 weeks, leaving practically no residue. Persons most vulnerable to this type of ego disorganization were usually very superstitious and highly suggestible.

Combat exhaustion represented a very small fraction of cases (1% of all psychiatric admissions, with a peak of 1.8% in 1965 when the military situation was the most critical). Several theories have been advanced as possible explanation for this low incidence of combat fatigue. However, the existence of equally low figures in the US Army suggests that the nature of the war itself may be the most significant factor (Bourne and San, 1967). The type of combat is quite different from that which produced combat exhaustion in World War II and in Korea. The fighting is generally in brief, intensive, and sporadic episodes with interspersed periods of relative calm and safety, during which the soldiers can relax. Troops usually are not pinned down by enemy fire for prolonged periods of days and weeks (Tiffany and Allerton, 1967).

D. Personality Disorders

The statistics of neuropsychiatric hospital admissions do not give any accurate data about the number of personality disorders in the ARVN. This is due to the fact that character and behavior disorders, except for chronic alcoholism and drug dependence, are considered as disciplinary problems within the units, and are therefore rarely sent to the hospital (Table IX).

TABLE IX
Personality Disorders in ARVN in 1967

Disorder	Number of cases	Percent
Inadequate personality	31	27.5
Chronic alcoholism	63	55.7
Opium dependence	19	16.8
Totals	113	100.0

During the year of 1967, only 31 persons (or 3.5% of the total admissions) were admitted for psychiatric evaluation because they were a source of continual difficulty for commanding officers.

The majority of these patients were immature and emotionally unstable and fell into the diagnostic categories of antisocial or inadequate personality. Usually they were referred back with the findings to their units where an attempt was made to retain them in duty by means of special training and rehabilitation under strict military discipline. If they continued to become involved in repetitive offenses against military law, they would be sentenced to the army correction system by court martial. Only a few patients were recommended for administrative discharge from the service.

The actual incidence of alcoholism in the ARVN is not known, because drinking enjoys a high level of tolerance in the Vietnamese culture. Many poets and artists have devoted an important part of their works to praising the creative effects of alcohol and the pleasure of drinking. To the ordinary man, alcohol gives more strength, relieves anxiety and depression, and provides a transient escape from the frustrations of life. Many people regard their capacity to drink as a manifestation of their masculinity. A well known saying is commonly quoted by alcoholics to rationalize their habit: "A man without alcohol is just like a flag not moved by the wind."

It is safe to assume that alcoholism constitutes one of the major causes of mental illness in Viet Nam. Throughout the past 5 years, the number of alcoholics admitted to our department remained fairly constant at a rate of 7-10% of all psychiatric admissions. Our civilian colleagues recorded an even higher incidence among the nonmilitary population. The most commonly encountered clinical pictures were delirium tremens, alcohol hallucinosis, and Korsakoff's syndrome with variable degrees of physical impairment: liver damage, gastritis, and peripheral neuropathies. The majority of these patients were noncommissioned officers over the age of 35 and having usually more than 10 years of service. Generally, the recommendation for administrative discharge from the army was made only after several hospitalizations.

Drug dependence represented 2% of our 1967 psychiatric admissions. These were exclusively new draftees whose addiction had not been detected at the time of induction. At least one-third of them were Chinese, among whom the use of opium can still be regarded as a culturally acceptable activity without the usual psychopathological implications. The most frequent form of drug dependence was opium smoking. Some patients used morphine or a mixture of morphine and amphetamine which was usually administered by intravenous injections. Once diagnosed as opium dependents (mostly by Nalline test), all the patients were recommended for separation from the army. Some few cases of barbiturates dependence have also been reported.

Sexual deviations are practically unknown by the average Vietnamese and have not become a psychiatric problem in the ARVN. In Viet Nam, at the present time, there are only some rumors about homosexuality practiced among some intellectuals and artists, especially the group of jazz, rock and roll, and pop-rock musicians.

E. Mental Retardation

The number of mentally retarded soldiers constituted an average of 3% of our total psychiatric admissions. In the ARVN, psychological testing and screening are not done at the time of induction. As a result, many mentally retarded have been drafted. Usually, those mentally deficient soldiers are assigned by commanding officers to limited duty or unskilled tasks such as cutting grass, cleaning barracks, humping shells, filling sandbags, and setting defense bunkers. Therefore, many of them do serve effectively. Only those unable to perform the simplest unskilled jobs were actually sent to the hospital for psychiatric evaluation and disposition.

F. Posttraumatic Defect Conditions

Under this heading (Noyes and Kolb, 1968), we are referring to a group of organic brain syndromes with mental deterioration and personality changes following severe head trauma or wounds of the brain. The changes become manifest when the patient gradually regains consciousness after a period of traumatic stupor or delirium. In milder forms, the impairment of mental capacity consists only of memory deficits, loss of sense of responsibility and decrease in the ability to recognize abstract relationships. In more serious cases, memory is impaired, attention is reduced, reaction time is slowed, and defensive confabulation may occur. Judgment is impaired; social values are not appreciated. Tasks that were formerly performed easily become burdens and sometimes impossible. The degree of mental deterioration varies greatly according to the site of the lesion and the nature and extent of the injury. It may be associated with epileptiform seizures, paralyses, aphasia, and other neurological signs. In some instances, there is a change from the original personality makeup of the patient. The amiable, placid individual may become irascible, irritable, quarrelsome, and impulsive. Family and other obligations and responsibilities are disregarded. Some become morose, dull, and apathetic. Others lose interest in all activities and withdraw from social contacts.

In 1967, out of 27 of such patients, 19 cases (or 64.5%) required separation from service.

VII. Conclusions

Throughout its 4000-year history, Viet Nam has been a country under continual stress. However, perhaps never since its foundation has Vietnamese society undergone so much suffering as within the last three decades. Leighton (1965) has set forth ten criteria for social disintegration which has a casual relationship to the incidence of mental illness: (1) Economic inadequacy; (2) cultural confusion; (3) widespread secularization; (4) high frequency of broken homes; (5) few and weak associations; (6) few and weak leaders; (7) few patterns of recreation; (8) high frequency of crime and delinquency; (9) high frequency of interpersonal hostility; and (10) a weak and fragmented network of communications. It would seem that most of these criteria are present in South Viet Nam today. Consequently, one would expect an important increase in the incidence of psychiatric disorders. And yet, the statistics of psychiatric hospital admissions did not show a significant increase of the morbidity rate. Although there has been no systematic epidemiologic research, the study of NP casualties in the ARVN did point out the fact that the incidence of mental illness in Viet Nam is relatively low as compared with more civilized countries of the Western world. Several factors can be considered as operative: (1) The rather stoic, accepting and stable personality of the Vietnamese, fostered by strong ties to a solid family system; (2) the general lack of awareness in Vietnamese culture of the possibility of using psychiatric symptoms as a method of communicating emotional stresses a man is under; (3) the attitude of the society toward mental illness and the social sanction of the sick role, or more specifically, of the "psychiatric sick role" (Redlich and Freedman, 1966); (4) the state of underdevelopment of psychiatry and the limited scope attributed to psychiatry in Viet Nam. Above all, one can see the considerable influences of sociocultural factors on the determination of human behavioral patterns and mental illnesses. This is reflected clearly in the incidence and symptomatology of psychosis or psychotic behavior, and to a greater degree, in the manifestations and the selection of symptoms in the more subtle aspects of learned behavior of neurotic patients.

Although psychiatry in Viet Nam started some 50 years ago, it has remained underdeveloped both professionally and academically in comparison with other medical specialties. Despite the present overwhelming demands for treatment of nonpsychiatric medical and surgical problems, it is believed that the development of psychiatry should be given more consideration by those in authority, especially in the army, since human effectiveness in combat is largely determined by an interaction of both somatic and psychic forces. It would appear that emphasis should be first placed on the training of an adequate psychiatric personnel (McKinley, 1966). Not only are many more well-trained psychiatrists needed, but also mental health workers, occupational therapists, clinical psychologists, psychiatric social workers, and a nursing staff should be provided. Then the next steps would be the improvement and expansion of treatment facilities and the integration of psychiatry into medical education. Research to increase the general fund of knowledge can not be implemented, nor can a wider public understanding and acceptance of psychiatry be gained without the accomplishment of those fundamental requirements. We believe that the ARVN Medical Service, with its relatively favorable position and all its material and human resources, could bring about a major contribution in the solution of mental health problems in Viet Nam.

REFERENCES

Bain, C. A. (1967). "Viet Nam, The Roots of Conflict." Prentice-Hall, Englewood Cliffs, New Jersey.
Bourne, P. G., and San, N. D. (1967). A comparative study of neuropsychiatric casualties in the U. S. Army and the ARVN. *Military Med.* 132, 904–909.
Glass, A. J. (1953). Preventive psychiatry in the combat zone. *In* "Symposium on Stress." Walter Reed Army Med. Center, Washington, D. C.
Hickey, G. C. (1967). "Village in Viet Nam." Yale Univ. Press, New Haven, Connecticut.

Hollender, M. H., and Hirsch, S. J. (1964). Hysterical psychosis. *Am. J. Psychiat.* **120**, 1066–1074.

Leighton, A. (1965). Poverty and social change. *Sci. Am.* **212**, 21–27.

McKinley, R. A. (1966). Psychiatry in Viet Nam — 1966. *Am. J. Psychiat.* **123**, 420–426.

Menninger, W. C. (1948). "Psychiatry in a Troubled World." Macmillan, New York.

Noyes, A. P., and Kolb, L. C. (1968). "Modern Clinical Psychiatry," 7th ed. Saunders, Philadelphia, Pennsylvania.

Redlich, F. C., and Freedman, D. X. (1966). "The Theory and Practice of Psychiatry." Basic Books, New York.

San, N. D. (1963). Le choc amphetaminique en psychiatrie: Interet diagnostique et valeur therapeutique. *ARVN Med. J.* **8** and **9**.

San, N. D. (1966). Some Particular Aspects of Mental Illness in the Army of the Republic of Viet Nam. Presented at the ARVN 1966 Medical Convention, Saigon, South Viet Nam.

San, N. D. (1967). Psychiatry in ARVN. Presented at the Military Mental Health Conf., 6th Med. Center, Cam Ranh Bay, South Viet Nam.

Slote, W. H. (1966). "Observations on Psychodynamic Structures in Vietnamese Personality," Initial Rept. on Psychological Study, Viet Nam.

Tiffany, W. J., Jr., and Allerton, W. S. (1967). Army psychiatry in the mid-60's. *Am. J. Psychiat.* **123**, 810–821.

4 // Effects of Combat Stress on Hospital Ship Psychiatric Evacuees*

Robert E. Strange

I. Introduction

All psychiatrists deal with patients under emotional stress, but in civilian and peacetime military practice this stress is most often caused by threats that are more symbolic than real. Psychiatry in a combat zone, however, offers a unique opportunity to observe the effects of real and immediate stresses including threats of death and injury, direct responsibility for others' lives, and physical deprivations. This chapter presents the author's observations of the characteristics of psychiatric patients hospitalized aboard the US Navy Hospital Ship *Repose* while in medical support of combat operations in the "I" Corps area in the Republic of Viet Nam

*Portions of this chapter are reprinted from the *American Journal of Psychiatry*, volume 124, pages 281-286, Copyright 1967, American Psychiatric Association and *Military Medicine*, volume 133, pages 823–826, Copyright 1968, Association of Military Surgeons of the US.

during 1966. Previous publications (Strange and Arthur, 1967; Strange, 1968) have offered early demographic and general psychiatric data involving this patient population, and the present report is a compilation and expansion of this clinical and statistical material.

II. Functions and Facilities

During 1966, the hospital ship served two medical functions in the combat area. Much of the time she steamed in a scheduled pattern and received patients sent from major hospitals ashore. These patients were referred from those facilities by specialists who had initially received them from field medical units. Frequently, however, the ship furnished immediate support of Marine combat operations, and casualties were evacuated directly from medical units in the field without previous specialty evaluation. This latter type of operation occurred with increasing frequency during the latter part of the year as the severity and duration of combat increased.

The psychiatric unit aboard the hospital ship consisted of two wards in adjoining compartments, containing a total of 48 functioning beds. The staff was made up of one psychiatrist, one psychiatric nurse, and nine hospital corpsmen. This was an open, unlocked unit, and the patients were allowed freedom of movement about the ship commensurate with their degree of illness and responsibility. Treatment methods included individual and group psychotherapy and medications. No somatic therapy was performed, and psychotherapy was of a short term type.

III. Intake Statistics

During the period from mid-February through December 1966, psychiatric patients accounted for 5.5% of the total admissions aboard the hospital ship. Of these, 70% were Marines and 30% were Naval personnel. Repair and upkeep of the ship necessitated several lengthy departures from the war zone during this initial period of operations, and there was consequently great fluctuation in patient intake and census. Usually, however, there were 12–15 patients maintained on the psychiatric ward, although on occasion the census rose to as high as 35. Length of hospitalization was also quite variable, ranging between extremes of overnight and 60 days. Over a representative 2-month period, the mean length of inpatient care was 13.5 days.

The total patient population over the 10½ month period under study was diagnostically classified as follows:

Personality disorder:	36%
Psychoneurotic disorder:	21%
Psychotic disorder:	11%
Situational Reactions:	
Combat	15%
Other	11%
Miscellaneous:	
(Administrative and	
no disease)	6%

IV. Combat as a Precipitating Stress

In a previously published study (Strange and Arthur, 1967), demographic variables were extracted and compiled in relationship to diagnosis of those patients hospitalized during the ship's initial 7 months of operations, this group being 60% of the total population recorded above. An attempt was made to evaluate the relative importance of combat stress as a precipitating factor in the emotional disorders of these patients by establishing whether or not the patient had actually participated in active combat and whether or not such combat experience was an immediate precipitating stress as determined by careful psychiatric interviews. The following results were obtained:

Of those with diagnosis of personality disorder (including situational reactions in the initial survey population), 63% had been in combat and in 49%, combat was judged to be a primary factor in precipitating the symptoms which caused hospitalization. It is noteworthy, however, that the syndrome of combat fatigue occurred with increasing frequency during the latter months not included in the original study, and finally accounted for 15% of the admissions. Considering these factors, it appeared that approximately half of those with character and behavior disorders had been in combat and in slightly more than one-third, combat was a major precipitating stress. There were also other interesting characteristics of the personality disorder group. The group was characterized by a short length of service and a history of civilian and military disciplinary problems. Sixty-five percent were unmarried, and there was a mean age of 21.4 years with a disproportionate number in the pay grade of E-2. Excited, agitated, or violent behavior was noted in 45% of these cases.

Of the patients with diagnoses established as psychoneurotic disorder, 79% had been in combat, and it was judged to be a significant precipitating stress in 47%. These patients had a mean age of 25 years and were characteristically in the pay grade of E-4 and above with more than 3 years of service. Forty-eight percent were unmarried. Sixty-one percent reported somatic complaints, and 54% had significant depressive symptoms. Only 18% had a history of agitation or violence.

Study of the patients hospitalized with psychotic diagnoses indicated that only 32% had been in combat and that in only 16% did combat appear to be a factor in precipitating illness. These patients had a mean age of 22.6 years, a relatively high proportion were in the pay grades of E-3 and E-4, and 77% were single. Ninety percent manifested overt thought disorder, and 63% had perceptual disturbances to the point of hallucinations. Thirty-two percent had paranoid ideation; 53% showed hostility in their behavior; and 18% had a history of excited or violent behavior. Sixty-three percent were apathetic and withdrawn. There were no significant clinical differences between these psychotic patients who had been in combat and those who had not faced such stress.

It was apparent from these figures that in the psychotic patient the stress of combat was relatively unimportant. As was predictable from prior studies (Arthur, 1965), the incidence of hospitalization for psychosis was less influenced by external factors than that for other emotional disorders. Among other patients who had been in active combat, however, these stresses seemed to be the significant precipitating factors in 60% of those with neurotic diagnoses and 75% of those with personality disorders. By definition, of course, traumatic combat experience was the precipitating stress in all patients who were diagnosed as having combat fatigue.

V. Combat-Precipitated Psychiatric Syndromes

Clinical observation revealed interesting patterns of superficial similarities and diagnostically significant differences in this group

of combat precipitated emotional problems. The frequent symptomatic similarities could in fact provide a major diagnostic trap for
the uninitiated military psychiatrist seeing his first patients in the
war area. For purposes of study, therefore, these psychiatric problems from combat may be conceptualized as falling into three distinct groups. These three categories of combat precipitated psychiatric syndromes are: *(1)* combat fatigue, *(2)* pseudocombat fatigue,
and *(3)* combat neurosis. Of these terms only combat fatigue is an
official diagnostic label; the others have been utilized by the
author strictly for emphasis and instructional value.

A. Combat Fatigue

The syndrome of combat fatigue or combat exhaustion is a very
specific diagnostic category. It may be defined as the transient
pathological reaction of a basically healthy personality to severe
stress of combat and is included in the American Psychiatric Association nomenclature in the category of Gross Stress Reactions.
Regarding such reactions, the "Diagnostic and Statistical Manual"
of the American Psychiatric Association (1952) states: "This diagnosis is justified only in situations in which the individual has
been exposed to severe physical demands or extreme emotional
stress such as in combat or in civilian catastrophe. . . . In many instances this diagnosis applies to previously more or less 'normal'
persons who have experienced intolerable stress." Although the
presenting symptom complex varied, the following characteristics
were generally present in patients with this problem: *(1)* past history of comparatively healthy emotional and social adjustment, *(2)*
previously satisfactory military performance, and *(3)* severe and
prolonged exposure to traumatic combat experience. Also, they
usually had histories of marked physical exertion and fatigue,
sleep deprivation, inadequate diet, and other somatic as well as
emotional stresses. Other authors have previously described the
variable symptoms among these patients, including generalized
anxiety, depression, apathy and withdrawal, conversion reactions,
agitation and disorganization, and psychosomatic manifestations
(Glass, 1955; U.S. Department of the Army, 1952). Experience has
revealed that mild symptoms are normal among combat troops in
Viet Nam as in every other war. Such symptoms can be considered
to be pathological only when they become severe enough to im-
pair the patient's ability to perform his duties effectively or persist

inappropriately when the stress of combat is no longer present. In these cases a diagnosis of combat fatigue is indicated.

In the group of patients under discussion, cases of classical combat fatigue as described above were relatively uncommon. As noted above, this diagnosis was established in only 15% of the total number of psychiatric patients hospitalized aboard the ship during the 10½ month period under study, but it was considered nevertheless to represent a potentially significant loss of combat manpower. It is quite possible that this figure may not be representative of the actual incidence of combat fatigue among operational units, due to many variable selection factors operating in the admission of patients on the ship. Discussion with medical officers assigned to Marine units ashore, however, indicated comparable case loads during periods of heavy engagement. Significantly, the incidence of this diagnosis increased as the severity and duration of combat increased during the latter months of 1966. It is noteworthy that most of the patients hospitalized for combat fatigue aboard the ship were young men who had been in positions of considerable responsibility, most often junior noncommissioned officers, such as corporals assigned as squad leaders, or hospital corpsmen working with combat units.

There was, in fact, a strikingly disproportionate number of corpsmen with this diagnosis. It seemed difficult for certain such young men, still in adolescence, to handle the grave challenge of continuing responsibility for others' lives. Unlike the officers and more senior noncommissioned officers, their own maturation had not progressed to a level at which the burden of lengthy field leadership and traumatic medical care was tolerable. Fear for personal safety seemed much less important in the dynamics of these combat syndromes than did burden of responsibility. Invariably these patients' military records were excellent, their past histories that of healthy social adjustment, and their combat experience lengthy and harrowing. Characteristically they had been in the war zone for more than 6 months, had strong emotional investment in their units, and had functioned in a leadership or other responsible role. The most common symptom complexes were those of acutely or insidiously developing generalized anxiety and/or depression both with accompanying psychophysiologic manifestations. The following is an illustrative case of this combat fatigue syndrome and its treatment (Case I):

This 20-year-old CPL USMC was admitted aboard the hospital ship after approximately 2 weeks of outpatient supportive treatment by his battalion surgeon because of chronic anxiety, nightmares, and persistent headaches. History revealed that he was the product of an intact, happy family with no previous indications of emotional or social problems. He attended a trade school successfully then enlisted in the US Marine Corps. For 2½ years he had served quite satisfactorily, and during the 11 months prior to hospitalization he had been assigned to combat duty in Viet Nam. His competence was such that he became a fire team leader shortly after he arrived in the field, and very soon after that he was made a squad leader. Over a number of months he led his squad through many patrols, was involved in numerous fire fights and mortar attacks, and participated in several lengthy operations in which there was prolonged engagement with the enemy. During the month preceding his admission to the sick list, his unit suffered heavy casualties which included a number of his own squad members. On one occasion, he sustained superficial wounds as several of his men were seriously injured in a grenade blast. Shortly thereafter, his unit came under heavy mortar attack, this being the fifteenth such mortaring experience for the patient. He recalled that when this occurred "things seemed hopeless"; and although he felt he should have been active among his men, he remained in his foxhole all night because "I was just too scared and tired to get out." He was then evacuated to his local field medical unit but was immediately returned to duty because of apparent lack of overt symptoms. For 2 weeks, he noted increasing apprehension, startability, nightmares, insomnia, and headaches. He was seen on several occasions by his battalion medical officer and treated with analgesics and mild ataractic medication. His symptoms continued, however, and his effectiveness in his duties deteriorated. He was consequently transferred to the hospital ship for psychiatric treatment, at which time he exhibited marked anxiety with agitation, tremulousness, and pressure of speech. He was near tears and struggling to maintain emotional control. Thought content was dominated by combat apprehension and feelings of guilt both about this apprehension and the recent loss of men under his leadership. He reported sleeplessness, terrifying dreams, anorexia, and a sense of impending death. After initial examination he was treated with chlorpromazine, 100 mg intramuscularly, then given the same amount orally every 6 hours over a 24-hour period. He slept soundly during this time but was able to awaken for meals and self-care. The dosage of chlorpromazine was then decreased to 50 mg orally every 4 hours during the waking hours of the next 2 days, along with 75 mg in spansule form in the late evening. Initially, this was supplemented with oral barbiturates at night, but this was soon discontinued as a normal sleep pattern was reestablished. After the first 24 hours of heavy medication and sleep, the patient was ambulatory on the ward and his symptoms of anxiety were vastly relieved. His feelings of apprehension and guilt were discussed in both individual and group psychotherapy sessions with much ventilation and abreaction; and there were support, interpretation, suggestion, and reality emphasis by the medical officer, nursing staff, and patient group. Medication was gradually decreased and then discontinued. Although he remained ambivalent about combat, there was no recurrence of anxiety symptoms, and he was returned to full duty after 10 days of hospitalization. Followup information indicated that he served 2 more months under intermittent hostile fire and satisfactorily completed his tour of duty in Viet Nam.

B. Pseudocombat Fatigue

The majority of patients from combat did not show the classical syndrome of combat fatigue as described above, however. These were young men with personality disorders who developed overt symptoms in the environment of the war zone. Superficially, their presenting symptoms frequently resembled those of the true combat fatigue patients, but their histories and hospital courses were quite different. At the time of their hospitalization, it was often difficult to obtain information about their current situation and history; but when the facts became known, they revealed poor past adjustment. Usually there were indications of impulsivity, poor stress tolerance, tenuous emotional control, and/or previous psychiatric contacts and symptoms. Characteristically, these patients had been in the war zone less than 6 months, and the degree of combat stress had been less severe. They were rarely in positions of responsibility and leadership, and feelings of guilt were uncommon in their thought content. Even if these clues were not apparent, their responses to the supportive but highly directive, reality-oriented, shipboard therapeutic techniques were distinctive. Initial treatment was similar to that of true combat fatigue, but because of the deep-seated nature of their problems, inadequate motivation, and poor identification with their military group, these pseudocombat fatigue patients responded poorly to treatment, although their symptoms of anxiety, despondency, or somatic complaints usually improved in the comparatively sheltered environment of the hospital. The crucial test was the prospect of return to duty; at this point, symptoms frequently recurred, new ones appeared, or the patient for the first time frankly discussed his past emotional problems and inability to tolerate them. The following case is a typical example of this pseudocombat fatigue syndrome (Case II):

This 22-year-old LCPL USMC with 2 years of active duty and 4 months of service in Viet Nam was hospitalized aboard *Repose* after he "froze" while under enemy fire. At the time of admission he was grossly anxious, tremulous, and agitated. His speech was in explosive bursts, interrupted by periods of preoccupied silence; he reported only vague memory for his combat experiences of recent weeks and the incident which had precipitated his evacuation from the field. He was immediately treated with chlorpromazine in a dosage schedule similar to that of Case I, and 24 hours later his symptoms had remarkably improved. He was calm and communicative, and history could be obtained. This indicated longstanding problems with emotional and impulse control which had caused difficulties in social, family, and school relationships. He enlisted in the Marine Corps after impulsively quitting high school; and his 2 years of service had been marked by frequent emotional upheavals, marginal performance of duty, and a total of nine disciplinary actions for a variety of minor offenses. His initial 2 months of Viet Nam duty had been comparatively peaceful. As his unit made more contacts with the enemy over the next 2 months, however, he grew increasingly apprehensive, and this became more severe after he received a minor shrapnel wound. On the night prior to hospitalization, he was involved in a brief but intense fire fight, and he "froze" in a state of tremulous dissociation. He was sedated, maintained in the field overnight, and then evacuated to the hospital ship in the morning. There his treatment program was very similar to that of Case I, utilizing both chemotherapy and group and individual psychotherapy; he showed early good results with almost complete initial disappearance of anxiety symptoms. It was noted that some tremulousness and apprehension recurred, however, whenever new casualties arrived aboard or when combat ashore was visible or audible from the ship. He then demonstrated acute exacerbation of symptoms when confronted with the prospect of possible return to duty, and he was finally evacuated out of the combat zone with the diagnosis of emotionally unstable personality after 10 days of hospitalization.

C. Combat Neurosis

Less common than the above described category of pseudocombat fatigue was that of combat neurosis. This can best be defined as neurotic symptoms precipitated by combat stress in patients with chronic psychoneurosis which had not been previously obvious. Again, the presenting symptoms frequently were similar to those of combat fatigue cases, but history and hospital course were different. History, when obtainable after admission, indicated longstanding neurotic problems and patterns which had not previously interfered seriously with duty performance. These patients were hospitalized longer, as more sophisticated psychotherapeutic techniques were necessary to obtain remission of their symptoms than were required for combat fatigue patients. The prognosis for return to duty was significantly better than that for pseudocombat fatigue cases and, in fact, almost equalled that for true combat fatigue. This is not surprising, as most psychiatrists would agree that psychoneurotic problems are generally much more amenable to treatment than are personality disorders. Since there was reasonable hope of success, evacuation was delayed until it was absolutely clear that improvement to the point of return to duty would not be possible in the combat zone. With pseudocombat fatigue patients, however, those who had poor adjustment potential were earlier apparent and therefore were evacuated more rapidly. Combat neurosis was most commonly manifested by anxiety or depression accompanied by psychosomatic symptoms, similar to the manifestations of combat fatigue. Much less common were occasional patients with obsessive–compulsive reactions. Length of time in combat and degree of stress appeared to be of little significance, although compared to pseudocombat fatigue there was a trend toward a history of greater combat stress. A frequently occurring clinical picture was that of a competent noncommissioned officer in peacetime with previous compulsive patterns and chronic but not disabling anxiety who had acute neurotic symptoms exacerbated by combat. Another common case was that of the previously successful Marine with neurotic problems of dependency, guilt, and hostility who became overtly depressed under combat stress. Frequently, there were other major upheavals occurring in these patients' lives simultaneously with the stress of combat, these additional stresses involving some symbolic loss or threat. Information about all of these factors frequently did not become known until some time after admission, and initially the complex of symptoms could be easily misdiagnosed. An example of such a case of combat neurosis is the following (Case III):

This 30-year old S/SGT USMC was initially placed on the sick list by the division psychiatrist because of "nervousness," headache, and gastrointestinal complaints following several mortar attacks on his unit. He was retained in a medical facility ashore for 48 hours, and when his acute symptoms did not improve under treatment there, he was transferred to the hospital ship for further psychiatric care. At the time of admission his psychomotor activity was retarded and there was little spontaneity in his movement or speech. He manifested a tremor, and his mood was obviously depressed and apprehensive. Thought content was dominated by preoccupation with the mortar attacks and the resulting destruction and injury along with his own sense of worthlessness, hopelessness, and futility. He also complained bitterly of vague headache and abdominal discomfort. He said, "I used to be a good Marine but now there is something wrong with me and I can't do my job anymore." History indicated a comparatively unremarkable childhood and adolescent background marked only by compulsive traits and somewhat excessive dependency needs. He enlisted in the Marine Corps after successfully completing high school near the end of the Korean War, and he was not in combat during that conflict. He had an excellent military record, but there was evidence of excessive perfectionism, rigidity, and tenuous self-esteem, especially in his personal life. His first marriage failed, largely because of his neurotic needs and demands, and shortly before he departed for Viet Nam and his initial combat experience, his second wife had threatened separation. During his 3 months in the combat area he had been appalled by the uncertainties and seeming disorganization of actual war, and he began to be preoccupied with a sense of inadequacy in managing the responsibilities of his job. He was plagued with headaches and abdominal discomfort, and all of his symptoms became suddenly worse following the succession of mortar attacks. Aboard the ship he was treated with amitriptyline, gastrointestinal medications, and barbiturate sedation at night. In psychotherapy his concern about the mortar attacks and combat soon proved to be superficial, and his more significant problems of dependency, guilt, self-esteem, and perfectionism were explored. He was assisted in gradually reassuming his identity as a Marine Staff Sergeant. His improvement was slow, but over a 6-week period his depressive symptoms subsided, his self-confidence grew, and his brooding ruminations ceased. He was then returned to full duty, and followup indicated that he completed his combat tour successfully with no recurrence of symptoms.

D. Differential Diagnosis and Disposition

Although the presenting illness of anxiety symptoms while under enemy fire are similar in cases I and II described above, the differences are noteworthy and demonstrate the differentiating characteristics between true combat fatigue and pseudocombat fatigue as observed aboard the hospital ship. Case I had previously good adjustment and lengthy combat service with severe stress. Also his illness involved feelings of responsibility and guilt more than personal fear. His response to treatment was consistent, and he remained symptom-free when faced with return to duty, even though he had ambivalent feelings about this disposition. Seventy-eight percent of the young men with this situational reaction to combat were returned to duty from the hospital ship, usually after less than 14 days hospitalization. Case II, although he initially appeared to have a situational syndrome of combat, demonstrated historically his poor adaptive capacity and further indicated this in his responses to treatment and the prospect of return to the field. It is likely that he would have become a military psychiatric patient even if he had not been exposed to battle stresses. This case exemplifies the most common type of psychiatric casualty in Viet Nam. Approximately 50% of these patients were returned to duty after hospitalization, but it was in this group that some failures and rehospitalizations occurred. Case III in his depressive symptoms differed from the first two cases described above, but this presenting syndrome was nevertheless similar to many other cases of true combat fatigue and pseudocombat fatigue. Again, however, history and hospital course indicated the correct diagnosis. His long-term neurotic problems became apparent and were dealt with therapeutically. Approximately 75% of these patients were returned to duty after treatment, this figure being very close to the percentage of true combat fatigue patients who were returned to their units. There were, in fact, also many psychodynamic similarities in these two groups, particularly involving conflicts about responsibility, guilt, and self-esteem.

VI. General Characteristics of Psychiatric Evacuees from Combat

Relative infrequency of suicidal attempts and threats (8%) was characteristic of this psychiatric population from combat. In other military hospitals, these are more commonly encountered problems; for example, 24% of a recent patient sample in a large Naval hospital in the Continental United States had made suicidal threats, gestures, or attempts. It is speculated that the externalization of aggression in combat is important in decreasing the comparative frequency of self-directed violence. Thirty-nine percent of the total patient group had manifested agitated and/or violent behavior of an aggressive nature prior to admission. One of the most common stories was that of young Marines who became agitated and violently aggressive while under the influence of alcohol between combat episodes. Hostility was a common finding in all except psychoneurotic cases. Depressive symptoms were most common in psychoneurotic patients (54%) but also occurred in a large number of those with personality disorder. It is apparent that the management of aggressive problems is of particular importance in the treatment of combat zone patients. There is situational approval of external aggressive expression, and such aggressive behavior is apparently accompanied by a decrease in suicidal attempts and threats. Yet there are many who cannot tolerate such externalization of aggression or who develop a need for such an outlet and cannot tolerate its absence between combat operations, who then either internalize their hostility and develop a depressive syndrome or lose control and behave violently. The psychodynamics of aggression and hostility were the major area of therapeutic attention in both group and individual psychotherapy aboard the hospital ship.

In this group of patients there were comparatively few with homosexual problems or similar concerns (4%), and this finding coincided with the reports of psychiatrists stationed with the Marine units ashore. It appeared that this chronic military problem is less frequent in combat then in garrison. This may be a result of the realistic external stress of war and, again, the encouragement of overt aggressive activity which partially compensates for the lack of sexual outlet. Also the latent undertones in the intimate and socially acceptable "buddy" relationships among combat troops may decrease the need for more overt expression.

Symptomatically, somatic complaints were almost universal in the group of patients from combat, and the most frequently occurring single somatization was that of headache. This was the most common and most intractable symptom with which the psychiatrist was faced—a vague and stubborn malady reported by the patients with monotonous regularity, indicating their degrees of depression, guilt, anxiety, and ambivalence.

As would be anticipated, many psychiatric patients were evacuated from the field with initial organic diagnoses which were found to be in error when evaluated during and after admission to a medical ward. The commonest such mistaken physical diagnosis was that of heat exhaustion. The identification of acute anxiety symptoms and their differentiation from physical illness are always difficult, and reports indicate that psychiatrists who dealt with casualties in the Korean War (Mullen, 1955) had this problem, particularly with the diagnosis of blast concussion. It was the author's observation that in the tropical environment of Viet Nam, the most frequent medical differential diagnostic problem involved heat exhaustion rather than blast concussion. In many patients, of course, both emotional and physiological factors were significant; but aboard the hospital ship the discovery of primary psychiatric problems were so frequent in evacuees with alleged heat exhaustion that patients arriving with that diagnosis were almost routinely referred for psychiatric evaluation.

Another characteristic of these patients from combat was the increase of anxiety frequently to the point of death obsession in those approaching the end of their tour in the war area. This was noted to occur in nonpsychiatric patients also and appeared to be present to a greater or lesser degree in all combat personnel as the time for rotation grew near. The closer the 13-month rotation date became, the more obsessively concerned became the individual about the certainty of his death. This preoccupation and near delusional belief were quite incapacitating for occasional experienced personnel and caused their deterioration of functioning and eventual hospitalization. More often, it was an anxiety provoking but not disabling concern.

VII. Responses during Hospitalization and Treatment

These combat zone psychiatric patients demonstrated characteristic patterns of behavior and attitude while hospitalized. In group therapy, there was continuing discussion of combat experience with working through of feelings of guilt, fear, and anger. This was an ongoing process with much interaction stimulated anew by each new patient who arrived aboard. This need to discuss and work through was universally observed in nonpsychiatric patients, also. The need to talk about combat experiences resulted in endless discussion which was characteristic of surgical and medical patients, as well as those on the psychiatric ward. The participants in group therapy gave each other mutual support and reassurance and demonstrated great reluctance to direct any anger at the peer group. Anger, however, was a primary focus of discussions, always displaced to authority figures or the local indigenous population. There was little concern with abstract philosophical and political concepts. There was, however, massive concern with the microcosm of the patient's own unit and its problems, pointing up once again the significance of the small group and its tremendous influence on human behavior and tolerance for stress.

As previously noted, problems with control of aggression and aggressive acts prior to hospitalization were frequent among these patients. However, antisocial, rebellious, and violent behavior was uncommon after admission of patients to the psychiatric ward aboard the hospital ship, although such behavior did occur frequently in patients hospitalized psychiatrically in shore facilities. Such aggressive behavior is also commonly encountered in peacetime military hospital wards. Aboard the ship, however, there were no weapons or alcohol available to the patients, and the secondary gain of hospitalization was such as to discourage behavior that (in the patient's mind at least) might anger the authorities and speed return to the discomforts of the field. The general feeling tone on the ward was that of depression, much more so than on other psychiatric wards in the author's experience. This depressed ambience seemed to be due to a comparatively large number of patients with depressive symptomatology, pervading awareness of eventual return to possible death or injury, and general ambivalence of goals and attitudes. The patients were in painful conflict between apprehension about return to combat, conscious or unconscious desire to escape through medical channels, and guilt because of leaving their units for hospitalization and possible further evacuation. This ambivalence was particularly marked at the time of disposition. Regardless of whether the patient was being evacuated out of the country or returned to duty, his feelings about his disposition were very conflictual. Underneath this diffuse ambivalence and depression was an undercurrent of hostility which sometimes taxed the emotional resources of the psychiatric staff.

VIII. Treatment and Disposition

The principles of combat psychiatric treatment were well established in World War II, validated in the Korean Conflict, and have been revalidated in Viet Nam (Tiffany, 1967; Tiffany and Allerton, 1967). These principles of treatment can be summarized as (1) retention of the psychiatric casualty as close to the area of combat as possible; (2) adequate and early medication with sedation and tranquilization; (3) replenishment of physical deprivations with rest, food, and fluids; (4) opportunities for ventilation and supportive–directive psychotherapy; and (5) rapid disposition with return to duty as soon as possible before invalidism and the secondary gain of hospitalization become too entrenched. These principles were utilized aboard the hospital ship, where it was attempted to maintain a strong back-to-duty orientation. Those patients who were psychotic or grossly immature and who obviously needed to be evacuated were transferred from the ship as soon as possible. An attempt was made to have patients who were potential candidates for return to duty in the majority on the ward at any given time. Group therapy sessions were held daily, led alternately by the psychiatrist and the senior corpsmen, and individual short term psychotherapy was done. Ventilation, discussion, suggestion, persuasion, confrontation, and support were the major therapeutic devices employed, and all discussions were strongly reality oriented. Drug therapy was employed quite successfully. This was the first war since phenothiazine drugs were introduced, and they proved to be very useful indeed. A wide variety of acute symptoms, including agitated depressive states, anxiety reactions, hysterical episodes, and psychosomatic problems, were largely ameliorated within 48 hours by the use of chlorpromazine, sometimes supplemented by nighttime barbiturate sedation. During this period, the patient could care for his own physical needs and be awake when necessary, while continuing to have maximal sedative and calming effects. Then medication could be drastically reduced or even discontinued and psychotherapy begun without serious symptomatic relapse. Minor ataractic drugs and antidepressant medications were also utilized.

It was in the matter of disposition that the most troublesome dilemmas faced the psychiatrist. Of the psychiatric patients hospitalized aboard the hospital ship, 62% were returned to duty and 38% were evacuated to out-of-country hospitals. As would be expected, the highest return-to-duty rate was in the patients diagnosed as combat fatigue; 78% of these patients were returned to their units after a brief period of hospitalization. Unfortunately, followup of patients after return to duty was difficult. It appeared, however, that most of them were able to complete their combat tours, although some were later seen by psychiatrists ashore and/or rehospitalized. It is of interest that contacts with patients after their return to duty indicated that tolerance and acceptance of returning psychiatric patients was greater in a combat unit than in noncombat situations. It seemed that units in the field and under fire, in which every man was especially valuable, considered psychiatric disorder to be more honorable and less prejudicial than did commands under more peaceful conditions.

The decision of which patient to return to duty and which to evacuate was always a difficult and highly individual one. The patient's clinical state, his response to treatment, his psychiatric history, his general military adjustment, and the local situation of his unit were all important factors in this decision. Motivation and response to treatment, along with historical and situational factors were much more significant than the type and severity of presenting symptoms. In the final analysis, problems of disposition with these patients from combat could be solved only by applying basic principals common to all psychiatric practice, civilian and military. The two most important fundamental ingredients for success in management and disposition of these patients were: (1) Accurate diagnosis and personality assessment and (2) retention of objectivity by the physician, with recognition of countertransference feelings and other irrational attitudes precipitated by combat zone duty. Experience indicates that diagnostic, therapeutic, and administrative problems notwithstanding, the latter factor of retention of his own objectivity is the most difficult problem which must be solved by the psychiatrist treating combat zone psychiatric patients.

IX. Summary

A review has been presented of the characteristics of psychiatric evacuees from combat treated aboard the U.S. Navy Hospital Ship *Repose* during her initial year in Viet Nam operations. Diagnostic and dispositional statistics were reported, and the apparent effects and significance of combat stress were discussed. For purposes of study, the patients were categorized in three groups: (1) combat fatigue (combat situational reactions in healthy personalities), (2) pseudocombat fatigue (combat-precipitated symptoms in basic personality disorders), and (3) combat neurosis (combat-precipitated symptoms in basic psychoneuroses). Similarities and differences in these categories were presented as they related to diagnosis, therapy, and disposition. Other general clinical observations of these psychiatric patients from combat were noted. Treatment methods in accordance with established principles of combat psychiatry were described, and the important problem of psychiatric disposition in a combat zone was briefly discussed.

REFERENCES

American Psychiatric Association (1952). "Diagnostic and Statistical Manual — Mental Disorders." Washington, D.C.
Arthur, R. J. (1965). Stability in psychosis admission rates: Three decades of navy experience. *Public Health Rept. (U.S.)* **80**, 512–514.
Glass, A. (1955). Principles of combat psychiatry. *Military Med.* 177, 33.
Mullen, C. S. (1955). "Combat Psychiatry in the Field," Training Bull. U.S. Dept. of the Navy, Bureau of Medicine and Surgery, Neuropsychiatric Branch, Washington, D.C.
Strange, R. E. (1968). Combat fatigue versus pseudo-combat fatigue in Vietnam. *Military Med.* 133, 8.

Strange, R. E., and Arthur, R. J. (1967). Hospital ship psychiatry in a war zone. *Am. J. Psychiat.* **124**, 3.

Tiffany, W. J., Jr. (1967). The mental health of army troops in Vietnam. *Am. J. Psychiat.* **123**, 1585–1586.

Tiffany, W. J., Jr., and Allerton, W. S. (1967). Army psychiatry in the mid-60's. *Am. J. Psychiat.* **123**, 810–821.

U.S. Department of the Army (1952). Psychiatric treatment in combat areas. *TB Med.* **238**.

5 // Urinary 17-OHCS Levels in // Two Combat Situations

Peter G. Bourne

I. Introduction: Endocrinology and Stress

A. Historical Background

The concept of stress has been widely accepted as a specific somatic response to damage or threat of damage by a wide variety of environmental agents, including events having a psychological rather than a physical impact. This concept was first suggested by the observation made in 1911 by Cannon and de la Paz that the adrenal medulla releases hormone in the cat during the emotional excitement associated with exposure to a barking dog (Cannon and de la Paz, 1911). In 1936 Hans Selye demonstrated evidence of a second endocrine system, the pituitary-adrenal-cortical axis. This system responding often to more subtle aspects of psychic and physical stress induced even more global and profound influences on metabolic function (Selye, 1936). The work of Cannon and the proposal by Selye of a "General Adaptation Syndrome" led to the expectation by some investigators that these hormones could provide an easy and tangible measure of the degree of stress to which an organism was exposed.

The emphasis on the adrenal glands proved most useful for stimulating research, since it offered a specific structure for the center of attention. However, with further work in the field and the development of improved biochemical techniques, evidence has accumulated that other endocrine systems in addition to those involving the adrenals can respond to psychological stimuli. In light of recent work, it would now appear that no endocrine system is entirely free from the influences of psychological stress (Mason, 1964).

Despite these recent advances implicating virtually all endocrine systems, altered adrenal function in relationship to behavior and to the handling of stress has remained the central focus for research in the field during the last 15 years. Early studies concentrated on observed elevations in adrenal cortical secretion produced by acute stimuli in the environment in both experimental and naturally occurring situations. Endocrinological reactions to movies (Wadeson *et al.*, 1963), final exams (Bliss *et al.*, 1956), and hospital admission (Mason *et al.*, 1965) were studied in human subjects as well as the responses to threatening and demanding stimuli in monkeys (Mason *et al.*, 1957a,b). It was also shown that calming influences in the environment, such as movies with a benign content and hypnosis, produced an acute decrease in the level of secretion (Sachar *et al.*, 1966; Wadeson *et al.*, 1963). These studies, however, dealt only with the response of the organism to an acute and well-defined event. Subsequently, investigations of more chronic situations have shown that under circumstances of prolonged stress both elevations and depressions in the mean adrenal steroid secretion level can occur (Friedman *et al.*, 1963; Mason, 1959).

More recently it has been appreciated that the degree of stress which an event in the environment is considered to provide, whether it be automobile racing or cardiac surgery, is based entirely on the subjective assessment of the event by the investigator. The problem has thus become more complex, necessitating a reexamination of the earlier conceptualization of stress as a stimulus–response or threat–defense phenomenon. Instead, it is now appreciated that stress can only be defined in terms of man's inter-action with his environment, and that an event is stressful for an individual only if he perceives it as such. By contrast with the ear-lier viewpoint, it is clear that no component of the stress reaction can be considered constant. Most important in producing this shift in emphasis was the work of Fox *et al.* (1961), Wolff *et al.* (1964), and Sachar *et al.* (1963), all of whom demonstrated the sig-nificance of individual difference in the psychological and physio-logical handling of similar events in the environment. Specifically, they demonstrated that there was a relationship between the adre-nal secretion of 17-hydroxycorticosteroid (17-OHCS) and an indi-vidual's characteristic style of dealing with the day to day stresses of living. The concept of ego defenses and the manner in which they were utilized to handle the perception of threatening stimuli was used to explain the differences they observed. As a result, it became experimentally feasible on the basis of observed behavior to predict the chronic mean level of 17-OHCS secretion in a given individual over a period of weeks or months (Wolff *et al.*, 1964). It was also demonstrated in certain clinical situations that over more extended periods of time, with therapy or other factors which alter the efficacy of the individual's defenses, changes occur in this characteristic mean level.

B. Present Concepts

There is now strong evidence that in addition to individual dif-ferences social factors may exert a significant effect in altering an individual's perception of stress, and hence his level of adrenal-cortical secretion (Mason and Brady, 1964). In small groups with free communication among members of equal standing, there is a tendency for a consensus to develop as to how a stress should be perceived, which in turn minimizes individual differences in adre-nal-cortical response. The group support also serves to reinforce avoidance of prolonged feelings of arousal or uncertainty. As a result, members of a group, when presented with a threatening event, will tend to have more similar levels of steroid excretion than if they were presented with the same event as isolated sub-jects. It is also becoming increasingly apparent that, aside from mere group consensus in the perception of stress when all members are equal, there is also an important potential influence of assigned role when some members assume positions as leaders (Marchbanks, 1958). This has been shown to be particularly true in primate societies, where animals high in the social hierarchy of the troop present entirely different endocrinological profiles in response to a given stress than do animals who are low in the dominance order (Rose and Levine, 1968). Current concepts suggest that in the investigation of man's response to stress attention must be paid to the threat itself, the psychological style of the individual in coping with his environment, and the social context in which he exists.

C. Stress Studies in Combat

Following the first indications that levels of steroid secretion from the adrenal gland could be a measurable parameter of an organism's response to stress, investigators sought out naturally occurring events which appeared to pose extreme threats to those involved. Race drivers, long distance runners, college oarsmen, and patients prior to open-heart surgery, as well as persons in a myriad of other pursuits, had their rates of steroid excretion measured to assess their "level of stress." Workers in the field were aware that combat with its very real threat of death or mutilation might represent the ultimate in naturally occurring events of stress, and many assumed that steroid levels could be anticipated that would far exceed those previously observed in any civilian circumstance. The historically high incidence of psychiatric casualties in combat seemed to support this point of view, and it was presumed that even those who functioned successfully would have significant biochemical evidence of their ordeal.

Even at the time of the Korean conflict, logistical problems and the relatively unrefined biochemical techniques then available for measuring endocrine excretion limited research in this area (El-madjian, 1955). It is also true that the greatest period of interest in the biochemical aspects of behavior came after the Korean war was concluded. Fifteen years later, with improved methods of measuring steroid excretion and, specifically, 17-OHCS levels as well as the greater mobility provided by the helicopter, the naturally occurring stress laboratory of combat was ready to be taken advantage of in Viet Nam.

II. Collection of Data

The study was carried out in two separate phases. In each, a group of United States soldiers in a distinct combat situation in Viet Nam were investigated. The men in the first group were helicopter medics who were exposed to periods of brief and acute stress interspersed with relative security and relaxation. The second group was comprised of the 12 members of a Special Forces (Green Beret) "A" Team defending an isolated outpost in the Central Highlands of Viet Nam. This latter group, as distinct from the former, were exposed to prolonged stress without any significant periods of relief, and with the state periodically accentuated by outbreaks of fighting.

A. Phase 1: Helicopter Ambulance Crews

1. *Subjects*

The subjects in the initial phase of the study consisted of seven medical aidmen serving on helicopters evacuating combat casualties in South Viet Nam. All were Caucasian, and five of the seven were married. Age ranged from 19 to 39 years (median 28.5). Education ranged from 11 to 13 years (median 12). Years of military service ranged from 2½ to 19 (median 18). The subjects came from two different helicopter ambulance units stationed together in South Viet Nam, and had been performing duties picking up and air evacuating combat casualties for 3–9 months at the time the measures began. These were frequently carried out under heavy enemy fire, and several of their colleagues had been killed. The situation, however, although clearly threatening, was not novel to the subjects.

One subject, No. 3, was taken off flight status for disciplinary reasons the day after the study was initiated. However, he had been flying regularly up until that point, and he was retained as a subject.

All the subjects were free of evidence of clinical disease during the study, with the exception of No. 3. This subject sustained a severe scalp laceration which became infected, and his steroid measurement for that day, to be discussed later, was therefore excluded from general consideration.

2. *Sample Collection*

Fourteen separate 24-hour urine collections were made on each man. These were made almost continuously during the 3-week study period. Some of the days during which urine collections were made were days when the men engaged in intense combat, some were days when they flew only in highly secure areas, and some were days when they did not fly at all or had the day off. A technician followed the subjects both on and off duty to insure completeness of the samples. The collected urine was frozen at 6-hour intervals, and at the end of 24 hours the collection for that day was thawed. It was then pooled for each subject, the total volume was measured, and appropriate aliquots for various biochemical measurements were taken and refrozen. Analyses of these 24-hour pools for 17-hydroxycorticosteroid concentration were performed by a modification of the Glenn-Nelson method (Rosenthal and Mason, 1959). A number of collections were known to be incomplete and were discarded. Seventy-six were considered complete and comprise the data presented. Each man was also weighed at the start of the study.

3. *Psychological and Behavioral Observations*

Shortly after selection each subject was asked to fill out a 75-item personal history questionnaire, as well as a copy of the Minnesota Multiphasic Personality Inventory. The study extended for a 3-week period, from January 10 through January 31, 1966, except for the seventh subject for whom it was continued an additional week. Each evening throughout the period of the study the subjects were asked to fill out a copy of the Daily Multiple Affect Adjective Check List (D-MAACL). The results of this aspect of the study are reported elsewhere (Bourne *et al.*, 1966). During the course of the investigation each man was interviewed individually and a psychiatric history was obtained. Particular emphasis was placed on the subject's general modes of handling stress, as well as on his conceptualization of the specific threat posed by his daily exposure to the danger of death or mutilation. Every third day during the study, the man was asked to fill out a self-report form in which he listed anything unusual that had happened to him in the previous 72 hours, as well as any significant affective experience.

During the 3-week period that the study lasted, a careful record was kept of each subject's activities, including details of the missions he flew as well as events in his private life. Close contact was maintained with each of the men, and additional information was obtained through informal interviews regarding responses to various combat events. Periodically, the author also accompanied the subject on his missions to record his behavior and performance.

B. Phase 2: Special Forces (Green Beret) "A" Team

1. *Subjects*

The subjects in the second phase of the study consisted of the 12 members of a Special Forces "A" team in an isolated camp near the Cambodian border in South Viet Nam. Two of the subjects were officers and ten were enlisted men. All of these subjects were Caucasian; two were married and ten were single or divorced. Ages ranged from 22 to 41 years (median 26). Education ranged from 10 to 16 years (median 12). Years of military service ranged from 1½ to 20 years (median 5½). Time in Viet Nam ranged from 5 to 36 months (median 8.5), and time in the camp ranged from 1 to 10 months (median 8).

2. *Location and Mission*

The camp was located in territory controlled by the Viet Cong. It was situated so as to provide significant obstruction to the free flow of arms and men from the Ho Chi Minh Trail into the Central Highlands of South Viet Nam. The mission of the 12 man team was to train locally recruited villagers and tribesmen, defend the camp against attack, and make frequent patrols into the surrounding countryside. The constant threat of attack by an overwhelmingly superior force was always present but was considerably increased at the start of the monsoon season in early May. On May 10, 1966, the men in the camp were notified that an attack was imminent. Intelligence sources indicated that the attack would come between May 18 and May 22, but most probably on the night of May 19. Although this particular attack failed to occur, there was mounting stress caused by this realistic external threat up to May 19, which then tapered off gradually during the following few days. A more colorful description of life in this camp has appeared elsewhere (Mason, 1967).

3. *Sample Collection*

Twenty-four hour urine collections were made on each of the 12 subjects. The number of collections ranged from one to seven. These were collected over an 18-day period from May 9 through May 27, but with the majority collected during the critical period of May 18 through May 22. The urine was handled in the same manner as in the first phase of the study with the helicopter ambulance crew members. It was stored in a field refrigerator run on a portable generator, and was kept frozen until it could be removed from the camp by helicopter. Analyses were again made on the 24-hour pools for 17-hydroxycorticosteroid concentration. Collections known to be incomplete were discarded. Fifty-five collections were considered complete and comprise the data presented. A record of each man's weight was obtained.

4. *Psychological and Behavioral Observations*

Because of the nature of the military operation that these men were engaged in, it was not possible to conduct the same type of formal psychological evaluations that were carried out with the helicopter ambulance medics. The personal history questionnaire and the Minnesota Multiphasic Personality Inventory were not used in this instance. However, the weekly form of the Multiple Affect Adjective Check List (W-MAACL) was administered for a 1-month period. The results of this aspect of the study have been reported previously (Bourne *et al.*, 1968). Informal interviews were conducted with each of the subjects at intervals during the study. In addition, the author and an assistant lived in the camp as participant observers for the duration of the study from May 1 to July 6, 1966. A daily log was maintained for all activities in the camp, as well as the significant events in the lives of each of the subjects. Records were also kept of all military activity in the area which altered the level of perceived stress in the camp.

III. Results: Urinary 17-Hydroxycorticosteroid Excretion

A. Phase 1

Daily 24-hour urinary 17-OHCS levels for each of the seven helicopter ambulance medics are shown in Fig. 1. In all, 76 24-hour collections were analyzed.

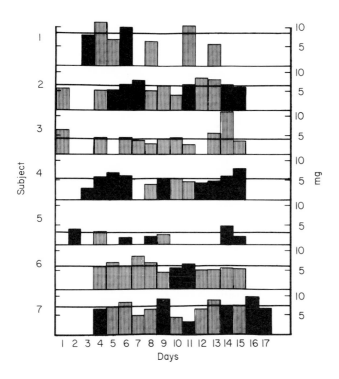

FIG. 1.   *Daily 24-hour urine 17-OHCS levels in seven helicopter ambulance medics, showing the mean for each subject. Solid areas indicate flying days; striped areas indicate nonflying days.*

It will be noted that in all subjects there is remarkably little difference in the observed level of 17-hydroxycorticosteroid obtained on flying and nonflying days. In half the instances, the highest levels of excretion were found on days when the subjects did not fly at all. A graphic example of this is seen in subject No. 1, who on January 14 flew five missions totalling 4 hours and encountered considerable enemy fire. His level of 17-OHCS excretion on that day was 7.8 mg in 24 hours. The same subject on January 17, when he remained at his billet, had a level of 11.2 mg in 24 hours.

The levels obtained on each day, whether the subject was flying or not, also differ very little from the overall mean obtained for each individual during the time of study. For the group as a whole, the coefficient of variance (standard deviation as percent of mean) was 27%. This is true despite the highly episodic nature of the danger they were exposed to and the markedly different behavior required of the subjects on flying and nonflying days.

Figure 2 shows the mean 24-hour urinary 17-OHCS levels obtained on each of the seven subjects during the period of the study. In addition, it shows the predicted levels for each subject calculated on the basis of weight alone, described by Rose *et al.* (1968) in a group of healthy young adult males in basic training. The mean of these two groups adjusted for sample size were significantly different. In each instance the level obtained falls at least one standard error below the weight predicted figure. They are also well below the figures of Mijeon *et al.* (1963) and Sachar *et al.* (1965), which have been considered as means for the population as a whole.

B. Phase 2

The chronic mean 24-hour levels of 17-hydroxycorticosteroid excretion for the members of the Special Forces "A" team are shown in Fig. 3. Insufficient complete collections were obtained on one subject, who was therefore excluded from consideration.

The mean level for the two officers (subjects A and B) is significantly higher than the mean of the nine enlisted men (subjects F through N), as determined by the *t* test; $t = 4.5$, $p < 0.02$. It is also

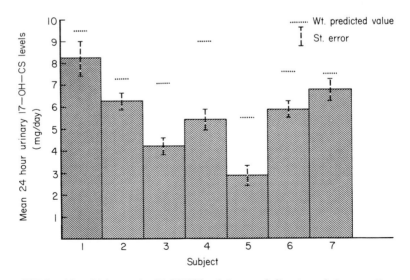

FIG. 2.   *Mean 24-hour urine 17-OHCS levels in seven helicopter ambulance medics.*

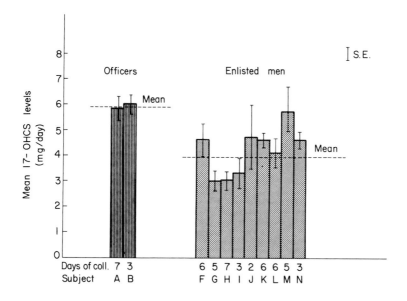

FIG. 3.   *Mean 24-hour urinary 17-OHCS levels for eleven Special Forces soldiers.*

apparent that there is relatively little deviation in the level of excretion by individual members from the mean of their respective
groups. An apparent exception is subject M. However, this man
had a body weight of 230 pounds as compared to the mean body
weight of 173 pounds for the entire group of subjects. If a correction is made for his large body size, then his level falls very close
to that of the group mean.

Adequate collections on the day of anticipated attack were obtained from one officer and six enlisted men (Fig. 4). The mean
level before attack was determined as a mean of 2 or 3 days' excre-
tions, except for one enlisted man who had only 1 day of collection
immediately prior to the day of anticipated attack. The postattack
levels were determined over a mean of 3 days for all seven men.
The responses of the officer and radio operator as compared to that
of the five enlisted men were found to be significantly different,
determined by a rank order comparison of the percent change in
17-OHCS excretion, Mann-Whitney U Test, $p < 0.028$.

The role of the senior radio operator in the camp while it was
under threat of attack was quite different from that of the other

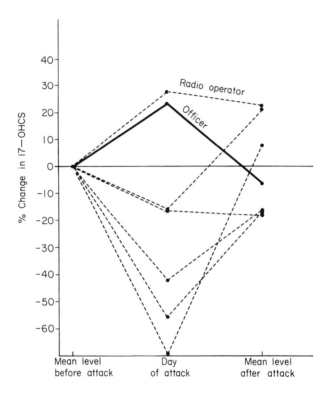

FIG. 4.   *Percentage change in 24-hour 17-OHCS levels. (——) officer; (_ _ _) enlisted*
men.

enlisted men. He worked very intimately with the officers and
spent most of that 24-hour period transmitting and receiving the
very large volume of communication which took place between
the officers and the higher command in Pleiku, 40 miles away. In
terms of the type of demands placed on him, his role was much
closer to that of the officers than to the other enlisted men, who
were not at all involved in the command interactions and decision
making process.

IV. Discussion

It appears from the data presented in the first phase of the study
that there are two major findings. First, for these subjects the vari-

ation in the level of 24-hour urinary 17-hydroxycorticosteroid excretion deviates very little from the overall mean and bears no direct relationship to whether the man was flying combat missions
or not. Second, the chronic mean level of 17-hydroxycorticosteroid
excretion for the entire period of study on each subject was considerably lower than that predicted by body weight alone, compared with a group of basic trainees at Fort Dix, New Jersey (Rose
et al., 1968). These two features, stability over time and the chronic
low level of 17-OHCS excretion, suggest that flying versus nonflying cannot be interpreted alone as stress versus nonstress, nor can
the objective threat of death and mutilation be interpreted as a
stress without consideration of the manner in which each individual perceives the threat. It appears that each subject utilizes very
extensive and effective psychological defenses to handle the
events with which he is faced. These defenses enable the man to
perceive reality in such a way that he minimizes the danger it represents, as well as to create for himself a feeling of invulnerability
and omnipotence.

Interviews with the subjects revealed that they tended, in general, to stress the considerable gratification they received in their
job which tended to balance the threat of danger to which they
were exposed. This was expressed particularly in terms of the
prestige they obtained among other troops because they were helicopter ambulance medics, as well as by frequent expressions of
gratitude from the casualties they evacuated. With two exceptions,
the threat of death or mutilation was constantly minimized. This
threat was handled with a wide variety of defenses, but with
equally effective results. Whether the defenses tended to deny the
danger or bolster the individual's feeling of invincibility, they
provided an altered perception of reality with which the man
seemed to be able to function relatively comfortably.

One subject, No. 5, was a sincerely religious Catholic who believed that God would protect him no matter how great the danger. This feeling was considerably reinforced by his successful
survival throughout the Korean War, where at times he had been
exposed to even more hazardous conditions than he was now
exposed to in Viet Nam. However, despite his rigid defense, this
subject had a permanent tremor and described himself as nervous,
dating his problems from his experiences in the Korean conflict.

Another subject, No. 6, had carefully calculated from the number of flights he flew, the number of casualties in the unit during
the previous year, and the length of his tour in Viet Nam, a statis-

tical estimate of the chance of his being killed or injured on any given day. The result was reassuringly small. This subject, following a near miss in a mine explosion in Saigon, expressed far greater fear of going into the city, a situation he could avoid, than of flying, a situation he could not avoid.

In one subject, No. 1, who was perhaps the least intellectually capable of the group, there was evidence of considerable ritualistic compulsive behavior. This subject had experienced great difficulty in learning the skills the army had taught him and performed all of his tasks in a painstakingly systematic manner. While flying out to a combat area for a pickup, he would mentally review in minute detail every single action he would perform from the moment the helicopter touched the ground. It seemed that he had taken literally the old army adage that if you do your job right you will stay out of trouble, and had expanded it to cover even the intransigencies of combat.

Another clearly definable manner in which the combat situation was handled was demonstrated in subjects No. 2 and No. 7. Both of these men constantly described how near the bullets had come, how close they were to the Viet Cong, and how miraculously they had been saved. In the group, this was a socially acceptable way to behave, including the admission of having been afraid. These stories were accepted without question, even when everyone present knew them to be considerably exaggerated. When asked to explain what they gained from the job when it was apparently so dangerous, they both openly stated that they were considerably motivated by the medals they received, the increased pay for flying, and the prestige. It was also evident that these men utilized their exaggeration of the danger to reinforce their own sense of omnipotence and the belief that they could survive and handle any eventuality in combat. Interestingly, these two subjects were rated as the best performers in the group when evaluated by the pilots with whom they flew.

In most instances, the defensive maneuvers were considerably more complex than would appear from the present description, and no subject used just one type of defense to the exclusion of all others. However, it is apparent that the type of defense used is of minimal consequence in terms of the effect in lowering the level of steroid secretion. What seems of significance is the extent to which the type of defense is successful in providing the individual protection against having to face the danger in the environment as well as enhancing his own feelings of invincibility.

The concept of varying defenses being used to exclude overwhelmingly threatening events from conscious appreciation is not new. As long as 25 years ago Rado (1943) made the following statement in discussing the psychodynamics of combat stress:

> By far the most efficient technique at the soldier's disposal in resolving this conflict is completely to ignore the dangers surrounding him as though disregarding his own life, and thus stop the entire working of emergency control. Transformed from a sensitive man into an insensitive technician of war, he then interprets combat not as a continued threat of injuries but as a sequence of operational demands to be responded to by precise military performances. He is able to take this remarkable attitude because the situation touches off in the depths of his mind the eternal human illusion of one's invulnerability and immortality. With his self-love thus powerfully protected he can afford to lose his identity in the military unit, can give himself entirely to the job in hand and may even perform deeds of heroism.

What is new is the demonstration that such well-established behavioral concepts can be substantiated at a physiological level. That such a specific measure of stress as 17-OHCS excretion should remain relatively impervious to the clear-cut threat of death or mutilation suggests that when the threat in the environment achieves sufficient magnitude, altered perception of the situation becomes a necessary and indispensable method of adaptation. This is required when social pressures are so great that physical avoidance is totally unacceptable to the individual.

Both in his handling of the danger and the consequences of his own aggressive behavior, the individual is able to repress the usual component of affective arousal and induce in himself a state of psychological anesthesia. In his book, "Air War, Viet Nam," Harvey (1967) describes the phased initiation that pilots go through to permit a similar depersonalization during the dropping of bombs and strafing of those on the ground without incurring an emotional reaction. It seems, however, that the process of affective denial, once aroused, spills over to other areas of the man's life, leading to a generalized emotional repression and hence a lowering of steroid secretion.

In the second phase of the study, the data obtained on the 12 members of the Special Forces "A" team demonstrates several important findings. With these subjects, as with the helicopter ambulance medics, the mean levels of 17-OHCS excretion are considerably lower than might be anticipated on the basis of body weight and studies of nonlife threatening experimental stress situations. At the same time the levels for the officers and enlisted men deviate little from their respective group means.

It appeared that, as in the first phase of the study, these findings can be largely attributed to the similar manner in which the external threat posed by the dangers of combat was handled. For instance, one Special Forces soldier was again a very religious individual who would drive many miles in a jeep over treacherous jungle roads so that a Vietnamese Catholic priest who spoke little or no English could hear his confession. By making this hazardous journey with sufficient frequency, the man was able to maintain his strong belief in divine protection and felt he had little to fear in combat.

Although a wide variety of defenses were observed in these subjects, all of which are interpretable as effective ways of protecting each man from an overwhelming sense of threat, an additional factor appears to be operative among these men. More so than the helicopter ambulance medics, the members of this Special Forces team demonstrated an overwhelming emphasis on self-reliance, often to the point of omnipotence. This was true both for the individual and for the team as a whole. The members expressed the belief that the team was invincible, gaining for themselves considerable support by virtue of their membership. Most of the members had an inordinate faith in their own capabilities, the result of preexisting personality traits, their very comprehensive training, and their past successful survival through the most hazardous combat experiences. In some of the men, particularly those who had spent years in counterinsurgency operations in Laos and Viet Nam, their faith in their own invulnerability bordered on a feeling of immortality.

In addition, it was apparent that these subjects were action-oriented individuals who characteristically spent little time in introspection. Their response to any environmental threat was to engage in a furor of activity which rapidly dissipated the developing tension. Externally directed aggressive behavior which enjoyed a maximum of group condonence tended to relieve the individual of any feelings of vulnerability and particularly protected him from the fear of being challenged beyond what he believed to be the limit of his capabilities.

The second point of interest which the data raises is that there is a significant difference in the adrenal–cortical response demonstrated by the enlisted men and by the two officers in the camp.

Although all members of the group are equally exposed to the realistic dangers surrounding them, this suggests either an inherent difference in the psychological adaptive capacity of the two officers, or that their assigned role in the group provides additional stresses which cannot be as easily dealt with as those confronting the enlisted men. The data supports the latter hypothesis. The enlisted men are generally required to perform tasks in which they are highly trained and which tend to be of a mechanical nature, such as building defenses and maintaining equipment. Their concern in combat or in the event of an attack on the camp revolves around their satisfactory performance of these tasks and the preservation of their own lives. Their competence in the former leaves little room for ruminative apprehension, and the fear for their own survival is conveniently handled by their feelings of invulnerability and by a heightened industriousness at their tasks. Unlike the enlisted men, the officers are primarily influenced in their behavior by radio messages coming from the higher command outside the camp. This involves rapid decision making on their part and the tactful handling of commands made with the weight of superior rank but hampered by the ignorance of a 40-mile physical separation. The demands created by this situation, as well as the responsibilities inherent in their own command situation, cannot be as easily dealt with or defended against as can the more vaguely defined and distant threats of death or injury. These demands require immediate solutions and tend to keep the officer in a state of at least mild interpersonal conflict with either his superiors, his subordinates, or both. In addition, the very nature of his job limits the possible avenues available to him for the dissipation of tension. He rarely can engage in the more physical and less emotionally demanding chores around the camp, but must constantly remain on the alert for new instructions which may call for new and unique patterns of behavior that he can never be sure how he will accomplish.

The sense of responsibility felt by the officers for the lives and safety of the ten enlisted men under their command and the additional stress which this provides are hard to gauge. Although these were easily kept from immediate awareness by such rationalizations as the often heard statement "If they overrun us, it is every man for himself," there is no doubt that the traditional responsibility of rank creates a real social stress. Of greater significance is the constant demands on the generally young officers to reinforce their role as leaders. Despite their official position, they are in constant competition with older, often highly battle-scarred senior enlisted men for informal control of the group and the respect of the other members. This leads them to take extreme personal risks in order to gain acceptance as the rightful leaders. The temptation to prove themselves in this way is not always yielded to, but the social pressure to do so is always there.

The separation of roles between the officers and enlisted men in the camp which appears to explain the difference in levels of chronic 17-OHCS excretion were further accentuated when the expectation of an enemy attack on the camp arose. This was reflected also by an increase in the separation of 17-OHCS levels. The drop in the level of excretion shown by five out of six of the enlisted men coincided with heightened activity in the form of laying additional mines, reinforcing barbed wire defenses, checking ammunition stores, and preparing the medical bunker for casualties. All of these are well-practiced activities which they had been taught to carry out in response to this type of emergency. They remained so busy coping with the immediacy of the threat by practical measures that they had little time to ruminate about the impending danger. Group cohesion, often lacking at other times, was emphasized and accentuated, and a feeling of euphoric expectancy pervaded their preparations for the attack.

The officers at the time of the expected attack also experienced an intensification of their previous role behavior. They were in almost constant radio communication with their superiors, both relaying information from the camp and coordinating their plans with those of other units in the general area. They were very much aware that the ability of the camp to withstand an attack was in their hands and that they were facing a crucial opportunity to prove their capabilities. The rise in level of 17-OHCS excretion demonstrated by the one officer from whom urine could be collected at this time is consistent with these findings.

The observations in this second phase of the study reconfirm the initial findings with the helicopter ambulance crew men that individual psychological defenses and behavior patterns enable man to perceive his environment in such a way that he denies the very real threat of death or mutilation in combat. They also suggest the importance of group influences and assigned role in modifying the individual's adrenal–cortical response to a stressful environment. In group situations where the possible alternative methods for handling stress are limited, the group factors tend to minimize the effect of individual differences. The observations made in the present study are highly consistent with the findings of Marchbanks (1958) in his study of B-52 crews. He found that on a long and stressful flight the instructor pilot showed significantly higher levels of 17-OHCS excretion than the other members of the group, all of whom demonstrated lower but remarkably similar levels of excretion. It appears that in both instances the higher levels of 17-OHCS excretion shown by those in the leadership position are related more to their assigned role than to specific personality factors, and that they are responding to the demands imposed by the group rather than to the major threat in the external environment. The similarity of response seen in the other group members suggests that there is considerable conformity in the way any threat is perceived and in the manner in which it is handled.

A number of other possible explanations for the biochemical findings in this study must be considered.

All United States military personnel in Viet Nam are required to take weekly a tablet containing 300 mg of Chloroquine base and 45 mg of Primaquine base as prophylaxis against malaria. There are two ways in which ingestion of these antimalarial drugs might produce falsely low levels of 17-OHCS in the urine. First, the drugs might interfere at higher wavelengths with the spectrophotometric readings upon which determination of 17-OHCS in the urine is based. Second, there might be a direct pharmacological effect upon adrenal function. Careful examination of the absorption spectra on a number of the samples showed no evidence of a contaminating substance, thus ruling out the former consideration. To the present time, there has been no definitive study which would absolutely preclude the latter possibility, although we believe on the basis of a great deal of empirical evidence that there is no significant effect of these two drugs on the activity of the pituitary–adrenal axis.

An alternative explanation for the low level of 17-OHCS excretion might be that in a condition of chronic stress such as these subjects are exposed to, with constant stimulation of the pituitary–adrenal axis, a state of "adrenal exhaustion" develops. However, a naturally occurring event involving one of the subjects in the first phase of the study tends to refute this. During the period of the investigation subject No. 3 was involved in a fight and sustained a scalp laceration which became severely infected. At that time his level of excretion rose to more than three times what it had been prior to the infection, returning to the previous levels 24 hours after antibiotic therapy was instituted. This certainly suggests that a considerable adrenal reserve existed. Similar evidence to support this belief was obtained by Freidman *et al.* (1963) when studying a group under chronic stress. In that instance considerable adrenal reserve was demonstrated in response both to naturally occurring events and to challenge with ACTH.

An additional variable might be the necessary adaptation to heat which occurs in Viet Nam. However, although the helicopter crews were operating in a tropical environment, the Special Forces camp located in the highlands enjoyed cool and equitable weather conditions.

It might be suggested that the groups under study are highly selected and their responses are not representative of combat troops in general. It is true that both groups of subjects are highly trained and have learned to handle stress with a high level of military arousal while at the same time preserving broad emotional tranquility. However, we believe that the wide range of personality types, the variety of past histories, and the varying degrees of investment in the job tend to refute this hypothesis.

In conclusion it may be stated that the findings described in this chapter suggest that, both physiologically and psychologically, man is able to adapt to the stress of war. At least when the episodes of combat are relatively brief and other physical needs such as nutrition, warmth, and sleep are adequately met, the potential danger presented by the possibility of death in battle can be defended against psychologically over relatively long periods of time. Physiological stress as defined by the elevation of 17-OHCS excretion appears at the same time to be more sensitive to the demands of interpersonal relationships than to the less certain but more lethal potential of combat. Particularly, the social pressures of the leadership role appear to produce a more profound physiological alteration in the individual than the duel even to death with the impersonal weapons of modern warfare.

ACKNOWLEDGMENTS

The author wishes to express his appreciation to William M. Coli, B.A., for his assistance in the collection of data in Viet Nam and to John W. Mason, M.D., and

Robert M. Rose, M.D., of the Department of Neuroendocrinology, Walter Reed Army Institute of Research, for their invaluable support, including making possible the biochemical determinations on the specimens collected.

REFERENCES

Bliss, E. D., Migeon, C. J., Hardin-Branch, C. H., and Samuels, L. T. (1956). Reaction of the adrenal cortex to emotional stress. *Psychosomat. Med.* 18, 56–76.

Bourne, P. G., Coli, W. M., and Datel, W. E. (1966). Anxiety levels of six helicopter ambulance medics in a combat zone. *Psychol. Rept.* 19, 821–822.

Bourne, P. G., Coli, W. M., and Datel, W. E. (1968). Affect levels of Special Forces soldiers under threat of attack. *Psychol. Rept.* 22, 363–366.

Cannon, W. B., and de la Paz, D. (1911). Emotional stimulation of adrenal secretion. *Am. J. Physiol.* 27, 64–70.

Elmadjian, R. (1955). Adrenocortical function of combat infantry men in Korea. *Ciba Found. Colloq. Endocrinol.* 8, 627–655.

Fox, H. M., Murawski, J. G., Bartholomay, A. F., and Gifford, S. (1961). Adrenal steroid excretion patterns of 18 healthy subjects and tentative correlations with personality structure. *Psychosomat. Med.* 23, 364–376.

Friedman, S. B., Mason, J. W., and Hamburg, D. A. (1963). Urinary 17-hydroxycorticosteroid levels in parents of children with neoplastic disease. *Psychosomat. Med.* 25, 364–376.

Harvey, F. (1967). "Air War, Viet Nam." Bantam, New York.

Marchbanks, V. H. (1958). Effects of flying stress on 17-hydroxycorticosteroid levels. *J. Aviation Med.* 29, 676–682.

Mason, J. F. (1967). Whom the gods love. *Reporter* 37, 21–25.

Mason, J. W. (1959). Psychological influences on the pituitary-adrenal cortical system. *Recent Progr. Hormone Res.* 15, 345–389.

Mason, J. W. (1964). Psychoendocrine approaches in stress research. *In* "Symposium on Medical Aspects of Stress in the Military Climate" (D. Rioch, ed.), pp. 375–417. Walter Reed Army Inst. of Res., Washington, D. C.

Mason, J. W., and Brady, J. V. (1964). The sensitivity of psychoendocrine systems to social and physical environment. *In* "Psychobiological Approaches to Social Behavior" (P. H. Leiderman and D. Shapiro, eds.) pp. 4–23. Stanford Univ. Press, Palo Alto, California.

Mason, J. W., Harwood, C. T., and Rosenthal, N. R. (1957a). Influence of some environmental factors on plasma and urinary 17-hydroxycorticosteroid levels in the rhesus monkey. *Am. J. Physiol.* 80, 429–433.

Mason, J. W., Brady, J. V., and Sidman, M. (1957b). Plasma 17-hydroxycorticosteroid levels and conditioned behavior in the rhesus monkey. *Endocrinology* 60, 741–752.

Mason, J. W., Sachar, E. J., Fishman, J. H., Hamburg, D. A., and Handlon, J. H. (1965). Corticosteroid response to hospital admission. *Arch. Gen. Psychiat.* 13, 1–8.

Mijeon, C. J., Green, O. C., and Eckert, J. P. (1963). Study of adrenocortical function in obesity. *Metab. Clin. Exptl.* 12, 218–739.

Rado, S. (1943). Pathodynamics and treatment of traumatic war neurosis (traumatophobia). *Psychosomat. Med.* 43, 362–368.

Rose, R. M., and Levine, M. (1968). Personal communication.

Rose, R. M., Poe, R. O., and Mason, J. W. (1968). Combined influence of body size and psychological state in determining 17-hydroxycorticosteroid excretion. *Arch. Int. Medicine* 121, 406–413.

Rosenthal, N. R., and Mason, J. W. (1959). Urinary excretion in the normal rhesus monkey. *J. Lab. Clin. Med.* 53, 720–728.

Sachar, E. J., Mason, J. W., Kolmer, J. S., and Artiss, K. L. (1963). Psychoendocrine aspects of acute schizophrenic reactions. *Psychosomat. Med.* 25, 510–520.

Sachar, E. J., Mason, J. W., Fishman, J. R., Hamburg, D. A., and Handlon, J. H. (1965). Corticosteroid excretion in normal young adults living under "basal conditions." *Psychosomat. Med.* 27, 437–455.

Sachar, E. J., Cobb, J. C., and Shor, R. E. (1966). Plasma cortical levels during hypnotic trance. *Arch. Gen. Psychiat.* 14, 482–490.

Selye, H. (1936). Thymus and adrenals in the response of the organism to injuries and intoxications. *Brit. J. Exptl. Pathol.* 17, 234–248.

Wadeson, R. W., Mason, J. W., Hamburg, D. A., and Handlon, J. H. (1963). Plasma and urinary 17-OHCS responses to motion pictures. *Arch. Gen. Psychiat.* 9, 146–156.

Wolff, C. T., Friedman, S. B., Hofer, M. A., and Mason, J. W. (1964). Relationship between psychological defenses and mean urinary 17-OHCS excretion rates: A predictive study of parents of fatally ill children. *Psychosomat. Med.* 26, 571–591.

6 // Androgen Excretion in Stress

Robert M. Rose

I. Psychoendocrinology

A considerable body of information now exists documenting the influence of psychological state upon adrenal–cortical activity. Mason (1968a) recently reviewed some 200 studies done over the past 15 years, which, taken together, establish the sensitivity of the pituitary–adrenal–cortical system to wide variety of psychological stimuli. The adrenal–cortical response relates not only to characteristics of the stimulus, eg., electric shock, combat, novel situations, but also is determined by the past history of the individual, his unique perception of the events, and constitutional factors such as weight and body build (Rose *et al.*, 1968). We have come to view changes in the secretion of cortisol (man and monkey) or corticosterone (rat) as a rather sensitive barometer of the organism's response to changes in his environment. When the experience is one of threat or challenge, adrenal–cortical activity increases. When the environment is no longer so arousing, when one "copes" or "adapts," cortisol secretion falls to more basal levels, or even lower than normal levels. Low or suppressed levels are seen during hypnosis (Sachar *et al.*, 1966a), or in response to distracting stimuli such as watching Disney nature movies (Wadeson *et al.*, 1963). From these studies a psychoendocrine model has developed relating adrenal response to alterations in the environment.

The role of the central nervous system in mediating endocrine activity rests on firm anatomical and physiological evidence, which has been brought together in a two volume work edited by Martini and Ganong (1966–1967). Figure 1 depicts, in a most schematic manner, the hypothalamic–hypophyseal neuroendocrine relationship. Material classified as releasing factors, possibly of a polypeptide composition, is synthesized in hypothalamic neurosecretory cells and carried via a pituitary–portal system to the anterior pituitary (adenohypophysis) (Harris *et al.*, 1966; Reichlin, 1966). These releasing factors act in a way as yet unknown to promote the synthesis and/or release of the various tropic hormones. For example, with respect to the hypothalamic-pituitary-adrenal-cortical system, corticotropin releasing factor (CRF) elaborated in various hypothalamic nuclei, acts upon cells located in the anterior pituitary to release increased amounts of ACTH, which in turn stimulates adrenal production of cortisol and other adrenal-cortical hormones. More recent work (Eleftheriou and Church, 1968) has demonstrated the influence of environmental events on the concentration of gonadal hormone releasing factor in the hypothalamus. Again referring to Fig. 1, luteinizing hormone releasing factor (LHRF) acts on different anterior pituitary cells to release increased amounts of luteinizing hormone, which in males stimulates the secretion of testosterone.

Compared to the extensive literature on psychological influences on the adrenal cortical system, very little direct evidence has been obtained documenting psychological influences on testosterone secretion. This chapter, I hope, will serve to orient the reader to some of the complexities of androgen secretion and metabolism, and present some preliminary evidence in support of psychoendocrine control of androgen activity in man.

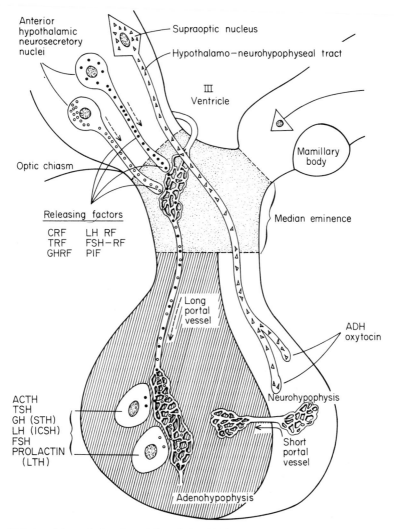

FIG. 1. *Schematic drawing of the relationship between hypothalamus, median eminence of infundibular stalk, adenohypophysis, and neurohypophysis. One set of neurosecretory cells elaborates releasing factors, which are picked up by the superior capillary plexus of the long pituitary portal system. These substances are carried to various cells in the adenohypophysis, where they stimulate the production and release of the trophic hormones. One exception is prolactin inhibiting factor (PIF), which exerts a tonic inhibition of prolactin synthesis in the adenohypophysis. Another set of neurosecretory cells originating in the supraoptic and paraventricular hypothalamic nuclei elaborates oxytocin and antidiuretic hormone (ADH). As the neurohypophysis is continuous with the hypothalamus, these hormones are released directly in the posterior pituitary, but may be carried anterior by short portal vessels. Abbreviations: CRF, corticotropin releasing factor; TRF, thyrotropin releasing factor; GHRF, growth hormone releasing factor; LHRF, luteinizing hormone releasing factor; FSH-RF, follicule stimulating hormone releasing factor; PIF, prolactin inhibiting factor.*

119

There are several lines of evidence which have directed our attention to investigate potential psychological influences on androgen secretion. We have briefly reviewed the anatomical relations which provide for brain influence on pituitary function, not only in control of ACTH, but also of gonadotrophin secretion. In a series of experiments, which initially demonstrated central nervous control of ACTH function, Mason *et al.* (1968) has obtained evidence of psychological influences on androgen activity. Animals which are required to avoid an electric shock by appropriate lever pressing over a continuous 72-hour period, show marked increases in plasma and urinary levels of 17-OHCS. During this period of increased adrenal–cortical activity, there is a concomitant fall in urinary testosterone and the excretion of two major 17-ketosteroids: androsterone and etiocholanolone. This suggests that during this period of arousal or stress, there may be a fall in the pituitary secretion of LH, while there is an increased secretion of ACTH. Many animals showed a rebound rise in testosterone above the baseline following termination of avoidance sessions, while the 17-OHCS levels fell to normal. As pointed out by Mason (1968b), the depression in testosterone followed by a later rise may reflect diminished anabolic activity during stress with an increase following the termination of stress. This has received tentative confirmation in a preliminary study in rats showing a fall in plasma testosterone levels following the onset of shock avoidance (Bliss, 1968). Evidence of the brain's control of potent metabolic regulators, such as cortisol and testosterone, may represent a mechanism involved in psychosomatic phenomena. Although there is no direct evidence to date, it is possible that psychologically induced alterations in androgen as well as adrenocorticoid activity may function in a causal or supportive role in the etiology of disease states.

In previous work on psychological influences on cortisol activity, it has been found that individuals differ significantly in their response to apparently similar environments. Not all parents are equally distressed during the terminal phase of their child's illness with leukemia (Wolff *et al.*, 1964a); not all men in a platoon engaged in basic combat training were equally threatened by this usually taxing experience (Rose *et al.*, 1968); not all men were equally aroused or challenged anticipating an imminent attack from the Viet Cong (Bourne *et al.*, 1968); not all rhesus monkeys maintain continued elevated levels of 17-OHCS excretion when forced to remain vigilant and avoid an electric shock by bar press-ing (Levine *et al.*, 1969). Individuals differ, and their different ad-renal cortical responses can be predicted and can provide a method of assessment that is independent of what individuals say they are experiencing, independent of how "stressed" they may appear to others. By grouping individuals in terms of their 17-OHCS response, we have been able to corroborate clinical impres-sions that individuals differ with respect to how they manifest their distress, for example, some tend to "suffer in silence" while others dramatize and exaggerate their difficulties. Some individu-als who exemplify this latter characteristic have been shown to have low 17-OHCS excretion, which may be interpreted as their experiencing less distress then their overt behavior might indicate (Wolff *et al.*, 1964b). It is possible that individuals may also differ in terms of androgen response; some may have significant altera-tions in gonadal hormone secretion during some provoking stim-ulus, while others may fail to have any alteration in hormone ac-tivity. It is possible that by extending the scope of psychoendo-crine research, we may further our understanding of how the environment influences psychological as well as physiological functioning.

II. Assessment of Androgen Activity

A. 17-Ketosteroids

Although investigators have been aware for some time of pos-sible psychological influences on androgen activity, research in the area has been hampered by the lack of specific techniques for measuring the various androgenic hormones. As methods for the specific and precise measurement of glucocorticoids-cortisol and its metabolites became available, it became possible to investigate issues of psychoendocrine control of the ACTH–adre-nal–cortical system. Up to most recently, parallel work in the an-drogens has been limited primarily to the measurement of 17-ketosteroids. Because of the complexity of the 17-ketosteroid story, it is important to digress somewhat and discuss in some detail the reasons which essentially invalidate the use of 17-ketosteroids as a precise index of androgen activity.

An outline of androgen metabolism is shown in Fig. 2. For the sake of the present discussion, let us consider only two of the ma-

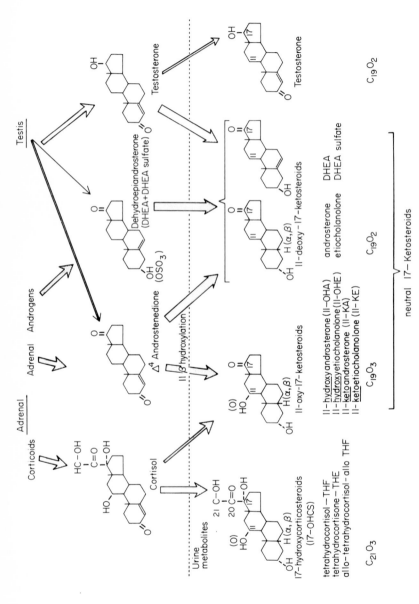

FIG. 2. General outline of androgen metabolism. Thickness of arrows denotes approximate quantitative importance of metabolic pathway. Positions of C-11 and C-17 on the steroid nucleus are labeled along with C-20 and C-21 of the side chain. These are crucial determinants of various classes of steroid metabolites. See text for discussion of outline.

jor classes of secretory products of the adrenal, the glucocorticoids–cortisol and cortisone, primarily in man, and the adrenal
androgens, hormones with relatively weak androgenic activity
compared to testosterone, the most potent androgen. The two
major adrenal androgens are Δ^4-androstenedione and dehydroepiandrosterone (DHEA), secreted unconjugated and as the sul-
fate. We will exclude progesterone, estrogens, and aldosterone as
not crucially related to the present discussion. The testis, under
normal conditions, is effectively the sole source of testosterone in
males, and also contributes to a minor degree to circulating
Δ^4-androstenedione and DHEA (Hudson *et al.*, 1967).

17-Hydroxycorticosteroids are characterized by the presence of
an additional two-carbon side chain (C-21) over the usual 19-car-
bon structure of the androgens (C-19). This carbon side chain attached to the ring at the C-17 position is one of the essential differences between the glucocorticoids and the androgens. The
presence of two hydroxy groups at the C-21 and C-17 positions
with a keto group in between yields a positive color reaction with
phenylhydrazine, the Porter–Silber reaction, and this reaction is
characteristic of the class designated as 17-hydroxycorticosteroids
(17-OHCS). The androgens do not possess this side chain, but
usually have a 17-keto group; hence the designation 17-ketoster-
oids. The major exception is testosterone with a 17β-hydroxy
group which is usually metabolized to a 17-keto group. The major
difficulty in utilizing 17-ketosteroids as an index of androgen activity is related to their diverse origins. The neutral 17-ketoster-
oids, those compounds with the 17-keto configuration minus the
estrogens, are derived from three major sources — glucocorticoids,
adrenal androgens, and testosterone. The 17-ketosteroids may be
subdivided into two groups, those with a hydroxy or a keto group
on the C-11 carbon — the 11-oxy-17-ketosteroids — and those without this additional oxygen — the 11-deoxy-17-ketosteroids. The 11-
oxy-17-ketosteroids are derived from two major sources. One is
from cortisol and cortisone, although less glucocorticoid is metabolized to 11-oxy-17-ketosteroids than to the 17-OHCS, composed
primarily of tetrahydrocortisol (THF), tetrahydrocortisone (THE),
and allotetrahydrocortisol (allo-THF) (Fukushima *et al.*, 1960). The
other source of the 11-oxy-17-ketosteroids is from Δ^4-androstene-
dione, via 11β-hydroxylation. The 11-deoxy-17-ketosteroids
comprise the major portion of urinary 17-ketosteroids and include androsterone, etiocholanolone, and dehydroepiandrosterone

(DHEA). The 11-deoxy compounds are derived from Δ^4-andro-stenedione, DHEA, as well as testosterone itself. In summary, taken as a group, the neutral 17-ketosteroids may be effected by changes in cortisol secretion, adrenal androgen secretion, and changes in testosterone secretion, and provide no clue as to specifically what has occurred.

In addition to representing metabolites of several quite different steroid hormones, problems with the chemical determination of the 17-ketosteroids further diminish their usefulness. Goldzieher and Axelrod (1962) analyzed a large number of urine samples for their 17-ketosteroid content. They compared the values obtained by measuring the 17-ketosteroids as a group, utilizing the usual Zimmerman color reaction, with that determined by estimating the individual ketosteroids and adding these individual values to get total 17-ketosteroid content. If the method for analyzing the 17-ketosteroids as a group was valid, it should compare closely to that obtained by summing the individual components. They found that in many cases the value obtained by measuring 17-ketosteroids as a group far exceeded the sum of individual compounds, and concluded that nonspecific interfering substances often comprise a significant proportion of the total 17-ketosteroid value. In other words, methods that attempt to estimate urinary 17-ketosteroids often measure substances that are not 17-ketosteroids, and this is not a constant source of error. The fact that 17-ketosteroids are composed of metabolites from cortisol, adrenal androgens, and testosterone, as well as the relative unreliability of the methods used to estimate total 17-ketosteroids, essentially invalidate utilizing this group to reflect changes in adrenal or gonadal secretion.

B. Testosterone Production

Testosterone is believed to be the most potent androgen secreted in the body. There is recent evidence that it may have to be reduced to dihydrotestosterone intracellularly to exert its endocrine effects (Mauvais-Jarvis *et al.*, 1968). Besides stimulating the development of male secondary sex characteristics, testosterone is known to have potent effects on nitrogen balance and protein metabolism. Recent work has also demonstrated the importance of testosterone in modifying social and sexual behavior in animals, not only at the time of administration, but later in life if given during a certain crucial period in neonatal development (Brown-Grant, 1966).

The ideal method of measuring testosterone should provide information on how much hormone in its active form is available to the tissues during any specified period of time. This availability is determined by two major factors. The first is how much testosterone is secreted or converted from various precursors; the amount secreted plus that which is converted equals the production rate of the hormone. The second factor relates to the binding of testosterone in plasma (Mercier *et al.*, 1966). Approximately 90–95% of testosterone in normal males is bound to α- and β-globulins (Forest *et al.*, 1968). As it is felt that only unbound testosterone is available for cellular uptake, the functional role of bound steroids in plasma is still unclear (de Moor *et al.*, 1968).

There are two methods of estimating the production rate of testosterone, one in blood and the other in urine. Neither attempts to assess any alteration in free versus bound testosterone. As the percent binding appears to be relatively constant, this may not be a crucial factor in determining the influence of potential psychoendocrine stimuli. However, this remains to be determined. The blood production rate estimates the metabolic clearance rate of the hormone by measuring the rate of disappearance in plasma of administered radioactive testosterone. The metabolic clearance rate times the plasma concentration equals the blood production rate. This provides the most precise estimate of the amount of testosterone produced over a relatively short period of time (1–2 hours). As the blood production rate has been shown to vary during the day (Southren *et al.*, 1968) this method has limitations in assessing changes over 1 or more days, unless blood production rate measurements are repeated during this period. In addition, blood production rates involving administration of labeled hormones and frequent blood samples do not regularly lend themselves to measurements in subjects engaged in routine activities, let alone combat or basic combat training. Urinary production rates are somewhat more practical, and rely on the collection of 24–48 hour urines, and the measurement of the excretion of testosterone glucuronide, as well as estimating the specific activity of this metabolite. However, this technique is based on the assumption that testosterone glucuronide is derived only from testosterone. It has been shown by several groups of investigators that this is not the case (Camacho and Migeon, 1964; Korenman and Lipsett,

1964; Horton and Tait, 1966). In females, blood testosterone and even larger amounts of urinary testosterone are derived from Δ^4-androstenedione, and this falsely elevates estimates of testosterone production by the urinary method (Horton and Tait, 1966). In males, the secretion of Δ^4-androstenedione is much less than in females, and this is not as important a source of circulating testosterone. Korenman and Lipsett (1964) have shown that small amounts of Δ^4-androstenedione are conjugated directly in the liver to testosterone glucuronide, and demonstrated that urinary testosterone in males has more than one source. However, as they, along with other investigators, generally find close agreement between blood and urinary production rates in males, it is felt that the urinary method is useful for physiological studies. One exception to this may be that when the adrenal responds to ACTH stimulation with a large increase in Δ^4-androstenedione secretion, the urinary method may give values in excess of that estimated by blood production methods (Saez and Migeon, 1967). However, this is not a constant or totally predictable response to ACTH (Rivarola *et al.*, 1966). Figure 3 summarizes the relationship between the secretion of testosterone, Δ^4-androstenedione, and DHEA and the excretion of testosterone, androsterone, and etiocholanolone in the urine.

C. Urinary Testosterone

The measurement of urinary testosterone glucuronide itself, without estimating production rate by isotope dilution techniques, is possibly the last compromise from the ideal that may still provide valid information about changes in testosterone production. Approximately 1% of secreted testosterone is excreted unchanged save for conjugation with glucuronic acid (Baulieu and Mauvais-Jarvis, 1964). Approximately 25–50% of secreted testosterone is metabolized to androsterone and etiocholanolone, two major 11-deoxy-17-ketosteroids (Prunty, 1966). However, there is evidence that the absolute percentage of secreted testosterone that is excreted unchanged may vary from individual to individual, thus making comparison between individuals more difficult (Camacho and Migeon, 1964). It does appear however, that the percentage of testosterone excreted unchanged remains constant for the individual, even in the face of large increases in secretion rate (Horton *et al.*, 1965) or following exogenously administered testos-

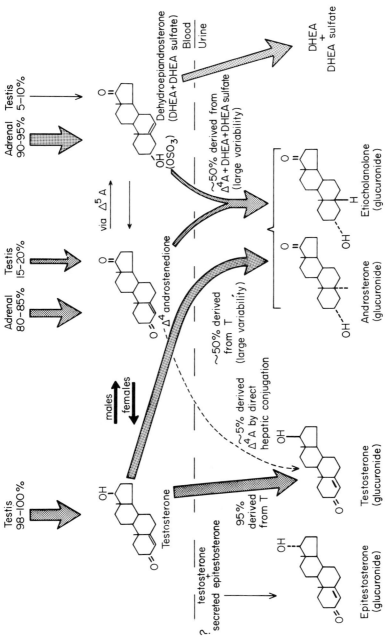

FIG. 3. *Major sources of urinary testosterone, androsterone, and etiocholanolone. The lower set of arrows represent the major precursors of these urinary metabolites, and do not indicate quantitative importance of the pathway. For example, although only a small percent of produced testosterone is excreted as testosterone glucuronide, approximately 95% of testosterone glucuronide is derived from this source.*

terone (Baulieu and Marvais-Jarvis, 1964). This would tend to support the use of testosterone glucuronide for measuring changes in testosterone secretion over time, utilizing the individual as his own control.

There is considerable evidence that the excretion of urinary testosterone reflects changes in the amount of testosterone produced in the body. Males excrete 10-20 times more testosterone glucuronide than females (Vermeulen, 1966; Ismail and Harkness, 1966). Testosterone glucuronide is very low to undetectable in castrates, hypogonadal males (Ismail and Harkness, 1967), and boys before puberty (Gupta, 1967). Testosterone glucuronide is suppressed by substances known to decrease testosterone secretion, such as estrogens (Forchielli *et al.*, 1965), and elevated after the administration of human chorionic gonadotrophin (Tamm *et al.*, 1966a). In the present study, androgen activity was assessed by the excretion of testosterone, epitestosterone, androsterone, and etiocholanolone. Although the origin of epitestosterone, the α-epimer of testosterone, is unclear, it may reflect alterations in endogenous testosterone activity (Tamm *et al.*, 1966b). As mentioned above, androsterone and etiocholanolone are derived from testosterone as well as Δ^4-androstenedione and DHEA. However, it was felt that if changes in excretion of these two major androgen metabolites paralleled those seen in urinary testosterone, they would provide additional evidence for altered testosterone production.

The data to be presented in the following sections of the chapter represent the collaborative effort of the author and several coworkers. A more complete description of the analytic methods employed, some of which were developed for these studies, along with more information of the subject groups, can be found in a separate report (Rose *et al.*, 1969).

III. Methods

A. Chemical Determinations

All values reported are based on chemical determinations of individual compounds, utilizing gas–liquid chromatography (GLC) for final separation and quantification. Androsterone, etiocholanolone, and the 11-oxy-17-ketosteroids were determined by modification of the method reported by Kirschner and Lipsett (1963). The urine is hydrolyzed, the androgens are extracted and purified by thin-layer chromatography (TLC), the derivatives are formed, and then run on GLC. Testosterone and epitestosterone glucuronide were measured by the method of Mougey *et al.* (1968) developed in our laboratories. This entails hydrolysis, extraction, first TLC, derivative formation, second TLC, and then injection on GLC. The method is capable of measuring levels of testosterone glucuronide excretion as low as 0.5 μg/day. It has a coefficient of variation of 6.8% based on 22 replicates of a single urine pool run repeatedly over a 3-month period.

B. Subjects

Androgen excretion in three groups of males is reported. The first group consists of 27 men, aged 17–26 years, in a platoon in the first months of basic combat training at Fort Dix, New Jersey. We have previously reported on individual differences in excretion of 17-OHCS among this group (Rose *et al.*, 1968). We were able to predict an individual's level of 17-OHCS based on estimates of his body size and assessments of his psychological state. The perception of being threatened or challenged beyond one's estimated capacity was associated with increased 17-OHCS excretion. For most men, basic training was a novel and taxing situation, involving many changes in the style of daily living, participation in intense group activity, and marked increases in physical activity. From the psychoendocrine point of view, the most interesting finding was the number of men who apparently adapted well to this situation and whose excretion of 17-OHCS was not markedly elevated. In other words, there was good evidence from both observations and measurement of adrenal cortical activity that the majority "coped" well in this environment. Androgen values in this group of men were derived from analyses of urine collected 3 days a week over a 3- or 4-week period and are reported as a mean monthly value.

The second group consists of seven men, aged 22–41 years, in a Special Forces A team located in an isolated camp in the mountain highlands in Viet Nam. Urine from these men was collected for 5–6 days over a 3-week period during which they were anticipating an imminent attack from the Viet Cong. The surprising fact was that most individuals did not respond to this threat of mutilation or death with elevated excretion of 17-OHCS. A much more complete discussion of the characteristics of these individuals as well as the unique nature of the events surrounding this study can be found in a recent report by Bourne *et al.* (1968) as well as in Chapter 5 in this volume. The androgen values for this group are based on a mean of 5–7 analyses of 24-hour urines collected before, during, and after the anticipated attack.

For the normal or comparison group, there were two subgroups of subjects used. One consisted of eight enlisted men, whose ages corresponded closely to the recruits at Fort Dix. These eight men were engaged in their usual activities during the 3 or 4 days of continuous urine collection. The other four men, also involved in their usual daily routine, contained two older individuals, aged 36 and 41 years, similar in age to some Special Forces personnel in Viet Nam. Urine was also collected 3–4 days continuously, and analyses were performed on a 3–4 day pool for all 12 men. Since there were no differences in androgen excretion between these two subgroups, they were combined to give a single group of normal male controls.

There are many hazards in making group comparisons. Differences discovered between groups may reflect the influence of many variables such as diet, activity, and climate, to name only a few. Our study is further complicated by the fact that the schedule of urine collection differs for the three groups. In the Fort Dix subjects, determinations are based on a monthly value, representing 9 or 12 days of collection. In Viet Nam, the values are based on a mean of five or six daily determinations during a particularly eventful period. For the normal group, androgen values are derived from a single 3-day pool. Because of the possible influence of several uncontrolled variables in addition to the impact of the environment, the results to be presented must be considered as tentative, and at best reflect possible trends of altered androgen activity. We feel these findings are worth presenting at this time because of the paucity of work in the literature on potential psychological influences on androgen secretion in men from whom sufficiently specific measurement of individual androgens were obtained.

IV. Results

A. Androsterone and Etiocholanolone Excretion

As explained previously, androsterone and etiocholanolone are derived primarily from both adrenal androgens as well as testosterone. However, it is possible that when considered in conjunction with the excretion of testosterone glucuronide, these individual ketosteroids may reflect alterations in androgen activity. Figure 4 presents a comparison between the three groups in their excretion of these two major 11-deoxy-17-ketosteroids. The group mean and standard error are shown along with the individual values presented as dots. It is immediately apparent that there is considerable spread of individual values in all three groups. This variability is well documented in the literature (see Table I). It also can be seen that the excretion of both androsterone and etiocholanolone is considerably lower in the Fort Dix group than in the normal group. These differences are statistically significant, utilizing a two-tailed Student t test, 37 df; for androsterone, $t = 3.66$, $p < .001$; for etiocholanolone $t = 2.10$, $p < .05$. The same trend may be observed in comparing the Viet Nam and normal groups. However, there are only seven men in the Viet Nam group, which makes group comparisons even more difficult. There is a statisti-

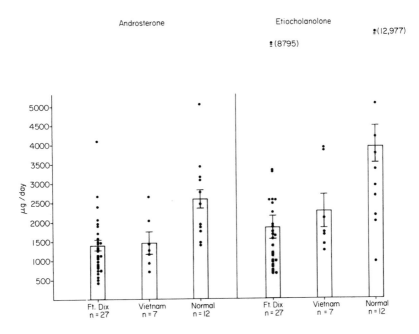

FIG. 4.   *A comparison of the excretion of androsterone and etiocholanolone among the three groups studied. Mean ± S.E. and individual values are shown.*

cally significant difference in androsterone excretion; $t = 2.23$, 17 df, $p < .05$, but no significant difference in etiocholanolone excretion. It can be seen that the range of etiocholanolone excretion is very large, 960 to 12,977 μg/day. This extreme range is primarily related to a few very high values, such that the distribution becomes log normal in configuration, also reported by Coppen *et al.* (1967).

Figure 5 shows the correlation between androsterone and etiocholanolone excretion for all 46 subjects. The correlation between these two metabolites is quite high; Pearson's $r = 0.62$, $p < .001$. This correlation obtains for all three groups, and the relationship between androsterone and etiocholanolone appears to be relatively independent of either the absolute level of excretion or the influence of different environments.

It is possible that the values seen in the Fort Dix and Viet Nam groups are low only in comparison to unusually high values obtained from the normal subjects. Table I compares the excretion of androsterone and etiocholanolone obtained from various groups of normal males as reported in five different studies. All these

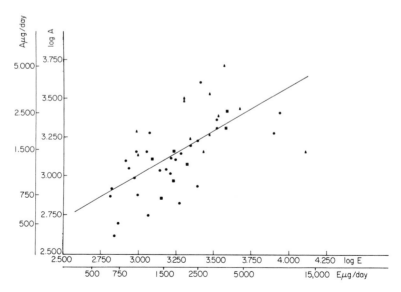

FIG. 5.   *Scattergram of etiocholanolone (E) versus androsterone (A). As the distribution of values is log normal, they are plotted in this fashion. Values in μg/day are also shown. Correlation obtained:* $r = 0.62$, $n = 46$, $p < .001$. (●) *Fort Dix;* (■) *Viet Nam;* (▲) *normal.*

TABLE I

Comparison of Excretion of Androsterone and Etiocholanolone in Normal Males

Author	No. cases	Age range (yr)	Andros- terone (mg/24 hr)	Range	Etiocho- lanolone (mg/24 hr)	Range
Beas *et al.* (1962)	5	28–45	4.44	*a*	5.24	*a*
Kirschner and Lipsett (1963)	9	20–40	2.40	(1.34–3.10)	2.18	(1.23–4.14)
Cawley *et al.* (1967)	10	*a*	4.4	(0.6–7.9)	5.0	(1.3–11.4)
Keutmann and	8	15–19	5.44	(S.D. ± 1.95)	3.16	(S.D. ± 1.83)
Mason	14	20–29	6.65	(S.D. ± 2.17)	5.14	(S.D. ± 1.37)
(1967)	9	30–39	4.47	(S.D. ± 2.76)	2.99	(S.D. ± 1.25)
Tanner and Gupta (1968)	26	19–21	4.01	(1.49–7.06)	2.87	(0.87–5.22)
Present study	12	18–41	2.49	(1.40–5.09)	3.44	(0.96–12.98)

*a*Data not given.

studies employed the necessary chemical techniques for separation and measurement of individual 17-ketosteroids, and most
utilized gas–liquid chromatography. Each study reports a wide
range of individual values, although mean values are in reason-
ably close agreement; for androsterone, 2.40–6.65 mg/24 hours and
for etiocholanolone, 2.18–5.24 mg/24 hours. The value obtained
from our normal subjects of 2.49 mg/24 hours for androsterone and
3.44 mg/24 hours for etiocholanolone are not elevated compared to
other studies but fall within the reported normal range. What is
striking about the Fort Dix and Viet Nam groups is not that there
are occasional individuals whose excretion of androsterone and
etiocholanolone equals the lowest values reported in many studies
of normal male subjects but that so many men demonstrate such
depressed levels. This provides additional support for the interpretation that these men had depressed excretion of these two
major androgen metabolites.

B. Creatinine Variability

One possible explanation for the diminished excretion of androsterone and etiocholanolone seen in the Fort Dix and Viet Nam
groups is that the urine collections were incomplete. One might

argue that under the stressful conditions of basic training or preparing for an imminent attack, complete 24-hour urine collection
would be most difficult, if not impossible. In the Fort Dix study,
the subjects were accompanied everywhere they went with supervisory technicians and their urine bottles. A technician was stationed at the latrine throughout the night to assure completeness
of collection. The normal subjects were individuals who had functioned as supervisory personnel in various psychoendocrine studies and were aware of the importance of complete collection. Urine
collection from the Special Forces men was supervised by Dr.
Bourne and SP Coli who were living with them during the time of
collection. The preceding description is necessary because there is
no way one may be certain of completeness of 24-hour collections.

It has been widely assumed that the excretion of creatinine is
constant from day to day and may be used to monitor the completeness of urine collection. As creatinine is derived from muscle
creatine, it has been postulated that some variability in the excretion of creatinine accompanying increased muscular excretion
may reflect an increase in breakdown of creatine during this period. It is of note that there were significant differences in the excretion of creatinine between the Fort Dix group, $2.40 \pm .41$ g/day
and normals, $1.63 \pm .27$ g/day. However, Consolazio et al. (1963)
report variability in creatinine excretion even after diet, exercise,
and environment are controlled. Keys et al. (1950) also report unex-
plained variability of creatinine excretion in control groups and
during starvation. Pscheidt et al. (1966) report considerable variation of creatinine excretion in groups of mental patients whose
voiding was constantly supervised, and that creatinine was correlated with the excretion of various indole metabolites. In a study
of 18 normal males and females, Vestergaard and Leverett (1958)
report that individuals differ significantly in the constancy of
creatinine excretion. Four subjects had a coefficient of variation of
greater than 10% in repeated 24 hour collections. The range of
daily values was much greater. Variability increased when 2- or 4-
hour urine collections were made. These authors suggest that as
blood levels of creatinine are reported to be most constant, the
inconsistency of creatinine excretion may reflect alterations in
glomerular filtration rate. The presumed constancy of creatinine
excretion is derived primarily from studies of hospitalized patients, those most likely to have urine collected continuously
through a catheter. The studies cited above, and our own experi-

ence, involve ambulatory individuals. There may be greater variability in glomerular filtration in this group compared to those continually in the supine or resting position. Whatever the explanation, individuals do vary in the constancy of creatinine excretion. It is hazardous to adjust the level of excretion of various substances per gram of creatinine, unless there is good evidence urine has been lost. The Fort Dix group showed depressed excretion of androsterone and etiocholanolone compared to normal subjects when results are expressed per gram of creatinine. This comparison, reflects not only the lowered excretion of metabolites but also the elevated creatinine excretion in the Fort Dix group. At any rate, it is highly unlikely that the lowered androgen excretion is due to urine loss.

C. Testosterone and Epitestosterone Excretion

The excretion of testosterone and epitestosterone for the three groups of subjects is shown in Fig. 6. The men at Fort Dix and those in Viet Nam had significantly diminished testosterone excretion compared to normal: Fort Dix versus normal; $t = 4.30$, 37 df, $p < .001$; Viet Nam versus normal; $t = 3.65$, 17 df, $p < .01$. The same relationship is observed if values are corrected per gram of creatinine, except that in Viet Nam versus normal the difference failed to reach statistical significance: $t = 1.99$, 17 df, $.05 < p < .1$. It is difficult to assess the importance of the lowered epitestosterone excretion seen in the Fort Dix group. There are contradictory reports in the literature as to whether urinary epitestosterone is derived from testosterone (Tamm *et al.*, 1966b; Blaquier *et al.*, 1967) or whether it is just derived primarily from secreted epitestosterone (Wilson and Lipsett, 1966). Although there is no significant correlation observed between the excretion of testosterone and epitestosterone, epitestosterone is clearly diminished in the Fort Dix group compared to normal: $t = 4.47$, 37 df, $p < .001$. This decrease in epitestosterone excretion may also be a reflection of a depression in testosterone production, as suggested by the lowered testosterone, androsterone, and etiocholanolone excretion seen in this group.

Various reports of the excretion of urinary testosterone and epitestosterone in normal males are listed in Table II. All these studies separated epitestosterone from testosterone itself. Similar to

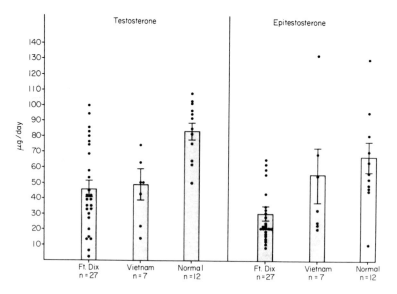

FIG. 6.   *A comparison of the excretion of testosterone and epitestosterone among the three groups studied. Mean ± S.E. and individual values are shown.*

TABLE II
Excretion of Testosterone and Epitestosterone in Normal Males

Author	No. cases	Age (yr)	Testosterone (μg/24 hr) Mean	Testosterone (μg/24 hr) Range	Epitestosterone (μg/24 hr) Mean	Epitestosterone (μg/24 hr) Range
Rosner *et al.*	5	17–24	151	113–193	—	—
(1965)	20	30–40	88	28–143	—	—
Vermeulen	8	puberty	159	102–245	—	—
(1966)		to 25				
	9	25–35	164	47–323	—	—
	10	35–45	133	59–352	—	—
Ismail and Harkness	20	21–63	52	40–64	—	—
(1966)						
de Nicola *et al.*	12	17–46	58	10–173	166	9–396
(1966)						
France and Knox	5	19–29	67	37–133	28	18–47
(1967)						
Present study	12	18–41	85	50–108	66	10–137
(Normals)						

androsterone and etiocholanolone, there is great variability in the excretion of both testosterone and epitestosterone from normal subjects. Part of the variability seen in the excretion of various hormone metabolites may relate to various differences between the subjects studied; that is, "normal" is not necessarily basal. We also know that for androsterone and etiocholanolone part of this variability may relate to their diverse origins, possibly reflecting changes in the secretion of any one of their adrenal or testicular precursors. This is probably not a source of variability of excreted testosterone, as it is almost totally derived in the urine from circulating testosterone, save for the small amount conjugated directly in the liver from Δ^4-androstenedione. As noted, the percent of secreted testosterone that is excreted as testosterone glucuronide varies between individuals. A range of 0.1% to 2% was reported by Camacho and Migeon (1964). This may account for some of the variability reported in Table II. The values obtained from our group of normal subjects lie clearly within the range reported by the other studies listed.

The lowered excretion of androsterone, etiocholanolone, and testosterone seen in the subjects at Fort Dix is suggestive of diminished androgen activity. However as has been pointed out, due to the complexities of androgen metabolism, neither measure offers conclusive evidence that these individuals were secreting or producing less testosterone during the period of study. It might be argued that the Fort Dix group fortuitously included many individuals who metabolize very small amounts of secreted testosterone to testosterone glucuronide and excrete it in this form. Further evidence of an actual depression in testosterone production is obtained when the excretion of both testosterone and androsterone plus etiocholanolone are considered together. Figure 7 is a histogram of the excretion of testosterone and androsterone plus etiocholanolone observed in the Fort Dix group. Of the 17 individuals whose excretion of testosterone fell below the group mean of 46 μg/24 hours, 13 men, or 76%, also had diminished excretion of androsterone plus etiocholanolone. Viewed in another way, 13 of the 27 men studied, or almost half of the group, had diminished excretion of both indices of androgen activity. As mentioned, the excretion of testosterone represents only a small fraction of secreted testosterone. However, if this is low in addition to low androsterone plus etiocholanolone which account for 25–50% of secreted testosterone, the most parsimonious explanation is that

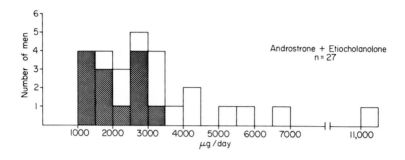

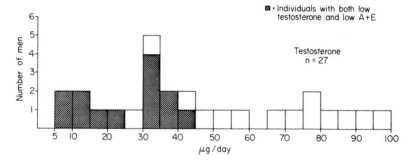

FIG. 7.   *The distribution of values in the Fort Dix group are plotted in the two histograms shown above, A + E on top, testosterone on the bottom. Most of the men who had lowered testosterone excretion also had lowered excretion of A + E.*

there was less testosterone produced in these subjects during this period of time.

D. Individuals' Androgen Responses

The data presented so far have been restricted to describing differences between groups of subjects as evidence of diminished androgen activity in response to environmental challenge or threat. As discussed, there are difficulties in making group comparisons, and longitudinal studies utilizing the individual as his own control provide clearer evidence for potential psychological influences on endocrine function. The endocrine responses of two men in the Special Forces group threatened by attack are shown in Fig. 8. As collection of samples in the field was severally limited; urine was saved for only 5 or 6 days per man during the period

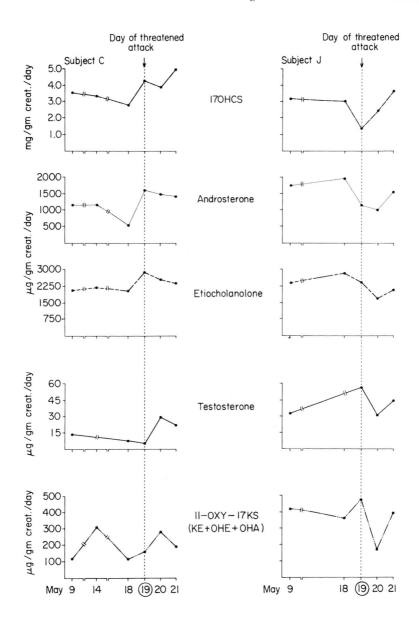

FIG. 8.　*17-OHCS, androsterone, etiocholanolone, testosterone, and 11-oxy-17-keto-steroid response of two subjects anticipating Viet Cong attack on May 19. Testosterone appears independent of 17-OHCS and androsterone and etiocholanolone excretion.*

from May 9 to May 21. For several men, these samples fortunately included days before, during, and after the anticipated attack. The urinary 17-OHCS shown at the top of the figure provide comparison with changes in androgen excretion. The sum of three individual 11-oxy-17-ketosteroids (11-KA is not usually detectable) is shown at the bottom of the figure. These results are all expressed per gram of creatinine. Correcting per gram of creatinine may distort changes seen in various days, not only because its excretion is not constant but because the method of analysis of creatinine is far less precise than that employed in the measurement of the hormones. However, it was known that under these most difficult circumstances some men lost small amounts of urine.

Subject C, the team's commanding officer, had a significant rise in 17-OHCS in response to the threatened attack, while subject J showed a fall in 17-OHCS excretion during this time. For both subjects, androsterone and etiocholanolone seem to parallel the 17-OHCS response, while testosterone appears to be independent of both corticoids and 17-ketosteroids. The 11-oxy compounds show no pattern of response during this period. It is possible that the changes in androsterone and etiocholanolone, parallel with the 17-OHCS response, reflect a change in the secretion of adrenal androgen precursors, especially as testosterone excretion appears to go in an opposite direction. However, this is highly speculative, as we have insufficient number of days prior to the threatened attack to adequately interpret the changes on May 19 and the 2 following days. These data are presented not as conclusive evidence, but along with the group differences observed, may serve to reflect potential psychological influences on androgen secretion.

V. Discussion

Almost all the studies reporting psychological influences on androgen production, utilize 17-ketosteroids as the index of hormone activity. This may account for the conflicting conclusions as to whether androgen secretion is increased or decreased secondary to threat or arousal. Because of the extremely limited value of 17-ketosteroid determinations, a review of studies employing this method is not warranted. There have been a few studies, most of them recent, which have measured individual ketosteroid excretion. Elmadjian (1955) in one of the earliest reports of alterations in adrenal cortical activity in combat, did analyse the excretion of individual ketosteroids in a few individuals along with determinations of 17-ketosteroids and 17-OHCS. Although the data were limited, there was evidence of depressed excretion of androsterone and etiocholanolone in a few subjects immediately after having engaged in combat. In a study of changes in urinary steroids following pulmonary lobectomy, Uozumi *et al.* (1967) reported a decrease in androsterone excretion 3 weeks following the operation. This decrease in androgen excretion occurred in the face of an increase in 17-OHCS excretion. These findings are complicated by the fact that the subjects had tuberculosis during the course of the study.

There have been several recent reports of the excretion of individual ketosteroids in depressed patients. There are difficulties in interpreting differences in steroid excretion in this group of patients. Many factors such as admission to the hospital, drug regimen, and differences in the type of depressive illness may affect endocrine output. An excellent survey of the problems in assessment of corticosteroid changes in depressed patients can be found in a recent review by Sachar (1967). Ferguson *et al.* (1964) studied five female patients who had been chronically depressed from 2 to 36 months (mean of 17 months) before treatment with electroconvulsive therapy. Androsterone and etiocholanolone showed a low level of excretion prior to treatment followed by a rise to normal levels during clinical remission. The excretion of 17-OHCS was elevated before treatment and fell following treatment, opposite to that seen for androsterone and etiocholanolone. The elevation in 17-OHCS and lowered androgen excretion are difficult to interpret, as initial urine samples were taken within 3 days after admission and several patients were on medication when samples were collected. Coppen *et al.* (1967) failed to find significant differences in the excretion of androsterone and etiocholanolone in a group of 21 depressed patients or in a group of 21 schizophrenic patients compared to a group of 25 normal male controls. They did not study changes in steroid excretion following treatment. Brooksbank and Pryse-Phillips (1964) studied the excretion of androstenol (androst-16-en-3α-ol) from a group of 33 schizophrenic patients compared to 112 male controls. Androstenol is an androgen metabolite whose exact origin is unclear; it is not derived from injected DHEA or testosterone (Bulbrook *et al.*, 1963; Wilson *et al.*, 1963), but is formed in the adrenals and testes. Brooksbank and

Pryse-Phillips (1964) postulate that it may be a product of a side reaction of increased importance during high androgen production. What is of note is that they found significantly diminished excretion of androstenol in the schizophrenic patients, a mean of 0.63 mg/24 hours compared to 1.24 mg/24 hours in normals; $t = 4.2$, $p < .001$. There was no difference in the excretion of 17-ketosteroids between these two groups. It is not clear whether the decreased excretion of androstenol reflects a decrease of androgen secretion or parallels the depression in 17-OHCS, as reported in schizophrenic patients who have reached a stable equilibrium with their psychoses (Sachar *et al.*, 1966b). Hendrikx *et al.* (1966) reported significantly depressed excretion of androsterone and etiocholanolone in five patients suffering from anorexia nervosa. They also found that coincident with one patient's clinical improvement, there was a marked increase in androsterone and etiocholanolone excretion, although there was only a modest gain in weight of approximately 3 pounds.

There are very few studies of psychological influences on testosterone excretion. Ismail and Harkness (1967) reported severely depressed levels of testosterone excretion in three young males, ages 17, 17, and 21, suffering from "psychogenic undernutrition." It is difficult to separate the influence of psychological factors from those of malnutrition itself, which have been shown to depress 11-deoxy-17-ketosteroid excretion (Hendrikx *et al.*, 1966). These authors also documented a rise of about 75% in the excretion of testosterone in two male subjects coincident with the resumption of sexual activity following a period of 18 weeks abstinence in one and 7 weeks in the other. This rise in testosterone excretion was not accompanied by an increase in either 17-OHCS or 17-ketosteroid excretion.

A number of the studies cited report a fall in the excretion of androsterone and etiocholanolone while there is a concurrent rise in 17-OHCS levels. In the Fort Dix group, there is evidence of lowered androsterone, etiocholanolone, testosterone, and epitestosterone excretion despite the fact that many of these men had elevated levels of urinary 17-OHCS (Rose *et al.*, 1968). This increased excretion of 17-OHCS probably reflected ACTH stimulation of the adrenals, which for some individuals, may have caused increased secretion of Δ^4-androstenedione as well as elevations in cortisol. We have no direct evidence of this, but assuming this to be so, the increase in Δ^4-androstenedione secretion would tend to increase testosterone glucuronide excretion in these men. Therefore, our findings of decreased excretion of testosterone, androsterone, and etiocholanolone in the face of indices of adrenal stimulation, provide more support for the interpretation of diminished testosterone production. These findings replicate the fall in testosterone, androsterone, and etiocholanolone concurrent with the rise in 17-OHCS excretion seen in the rhesus monkey during 72-hour shock avoidance (Mason, 1968b). This probable depression in testosterone production may be secondary to diminished pituitary secretion of LH. This reciprocal relation of ACTH increase to LH fall in response to environmental confrontation or threat supports the concept of regulation of endocrine processes by the central nervous system and provides further insight into mechanisms of psychological influences on physiological function.

VI. Summary

The investigation of potential psychological influences on androgen activity has been hampered by the complexities of androgen metabolism and the use of nonspecific analytical methods. The use of urinary 17-ketosteroids as an index of androgen activity is invalidated by the diverse origins of this group of metabolites, representing potential contributions from secreted cortisol, adrenal androgens, and testosterone.

As testosterone is the most potent androgen secreted endogenously, techniques should be directed toward assessment of changes in testosterone production. Isotope dilution techniques in blood and urine represent the best methods available at present but present technical difficulties in field studies. However, the measurement of urinary testosterone glucuronide along with the separation and quantification of individual androgens, such as androsterone and etiocholanolone, may reflect alterations in testosterone production. We have reported significant decreases in the excretion of testosterone, epitestosterone, androsterone, and etiocholanolone in a group of men in basic combat training and in some individuals anticipating an imminent attack in Viet Nam. These levels were found to be low compared to a group of normal male controls as well as low in comparison to levels found in normal males as reported in the literature. The decrease in excretion of these testosterone metabolites occurs at the same time there is an increase in 17-OHCS excretion. This suggests a decrease in gonadal secretion while there is an increase in adrenal–cortical secretion, possibly reflecting a depression in LH while ACTH increases. If more direct measurements of cortisol and testosterone production confirm these results, these studies provide further insight into possible mechanisms of psychological influences on endocrine function.

REFERENCES

Baulieu, E. E., and Mauvais-Jarvis, P. (1964). Studies on testosterone metabolism. II. Metabolism of testosterone-4-^{14}C and androstene-4-ene-3, 17-dione-1, 2-^{3}H. *J. Biol. Chem.* **239**, 1579–1584.

Beas, F., Zurbrugg, R. P., Cara, J., and Gardner, L. I. (1962). Urinary C_{19} steroids in normal children and adults. *J. Clin. Endocrinol. Metab.* **22**, 1090–1094.

Blaquier, J., Dorfman, R. I., and Forchielli, E. (1967). Formation of epitestosterone by human blood and adrenal tissue. *Acta Endocrinol.* **54**, 208–214.

Bliss, E. (1968). Personal communication.

Bourne, P. G., Rose, R. M., and Mason, J. W. (1968). 17-OHCS levels in combat: Special Forces "A" team under threat of attack. *Arch. Gen. Psychiat.* **19**, 135–140.

Brooksbank, B. W. L., and Pryse-Phillips, W. (1964). Urinary Δ^{16}-androsten-3α-ol, 17-oxosteroids and mental illness. *Brit. Med. J.* **1**, 1602–1606.

Brown-Grant, K. (1966). The action of hormones on the hypothalamus. *Brit. Med. Bull.* **22**, 273.

Bulbrook, R. D., Thomas, B. S., and Brooksbank, B. W. L. (1963). The relationship between urinary androst-16-en-3α-ol and urinary 11-deoxy-17-oxosteroid excretion. *J. Endocrinol.* **26**, 149–153.

Camacho, A. M., and Migeon, C. J. (1964). Studies on the origin of testosterone in the urine of normal adult subjects and patients with various endocrine disorders. *J. Clin. Invest.* **43**, 1083–1089.

Cawley, L. P., Musser, B. O., and Tretbar, H. A. (1967). Gas-liquid chromatography of urinary 17-ketosteroids, pregnanediol, and pregnanetriol in normal individuals. *Am. J. Clin. Pathol.* **28**, 216–224.

Consolazio, C. F., Johnson, R. E., and Pecora, L. J. (1963). "Physiological Measurements of Metabolic Functions in Man," p. 262. McGraw-Hill (Blakiston), New York.

Coppen, A., Julian, T., Fry, D. E., and Marks, V. (1967). Body build and urinary steroid excretion in mental illness. *Brit. J. Psychol.* **113**, 269–275.

de Moor, P., Steeno, O., and Heyns, W. (1968). Possible role or significance of protein-steroid binding in plasma. *Ann. Endocrinol. (Paris)* **29**, Suppl., 119–123.

de Nicola, A. F., Dorfman, R. I., and Forchielli, E. (1966). Urinary excretion of epitestosterone and testosterone in normal individuals and hirsute and virilized females. *Steroids* **7**, 351–365.

Eleftheriou, B. E., and Church, E. L. (1968). Levels of hypothalamic luteinizing hormone-releasing factor after exposure to aggression (defeat) in C57BL/6J mice. *J. Endocrinol.* **42**, 347–348.

Elmadjian, F. (1955). Adrenocortical function of combat infantrymen in Korea. *Ciba Found. Colloq. Endocrinol.* **8**, 627–655.

Ferguson, H. C., Bartram, A. C. G., Fowlie, H. C., Cathro, D. M., Birchall, K., and Mitchell, F. L. (1964). A preliminary investigation of steroid excretion in depressed patients before and after electro-convulsive therapy. *Acta Endocrinol.* 47, 58–68.

Forchielli, E., Rao, G. S., Sarda, I. R., Gibree, N. B., Pochi, P. E., Strauss, J. S., and Dorfman, R. I. (1965). Effect of ethinyloestradiol on plasma testosterone levels and urinary testosterone excretion in man. *Acta Endocrinol.* 50, 51–54.

Forest, M. G., Rivarola, M. A., and Migeon, C. J. (1968). Percentage binding of testosterone, androstenedione and dehydroisoandrosterone in human plasma. *Steroids* 12, 323–345.

France, J. T., and Knox, B. S. (1967). Urinary excretion of testosterone and epitestosterone in hirsutism. *Acta Endocrinol.* 56, 177–187.

Fukushima, D. K., Bradlow, H. L., Hellman, L., Zumoff, B., and Gallagher, T. F. (1960). Metabolic transformation of hydrocortisone 4-C^{14} in normal men. *J. Biol. Chem.* 235, 2246–2252.

Goldzieher, J. W., and Axelrod, L. R. (1962). A study of methods for the determination of total, grouped and individual urinary 17-ketosteroids. *J. Clin. Endocrinol. Metab.* 22, 1234.

Gupta, D. (1967). Separation and estimation of testosterone and epitestosterone in the urine of pre-pubertal children. *Steroids* 10, 457–471.

Harris, G. W., Reed, M., and Fawcett, C. P. (1966). Hypothalamic releasing factors and the control of anterior pituitary function. *Brit. Med. Bull.* 22, 266–272.

Hendrikx, A., Heyns, W., Steeno, O., and de Moor, P. (1966). Influence of body size, changes in body weight and/or food intake on urinary excretion of 11-desoxy-17-ketosteroids. *In* "Androgens in Normal and Pathological Conditions." *Proc. 2nd Symp. Steroid Hormones, Ghent, 1965, Excerpta Med. Found. Intern. Congr. Ser.* 101, 63–70.

Horton, R., and Tait, J. F. (1966). Androstenedione production and interconversion rates measured in peripheral blood and studies on the possible site of its conversion to testosterone. *J. Clin. Invest.* 45, 301–313.

Horton, R., Shinsako, J., and Forsham, P. H. (1965). Testosterone production and metabolic clearance rates with volumes of distribution in normal adult men and women. *Acta Endocrinol.* 48, 446–458.

Hudson, B., Coghlan, J. P., and Dulmanis, A. (1967). Testicular function in man. "Endocrinology of the Testis." *Ciba Found. Colloq. Endocrinol.* 16, 140–155.

Ismail, A. A. A., and Harkness, R. A. (1966). A method for the estimation of urinary testosterone. *Biochem. J.* 99, 717–725.

Ismail, A. A. A., and Harkness, R. A. (1967). Urinary testosterone excretion in men in normal and pathological conditions. *Acta Endocrinol.* 56, 469–48^.

Keutmann, E. H., and Mason, W. B. (1967). Individual urinary 17-ketosteroids of healthy persons determined by gas chromatography: Biochemical and clinical considerations. *J. Clin. Endocrinol. Metab.* 27, 406–420.

Keys, A., Brozek, J., Henschel, A., Mickelsen, O., and Taylor, H. L. (1950). "The Biology of Human Starvation," pp. 428–432. Univ. of Minnesota Press, Minneapolis, Minnesota.

Kirschner, M. A., and Lipsett, M. B. (1963). Gas-liquid chromatography in the quantitative analysis of urinary 11-deoxy-17-ketosteroids. *J. Clin. Endocrinol. Metab.* 23, 255–260.

Korenman, S. G., and Lipsett, M. B. (1964). Is testosterone glucuronoside uniquely derived from plasma testosterone? *J. Clin. Invest.*, 43, 2125–2131.

Levine, M. D., Gordon, T. P., and Rose, R. M. (1969). Behavioral and endocrine correlates of adaptation to chronic shock avoidance. *Proc. 2nd Intern. Congr. Primat.* (in press). Karger, Basel.

Martini, L., and Ganong, W. F., eds. (1966-1967). "Neuroendocrinology," Vols. I and II. Academic Press, New York.

Mason, J. W. (1968a). A review of psychoendocrine research on the pituitary-adrenal cortical system. "Organization of Psychoendocrine Mechanisms." *Psychosomat. Med.* **30**, Suppl., 576-607.

Mason, J. W. (1968b). Organization of multiple responses to avoidance in the monkey. *In* "Organization of Psychoendocrine Mechanisms." *Psychosomat. Med.* **30**, Suppl., 774-790.

Mason, J. W., Kenion, C. C., Collins, D. R., Mougey, E. H., Jones, J. A., Driver, G. C., Brady, J. V., and Beer, B. (1968). Urinary testosterone response to 72-hr. avoidance sessions in the monkey. *In* "Organization of Psychoendocrine Mechanisms." *Psychosomat. Med.* **30**, Suppl. 721-732.

Mauvais-Jarvis, P., Floch, H. H., and Bercovici, J. P. (1968). Studies on testosterone metabolism in human subjects with normal and pathological sexual differentiation. *J. Clin. Endocrinol. Metab.* **28**, 460-471.

Mercier, A., Alfsen, A., and Baulieu, E.-E. (1966). A testosterone binding globulin. *In* "Androgens in Normal and Pathological Conditions." *Proc. 2nd Symp. Steroid Hormones, Ghent, 1965, Excerpta Med. Found. Intern. Congr.* **101**, 212.

Mougey, E. H., Collins, D. R., Rose, R. M., and Mason, J. W. (1969). The measurement of testosterone and epitestosterone in monkey and human urine by gas-liquid chromatography. *Anal. Biochem.*, **27**, 343-358.

Prunty, F. T. G. (1966). Androgen metabolism in man — some current concepts. *Brit. Med. J.* **ii**, 605-613.

Pscheidt, G. R., Berlet, H. H., Spade, J., and Himwich, H. E. (1966). Variations of urinary creatinine and its correlation to excretion of indole metabolites in mental patients. *Clin. Chim. Acta* **13**, 228-234.

Reichlin, S. (1966). Functions of the median-eminence gland. *New Engl. J. Med.* **275**, 600-607.

Rivarola, M. A., Saez, J. M., Meyer, W. J., Jenkins, M. E., and Migeon, C. J. (1966). Metabolic clearance rate and blood production rate of testosterone and androst-2-ene-3, 17-dione under basal conditions, ACTH and HCG stimulation. Comparison with urinary production rate of testosterone. *J. Clin. Endocrinol. Metab.* **26**, 1208-1218.

Rose, R. M., Poe, R. O., and Mason J. W. (1968). Psychological state and body size as determinants of 17-OHCS excretion. *Arch. Internal Med.* **121**, 406-413.

Rose, R. M., Bourne, P. G., Poe, R. O., Mougey, E. H., Collins, D. R., and Mason, J. W. (1969). Androgen responses to stress: II. Excretion of testosterone, epitestosterone, androsterone and etiocholanolone during basic combat training and under threat of attack. *Psychosomat. Med.* (in press).

Rosner, J. M., Conte, N. F., Briggs, J. H., Chao, P. Y., Sudman, E. M., and Forsham, P. H. (1965). Determination of urinary testosterone by chromatography and colorimetry: Findings in normal subjects and in patients with endocrine diseases. *J. Clin. Endocrinol. Metab.* **25**, 95-100.

Sachar, E. J. (1967) Corticosteroids in depressive illness: I. A re-evaluation of control issues and the literature. *Arch. Gen. Psychiat.* **17**, 544-553.

Sachar, E. J., Cobb, J. C., and Shor, R. E. (1966a). Plasma cortisol changes during hypnotic trance. *Arch. Gen. Psychiat.* 14, 484–490.

Sachar, E. J., Harmatz, J., Bergen, H., and Cohler, J. (1966b). Corticosteroid responses to milieu therapy of chronic schizophrenics. *Arch Gen. Psychiat.* 15, 310–319.

Saez, J. M., and Migeon, C. J. (1967). Problems related to the determination of the secretion and interconversion of androgens by "urinary" methods. *Steroids* 10, 441–456.

Southren, A. L., Gordon, G. G., and Tochimoto, S. (1968). Further study of factors affecting the metabolic clearance rate of testosterone in man. *J. Clin. Endocrinol. Metab.* 28, 1105–1113.

Tamm, J., Apostolakis, M., and Voigt, K. D. (1966a). The effects of ACTH and HCG on the urinary excretion of testosterone in male patients with various endocrine disorders. *Acta Endocrinol.* 53, 61–72.

Tamm, J., Volkwein, U., and Starcevic, Z. (1966b). The urinary excretion of epitestosterone, testosterone and androstenedione following intravenous infusions of high doses of these steroids in human subjects. *Steroids* 8, 659–669.

Tanner, J. M., and Gupta, D. (1968). Urinary levels of C_{19} and C_{21} steroids in healthy young men and their relation to muscle and limb bone widths. *J. Endocrinol.* 41, 157–159.

Uozumi, T., Tanaka, H., Hamanaka, Y., Seki, T., Matsumoto, K., and Akehi, A. (1967). Changes of urinary steroids following major surgical stress. *Endocrinol. Japon.* 14, 7–10.

Vermeulen, A. (1966). Urinary excretion of testosterone. *In* "Androgens in Normal and Pathological Conditions." *Proc. 2nd Symp. Steroid Hormones, Ghent, 1965, Excerpta Med. Found. Intern. Congr. Ser.* 101, 71–76.

Vestergaard, P., and Leverett, R. (1958). Constancy of urinary creatinine excretion. *J. Lab. Clin. Med.* 51, 211–218.

Wadeson, R. W., Mason, J. W., Hamburg, D. A., and Handlon, J. H. (1963). Plasma and urinary 17-OHCS responses to motion pictures. *Arch. Gen. Psychiat.* 9, 146–156.

Wilson, H., and Lipsett, M. B., (1966). Metabolism of epitestosterone in man. *J. Clin. Endocrinol. Metab.* 26, 902–914.

Wilson, H., Lipsett, M. B., and Korenman, S. G. (1963). Evidence that 16-androsten-3α-ol is not a peripheral metabolite of testosterone in man. *J. Clin. Endocrinol. Metab.* 23, 291–492.

Wolff, C. T., Friedman, S. B., Hofer, M. A., and Mason, J. W. (1964a). Relationship between psychological defenses and mean urinary 17-OHCS excretion rates: Part I. A predictive study of parents of fatally ill children. *Psychosomat. Med.* 26, 576–591.

Wolff, C. T., Hofer, M. A., and Mason, J. W. (1964b). Relationship between psychological defenses and mean urinary 17-OHCS excretion rates: Part II. Methodological and theoretical considerations. *Psychosomat. Med.* 26, 592–609.

7 // Heat Stress in Army Pilots in Viet Nam

Robert J. T. Joy

I. Introduction

Heat illness, most commonly heat exhaustion and heat stroke, is not usually a major cause of overall morbidity in troops operating in hot climates. However, in certain specific places or for particular jobs or climates, heat illness may be a local or temporary cause of considerable ineffectiveness and lost man hours.

In World War II, the overall rate for heat illness for the period between 1942 and 1945 for the total United States Army was 1.4 per 1000 men per year. In certain southern training bases in 1942, the rate was to 12 per 1000 men per year, and in the Persian Gulf Command in the summer of 1943, the rate rose to 88.6 per 1000 men (Whayne, 1951).

In Viet Nam, the overall rates of heat illness during 1966 and 1967 averaged 3.6 to 2.3 per 1000 men per year (Medical Statistics Agency, 1968) which, even though it probably represents underreporting by a factor of two or three, is still an insignificant cause of manpower loss. However, local effects in certain areas or specific man–machine–environment problems can continue to be a significant problem for some units. This was the case in May and June of 1966, in a group of army aviators in II Corps in Viet Nam, when fatigue, discomfort, and symptoms suggestive of heat illness were reported by Mohawk crews while flying certain missions, particularly low level visual reconnaissance surveys.

A report of a study of this unit is presented in this chapter. It illustrates the kind of local problem which can arise due to heat in military units, a way of evaluating heat stress problems in the field, and an approach to their solution.

II. Methods

The OV-1 (Mohawk) is a two place, twin engine aircraft with considerable maneuverability, capable of speeds in excess of 180 knots. It is used primarily for reconnaissance missions in support of ground operations.

A. Description of Mission Types

Visual Reconnaissance (VR) missions are flown at altitudes of from 50 to 100 ft, at speeds of 150 to 200 knots, for low level surveillance of enemy terrain. While there is a photographic capability, these missions are primarily flown for spot sightings and for visual observation of trails, movement areas, etc.

Infrared Reconnaissance (IR) missions are usually flown at night, with infrared equipment which can detect such heat sources as generators and vehicles. Depending on altitude, these can be demanding or routine missions.

Radar reconnaissance missions are missions which employ the Side Looking Airborne Radar (SLAR) System and are designed to locate moving targets such as vehicle convoys and sampans on rivers. They are flown at high altitudes, usually at night, and are considered by pilots to be routine missions.

B. Physiological Measurements

Immediately prior to each flight, nude body weights and the weights of all clothing worn were secured for the pilot and the observer or investigator. Weights were measured to ± 25 g with a Fairbanks-Morse beam balance. Ten milliliters of blood were taken from both the pilot and the observer and immediately re-frigerated at 5°C. On investigator-accompanied flights, both the pilot and the investigator inserted a thermistor catheter (Yellow Springs Instrument Company, Model 401) 10 cm into the rectum and taped another such thermistor catheter to the chest over the xiphoid process. Clothing was then donned, rectal (T_r) and skin (T_s) temperature measurements were made prior to leaving the platoon area, and the two subjects then went to the aircraft.

During flight, a time log was kept of all events by the investigator. T_r and T_s were read and logged at 15 min intervals from a battery-operated portable resistance bridge (YSIC Telethermometer, Model 43). At 30 min intervals, temperatures inside the cockpit were secured from a dry-bulb thermometer (T_{DB}), a naturally convected wet-bulb thermometer (T_{WB}) and a black-globe radiant temperature thermometer (T_G). Air temperature (T_A) external to the aircraft was recorded from a cockpit meter.

Upon return from a mission, the subjects were again weighed nude, clothing weights were again secured, and another blood sample was taken and refrigerated. Blood samples were allowed to clot under refrigeration, were then centrifuged, and the serum removed and frozen. Standard methods of estimating total and evaporative water loss and of calculating body heat content have been used (Joy and Goldman, 1964). Data expressed in terms of hourly rates have been adjusted using the time elapsing between the two data collections.

Ambient temperatures were recorded from a ground weather station in the platoon flight line area just prior to each mission. T_{DB}, T_{WB}, and T_G values were used to calculate the Wet Bulb Globe Temperature Index (WBGT) according to the formula: $0.7 \, T_{WB} + 0.2 \, T_G + 0.1 \, T_{DB} = \text{WBGT}$ (°F) (Yaglou and Minard, 1957).

A total of 17 missions were studied. On seven VR missions, the investigator replaced the enlisted technical observer. There were tactical requirements for the trained observer on all other missions, so that only water loss data were obtained. Except for comparative purposes and one correlation analysis (Figs. 1 and 2) in-

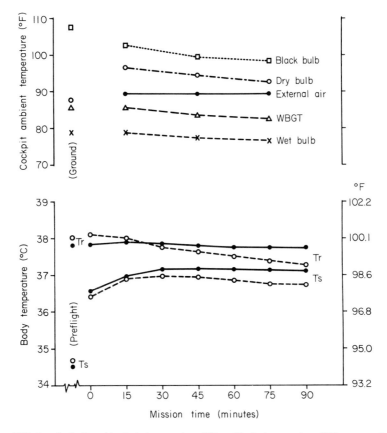

FIG. 1.   *Cockpit ambient air temperature (°F) and body temperature (°C) versus mission time. (●--●) Pilot, n = 5; (0---0) investigator. T$_R$ = rectal temperature; T$_S$ = skin temperature.*

vestigator data are not used to estimate water requirements, etc., in order to avoid bias of the data by overreplication of measurement on one subject. All missions reported here were flown over enemy controlled terrain.

These studies were performed during the periods between June 13 and 18 and between June 29 and July 2, 1966. VR missions are divided into "hot" missions, with starting times between 1100–1500 hrs, and "cool" missions, with starting times before 1100 hrs or after 1500 hrs.

Statistical analyses were performed by nonpaired *t* test, and the null hypothesis rejected at the 5% level of confidence (Croxton, 1959).

III. Results

A. Subjects

The 18 men studied had a mean age of 29.3 years (±S.D. 6.8), a mean height of 156.5 cm (±S.D. 5.4), a mean weight of 74.4 kg (±S.D. 9.6), and had been in Viet Nam an average of 7.6 months (±S.D. 3.9). Some men were studied in more than one type of mission. All subjects had been in Viet Nam long enough to be well heat acclimatized, and acclimatization was maintained not only by the physical work of regular duties but also by a vigorous athletic program.

B. Ambient Temperatures

Tables I and II present data on ground and cockpit temperatures. The similarity of ground and cockpit temperature measurements reflects the low altitude of flight and the "greenhouse" effect of the cockpit, which has a glass and plexiglass cover for approximately 230° of arc from side to side. In this report major attention is given to the WBGT index and correlations are per-

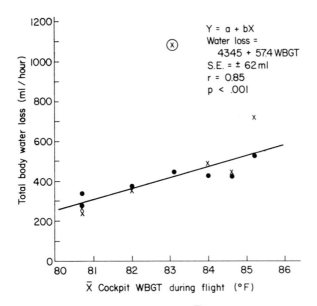

FIG. 2.   *Total body water loss (ml/hour) versus* $\bar{X}$ *cockpit WBGT (°F) during flight.* (●) *Pilot,* (×) *investigator. See figure for regression equation.* ⊗ *Value not used, as investigator was clinically ill (see Table IV).*

TABLE I

Ground Temperatures

Time (hr)	n	$T_{DB}{}^a$ (°F)	$T_{WB}{}^a$ (°F)	$T_G{}^a$ (°F)	WBGT^a (°F)
1100–1300	7	86.3 ± 2.9	78.4 ± 1.0	104.1 ± 8.0	84.4 ± 2.3
1300–1800	7	84.9 ± 3.1	77.7 ± 1.0	95.9 ± 9.4	82.1 ± 2.6

^{a}Mean ± S.D. See Table II for symbols.

TABLE II

Cockpit Temperatures^a

Date	Pilot	$\overline{T}_{DB}$(°F)	$\overline{T}_{WB}$(°F)	$\overline{T}_G$(°F)	$\overline{T}_A$(°F)	$\overline{\text{WBGT}}$(°F)
June 14 (1300 hr)	B.T.	95.0	77.3	97.5	92.0	83.1
June 15 (1300 hr)	R.J.	94.7	77.3	102.0	88.7	84.0
June 15 (1700 hr)	W.P.	91.0	76.3	90.7	89.3	80.7
June 16 (1300 hr)	R.S.	95.5	79.3	97.8	89.5	84.6
June 17 (1100 hr)	F.W.	90.7	76.7	96.7	85.3	82.0
June 17 (1600 hr)	J.M.	90.5	76.4	91.6	84.6	80.7
June 18 (1300 hr)	H.B.	96.7	78.3	103.7	89.7	85.2

^{a}Values for cockpit temperatures represent the mean value ($\overline{X}$) of three or more readings, depending on length of mission. WBGT was always calculated from simultaneous readings. T_{DB}, dry bulb; T_{WB}, wet bulb; T_G, black bulb; T_A, external air; $\overline{\text{WBGT}}$, wet bulb globe temperatures.

formed with it. This weighted temperature has been consistently found to be most representative of the conditions which produce physiological strain (Yaglou and Minard, 1957), for example, a WBGT greater than 85 is stated to be limiting for strenuous exercise or outdoor classes in the sun (Department of the Army Technical Bulletin, 1957).

C. Body Temperatures

Figure 1 and Table III present the rectal and skin temperature data secured during flight in investigator-accompanied VR missions and the calculated body heat storage estimates. Figure 1 is for five "hot" VR missions. These are not high rectal temperatures. The skin temperatures are high, but they were intentionally secured from the skin area expected to reach the highest temperatures—under the armored vest, where sweat evaporative cooling could not occur.

TABLE III

Heat Storage Data and Calculations on
Visual Reconnaissance Investigator-Accompanied Missions

Pilot	Takeoff T_r (°C)	Takeoff T_s (°C)	Landing T_r (°C)	Landing T_r (°C)	Body heat Content (H_c) (kcal) Takeoff	Landing	Difference	Estimated metabolic heat production (kcal)	Evaporative heat loss (kcal)	Environmental heat gain[a] (kcal)	Environmental heat gain[a] (kcal/hr)
B.T.[b]	38.0	36.8	37.8	37.1	2011	1972	−39	300	566	227	91
R.J.[b]	37.8	36.0	37.8	37.2	2653	2647	+6	320	522	208	78
R.S.[b]	37.8	37.0	37.7	37.0	2436	2397	+39	320	554	273	102
H.B.[b]	37.9	37.3	37.8	37.2	2648	2642	−6	370	754	278	90
W.P.	37.6	36.1	37.6	37.2	2222	2218	−4	300	392	88	35
F.W.[b]	37.7	35.7	37.5	37.2	2797	2794	−3	330	464	131	48
J.M.	37.5	36.0	37.5	36.7	2246	2229	−17	420	493	56	16

Per mission spans the Estimated metabolic heat production, Evaporative heat loss, and Environmental heat gain columns.

[a] Heat gain from the environment is calculated as: Environmental heat gain = total heat loss − metabolic heat production ± change in heat content.

[b] "Hot" missions.

D. Water Losses

Tables IV–VII present data for total sweat production, for total sweat evaporation, and for mission duration. The calculated rates are based on total elapsed time between weighings, which usually exceeded actual mission time by approximately 1 hr. The IR and SLAR missions (Tables VI and VIII) evoked much lower water losses.

Table VIII presents the average hourly water losses by type of mission. Statistical analysis gave the following comparisons of hourly water loss by type of mission: Water loss during IR missions was 200 g/hr, not significantly different from the 139 g/hr average loss during SLAR missions ($p > 0.05$). Hourly water losses on "cool" VR missions were 288 g/hr, which is significantly greater than the mean of IR and SLAR missions combined ($p < 0.001$). "Hot" VR missions resulted in average water losses of 405 g/hr, which is significantly greater than that which resulted from "cool" VR missions ($p < 0.001$).

Figure 2 is a predictive graph derived from least-squares analysis (Croxton, 1959) for water loss per hour as a function of cockpit WBGT.

E. Serum Chemistry

The paired serum samples were analyzed for sodium, chloride, osmolarity, blood urea nitrogen, and creatinine by Auto-Analyzer techniques. As anticipated from the dehydration incurred in the "hot" VR flights, there were mean increases of 3.4 meq/liter of sodium and 3.7 mosm/liter of osmolarity. Chloride, blood urea nitrogen, and creatinine showed similar small changes in the same directions. In "cool" VR and all SLAR and IR missions the measured serum chemistries were essentially unaffected.

IV. Discussion

The cockpit temperatures reported here are considered to be in the moderate range with respect to producing physiological strain. This is not to say that there is no heat stress associated with WBGT values of 81°–85°F, but rather that under the circumstances of this study the combination of work levels and environmental factors

TABLE IV

Water Losses on Visual Reconnaissance Investigator-Accompanied Missions

Date (June)	Mission start time (hr)	Subject	Mission time (hr)	Total elapsed time (hr)	Total sweat produced (g)	Total sweat evaporated (g)	Water loss[a] (g/hr)	Sweat evaporation (g/hr)	Water loss as % BWi (initial)
14[b]	1300	B.T.	1.67	2.50	1100	975	440	390	1.7
14	1300	Invest.	1.67	2.50	2725[c]	2175[c]	1090[c]	870[c]	3.5[c]
15[b]	1300	R.J.	1.50	2.67	1100	900	412	337	1.3
15	1300	Invest.	1.50	2.67	1300	1025	487	384	1.7
15	1700	W.P.	1.42	2.50	850	675	340	270	1.2
15	1700	Invest.	1.42	2.50	685	585	274	234	0.9
16[b]	1300	R.S.	1.58	2.67	1100	955	412	358	1.4
16	1300	Invest.	1.58	2.67	1140	990	427	371	1.5
17[b]	1100	F.W.	1.17	2.75	1000	800	364	291	1.1
17	1100	Invest.	1.17	2.75	975	925	355	336	1.3
17	1600	J.M.	2.08	3.50	1000	850	286	243	1.4
17	1600	Invest.	2.08	3.50	900	750	257	214	1.2
18[b]	1300	H.B.	1.42	3.08	1625	1300	528	422	1.9
18	1300	Invest.	1.42	3.08	2215	2015	719	654	2.9

[a] Sweat production per hour.

[b] "Hot" Missions.

[c] Values abnormal as investigator was clinically ill during the mission.

TABLE V

Water Losses on Visual Reconnaissance Investigator-Unaccompanied Missions

Date (June)	Subject	Mission start (hr)	Mission time (hr)	Total elapsed time (hr)	Total sweat produced (g)	Total sweat evaporated (g)	Water loss[a] (g/hr)	Sweat evaporation (g/hr)	Water loss as % BWi (initial)
14	J.M.[b]	1600	2.00	3.15	955	805	303	256	1.3
14	R.T.	1600	2.00	3.15	975	795	310	252	1.3
16	H.B.[b]	1000	1.66	2.40	700	650	292	271	0.8
16	J.G.	1000	1.66	2.40	650	625	271	260	0.8
30	J.S.	1800	1.33	2.08	450	200	217	96	0.8
30[c]	W.M.[b]	1500	2.00	2.66	925	725	348	273	1.2
30[c]	R.G.	1500	2.00	2.66	875	575	329	216	1.3

[a]Sweat production.
[b]Pilot.
[c]"Hot" Mission.

158

TABLE VI
Water Losses on Infrared Missions

Date (June)	Subject	Mission start time (hr)	Mission time (hr)	Total elapsed time (hr)	Total sweat produced (g)	Total sweat evaporated (g)	Water loss[a] (g/hr)	Sweat evaporation (g/hr)	Water loss as % BWi (initial)
14	R.M.[b]	1800	1.33	2.25	575	445	256	198	0.8
14	F.J.	1800	1.33	2.25	425	375	189	167	0.6
16	R.J.[b]	1830	1.66	2.40	500	475	208	198	0.6
30	W.M.[b]	2030	1.75	2.75	400	350	145	127	0.5
30	R.T.	2030	1.75	2.75	550	500	200	182	0.7

[a]Sweat production.
[b]Pilot.

159

TABLE VII
Water Losses on SLAR Missions

Date (June)	Subject	Mission start time (hr)	Mission time (hr)	Total elapsed time (hr)	Total sweat produced (g)	Total sweat evaporated (g)	Water loss[a] (g/hr)	Sweat evaporation (g/hr)	Water loss as % BWi (initial)
13	H.B.[b]	2300	2.50	2.75	250	230	91	84	0.3
14	W.P.[b]	2200	2.00	2.90	385	385	133	133	0.5
14	D.S.	2200	2.00	2.90	575	450	198	155	0.7
30	R.E.[b]	2045	2.10	3.75	750	750	200	200	1.0
30	A.W.	2045	2.10	3.75	275	275	73	73	0.5

[a] Sweat production.
[b] Pilot.

TABLE VIII

Average Hourly Water Loss for all Mission Types

Mission type	Number missions	Number subjects	$\overline{X}$ (g)	±S.D. (g)
VR "hot"	6	7	404.7	53.5
VR "cool"	5	7	288.4	38.2
IR	3	5	199.6	39.8
SLAR	3	5	139.0	59.0

was adequately compensated by physiological adjustments — at least for the period of time measured.

The investigator tended to cool (as measured by rectal temperature) more rapidly than did the pilots and did not reach as high skin temperatures. These findings probably reflect the fact that the investigator did relatively little physical work and also tended to have higher sweat rates (Table IV), and hence greater evaporative cooling. The two "cool" VR missions for which similar data were secured showed slightly lower values for T_r and T_s for both pilots and investigator and the same differential relationship.

In general, "hot" VR missions were the most stressful when assessed in terms of water loss. The pilots on these missions (Tables IV and V) became dehydrated to an average level of 1.4% loss of initial body weight. This is considered to be only a modest total loss and reflects the short duration of the missions. However, the rate of loss is moderately high and is nearly identical to that of infantry sitting in desert sun at comparable dry bulb temperatures and to that found in pilots operating over desert areas at altitudes of 1000–3000 ft (Adolf, 1947). Previous work at similar ambient temperatures has shown that only 1% more dehydration (to 2.4%) can cause an unusually rapid increase in the rectal temperatures of men, who after dehydrating while seated quietly then begin to work (Joy and Goldman, 1964). Hence, if mission times were to be doubled, dehydration and the accompanying hyperthermia could reach levels which might produce clinical illness.

The calculations for heat exchange reported here (Table III) contain two major sources of estimate error: T_s is available from only one "worst case" measurement site rather than the usual three to nine, and metabolic heat production is not measured but estimated from the literature at 120 kcal/hr (Altman *et al.*, 1958; Passmore and Durnin, 1955). These data are presented primarily to make available to engineers values which might be useful in cockpit design.

The mean heat loss to the environment of the pilots during the five "hot," investigator-accompanied VR missions is estimated as 572 kcal, or 209 kcal/hr. The heat gain from the environment by the pilots averaged 82 kcal/hr in these five missions. It must be emphasized that this environmental heat gain is a transient heat gain, acquired from the environment primarily by radiation and compensated for—i.e., transferred—back to the environment by sweat evaporation. The miniscule changes in body heat content, reflecting small increases in core (rectal) and skin temperatures, demonstrate this point.

While flying, the crew members wore the following ensemble: Combat boots, socks, cotton shorts, T-shirts, standard utility "fatigues" (cotton, sateen, OG 107) shirt and trousers, armored vest (infantry type—7½ pounds), flight helmet (painted OD), leather gloves, a weapon, and survival equipment.

From a physiological viewpoint, this ensemble contributes to the heat strain and discomfort problem of the air crews. A cotton T-shirt tends to hold warm sweat close to the skin, impedes air circulation across the skin, and favors wicking of sweat away from the skin rather than direct skin surface evaporation. The design of the standard utility uniform is such that air circulation is limited when worn while one is strapped into an airplane seat. A one piece, loosely fitting, light-weight coverall garment could contribute to increasing air circulation and decreasing pilot heat strain, if worn only with boots, socks, undershorts, flight helmet, and gloves. When flying with sleeves and gloves rolled down, the only bare skin surface directly exposed to the air is a portion of the face—thus there is little enough opportunity for the convective air movement across the skin essential for efficient evaporative heat loss.

The armored vest is a serious barrier to heat dissipation. It completely prohibits evaporative cooling and air circulation over the torso. Further, it contributes to ineffective water loss due to the higher local skin temperature underneath it. This produces a secondary increase in the local thermal drive to sweat production, but since evaporation is prevented, causes "wastage" of the sweat so produced. When worn by marching infantry (2.5 mi/hr) at these WBGT levels, vests of this type have reduced tolerance time in a heat stress situation by 40% (Goldman, 1963).

The pilots and technical observers were questioned about their reasons for wearing the armored vest. In general the answers were of three types. The vest was worn for protection, worn as a convenient garment to carry survival gear, and worn because of an order to wear it. There can be no objection to the first reason. However, the second and third reasons are specious. Survival gear can be carried in a mesh vest. If the armored vest is worn routinely only because it is an issued item, then the basis of issue and the actual need for the item require review.

The flight helmet when painted olive drab tends to favor radiant heat absorption instead of reflection. If white helmets were worn they could be expected to add to pilot comfort and contribute to a decrease in heat strain.

In the several aircraft in which this study was performed, the ventilating system yielded little or no air flow. The lack of ventilation was most likely due to the lack of a provision for air exit from the cockpit, and thus the ram jet of air intake was limited as positive pressure built up in the system. In the absence of an air exit, there could be little convective air flow through the cockpit.

Development and engineering studies are in progress which may result in the provision of a practical air conditioner for the Mohawk cockpit. Providing that parked aircraft can be shaded, and that the rate of cooling of such a unit can be rapid enough, this approach is a rational answer to the problem discussed here. However, it must be recognized that it would add weight, complexity, maintenance problems, and require additional engine power.

Air- or water-cooled garments have been evaluated in Viet Nam, but to date have not been acceptable to pilots and observers because the garments are hot when worn on the ground, are bulky and uncomfortable, and are another maintenance problem in an already complex system. The modest values for heat loss and environmental heat gain found in this study do not suggest a mandatory requirement for air conditioning or ventilated suits to handle the heat load. However, the data do emphasize the importance to the crew of evaporative cooling and hence the need for appropriate clothing and improved cockpit ventilation. The effective dissipation of the heat removed by water vaporization can be improved by increasing the convective air stream. In still air, an equilibrium is soon reached in which the water vapor pressure immediately above the skin approaches the vapor pressure of the sweat, evaporation is drastically reduced, and liquid sweat drips from the skin. At this point, body water is being "wasted," since in the absence of sweat evaporation no body cooling is being achieved, and body temperature, skin and rectal, must rise as heat accumulates in the body. A vicious circle begins — increased body temperature causes an increased sweat drive, body water is depleted more rapidly, and severe dehydration can occur if water is not replaced, with clinical illness occurring when body water losses approach or pass 5% of body weight (Adolf, 1947).

Certain recommendations were made to command at the conclusion of this study:

The crew members should replace their water loss by inflight drinking of water, approximately 1 pt/hr. This would prevent dehydration and eliminate any chance of a secondary hyperthermia. Measurement of the WBGT at a ground station would alert crews to days when climatic stress might be unusually severe and when water requirements might be increased (Fig. 2).

The cockpit should be ventilated by exit vents located at the top rear of the cockpit, allowing an air flow to pass through the cockpit.

Light-weight flying suits should be worn to increase convective air movement across the skin and allow for better evaporation, and white flight helmets should be worn to decrease radiant heat absorption.

The wearing of the armored vest should be reviewed to define those missions in which it should be worn and those missions in which it can safely be eliminated.

In short, the major heat problem of the Mohawk crew was found to be discomfort and dehydration with accompanying fatigue, both of which could be considerably alleviated with inflight water drinking and improved cockpit ventilation and clothing ensembles. There does not appear to be an urgent need for air conditioning or mechanically cooled overgarments.

V. Summary

The OV-1 (Mohawk) is a two place, twin engine, fast and maneuverable aircraft used for reconnaissance missions. Following reports of heat stress in Mohawk crews in June 1966 in Viet Nam,

17 missions and 24 subjects were studied for water losses; in seven of these missions seven pilots and the investigator also had rectal and skin temperature measured during flight. Ground and cockpit WBGT's were measured. Low level visual reconnaissance flights during the day were found to be the most stressful, with water losses (sweat) of 405 ml/hr/man, while rectal and skin temperatures and heat gains were well compensated by the high sweat rates. An average of 82 kcal/hr/man of transient heat gain was acquired from the environment, and an average of 209 kcal/man of heat was contributed to the cockpit environment. Evening and night missions were found to cause modest dehydration. It did not appear that the air crews were subjected to an uncompensable heat strain. These data are nearly identical to those secured by Adolf in 1944 in simulated tactical situations. At least for the variables measured, actual combat circumstances did not appear to cause additional physiological strain. Inflight water drinking, cockpit ventilation, and lighter clothing were recommended to reduce air crew discomfort and restore homeostatic conditions. These suggestions were implemented by command and appear to have alleviated the problem.

ACKNOWLEDGMENTS

Major John Ward, MC, USA, previously the Flight Surgeon, 11th Aviation Group, was the first to recognize and report this problem. Major Billy Taylor, USA, Commanding Officer of the Surveillance Platoon, 11th Aviation Group, 1st Cavalry Division (AM), his pilots and his crew members gave complete and cheerful cooperation throughout the study and willingly endured considerable personal discomfort and inconvenience. Colonel Allen Burdette, USA, and Colonel Howard Lukens, USA, successive Commanding Officers of the 11th Aviation Group, gave complete support to this study and implemented the recommendations.

LTC Richard Salcedo, MC, USA, presently Flight Surgeon, 11th Aviation Group, has kindly provided followup information since the rotation of the author from Viet Nam. The Mohawk cockpit has been vented by unit mechanics by adding two exit vents just above and aft of the cockpit. The uniform regulations have been changed to permit the use of flight suits, white helmets, and discretionary use of armored vests. The crew members now drink water in flight. According to Dr. Salcedo, the pilots and observers have noted less fatigue, are more comfortable, and believe they are considerably cooler during flights.

This material in this chapter was presented in part at the annual meeting of the Federation of American Societies for Experimental Biology, in Chicago, on April 18, 1967. A somewhat different version appeared in *Aerospace Medicine*, Vol. 38, p. 895 (1967).

REFERENCES

Adolf, E. F. (1947). "Physiology of Man in the Desert." Wiley (Interscience), New York.

Altman, P. L., Gibson, J. F., and Wang, C. C. (1958). "Handbook of Respiration," pp. 147–150. Saunders, Philadelphia, Pennsylvania.

Croxton, F. E. (1959). "Elementary Statistics With Applications in Medicine and the Biological Sciences." Dover, New York.

Department of the Army Technical Bulletin (1957). "Adverse Effects of Heat." *TB Med.* 175.

Goldman, R. F. (1963). Tolerance time for work in the heat when wearing CBR protective clothing. *Military Med.* 128, 776.

Joy, R. J. T., and Goldman, R. F. (1964). Microenvironments, modern equipment and the mobility of the soldier. *In* "Symposium on Medical Aspects of Stress in the Military Environment" (D. Rioch, ed.), pp. 101–126. Walter Reed Army Inst. of Res., Washington, D.C.

Medical Statistics Agency (1968). "The Health of the Army." Office of the Surgeon General, Dept. of the Army, Washington, D.C.

Passmore, R., and Durnin, J. V. G. A. (1955). Human energy expenditure. *Physiol. Rev.* 35, 801.

Whayne, R. F. (1951). History of heat trauma as a war experience. *In* "Army Medical Graduate School: Basic Science Notes." Pp. 1–38. Walter Reed Army Inst. of Res., Washington, D.C.

Yaglou, C. P., and Minard, D. (1957). Control of heat casualties at military training centers. *A.M.A. Arch. Ind. Health* 16, 302.

8 // Background Characteristics, Attitudes, and Self-Concepts of Air Force Psychiatric Casualties from Southeast Asia*

Vincent Wallen

*The views expressed herein are those of the author and do not necessarily reflect the views of the U.S. Air Force or the Department of Defense.

I. Introduction

The airman in the US Air Force is in large part an expression of his culture. During his youth and early manhood he has had only vicarious experience in the business of self-sacrifice for duty and honor. Life has generally not been precarious for him, nor ever dangerous. He has been conditioned to see aggressiveness and aggression only as fantasy, and within an entertainment media as an unwanted thing, dangerous, to be avoided, and largely external to his basic frame of reference and also to his behavior. He has also been led to believe that soldiering and that being a soldier are largely impersonal things and that the responsibility for the protection of his country is assumed by the government through selective service. Inculcated in him as well, is the strong belief that his duty assignment should be more or less appropriate to his civilian training and personal desires. All of these beliefs stem from the American culture and reflect the basic philosophy of a democratic society.

The hypothetical "average" American has learned to love liberty and to strive for independence. He is convinced that he can maintain his independence by hard work and by dedication to his job or profession. If he is not content with his job, he knows that he can quit and can find another. Politically, he feels free to choose his leaders and to make himself heard on issues both great and small. What he does not like he may criticize through the press, TV, personal humor, and through direct verbal attack. His independence is pursued through matters of dress, amusement, recreation, avocations, and through the selection of friends. He has license to study whatever and how much he desires and to enter an almost unlimited field of occupations. He has a wide lattitude in terms of responding to his wife and family as he pleases and to come and go as he desires. He has a repugnance for violence, for unyielding authority, and for ruthless strength. Although he tries to be realistic while still being idealistic, he believes with optimistic fervor that things will always get moving again and that with dedication, industry, patience, and fervor all things will improve for himself and everyone as well. This, then, is the hypothetical American character as found in the American airman.

What happens in wartime? How is the basic American character restructured? Perhaps it reaches its greatest test when it becomes transformed into a "combat personality." Under the new conditions of wartime, independence and freedom are largely surrendered to military authority and to the acceptance of restrictions, both public and private. Personal strength must yield to group strength for the greater good and the greater protection that it affords. Self-interest must become group interest. Aggressive energies, formerly directed into creative and socially accepted channels have to be directed toward open hostile, destructive, and what is more important, homicidal behavior. The rewards that are yielded are physical and emotional hardships fraught with anxiety and suffering. It is within such an arena that the personal reconstruction takes place.

The fear of unexpected death in wartime is unlike any other stress one can ever experience. It affects the soldier in a myriad of ways both physically and emotionally. It affects his homeostatic characterological and behavior equilibrium so that he either learns to adapt to the difficult stresses of the new reality or he begins to maladapt and to decompensate.

The "normal" citizen–soldier who has been functioning as a civilian prior to induction may find the stress of combat to be extremely traumatic. His personality may be laid bare both physiologically and psychologically. He may begin to exude psychophysiologic, neurotic, or other more serious symptoms, depending upon the balance between his strengths and his weaknesses.

There is also the factor of technological advancement which must be considered.

Since World War II, the rate of technological advancement has been accelerated to the point where it almost staggers the imagination. Almost as fast as new weapons systems have been developed, tested, and made operational, some of them have become obsolete. For example, the infantryman's rifle of World War II vintage, the M-1, was declared obsolete and replaced with the all-purpose M-14. The M-14 is now being replaced with a lighter rifle designed for jungle warfare in Southeast Asia, the M-16.

Not only does the technology but the amount of firepower available stagger the imagination; weapons systems have progressed so rapidly that it is difficult to conceive of their actual destructive potential.

World War I battles consisted chiefly of "trench warfare" where the adversaries charged and countercharged from their trenches and where battles were gauged in terms of trenches won or miles that troops were able to advance and hold.

World War II consisted of great battles that were largely impersonal, on land, on sea, and in the air. The scientific revolution in weapons made it a "massive firepower war" where adversaries no longer had direct personal contact with one another. It was in short, a war of "massive firepower annihilation." Battle lines, however, tended to be somewhat clearly defined by great rivers, deserts, mountains, coastlines, and cities.

On the conflict being waged in Southeast Asia today, boundaries are indefinite, the enemy is often unseen, and the firepower of automatic weapons, rockets, and artillery is not only formidable but highly accurate. In addition, one's unit or base may be in complete encirclement by the enemy forces. As an example, the US Marine Base at Khe Sanh, recently during a 77-day siege, encircled by the North Vietnamese who held most of the high ground, was continuously dazed by rocket and 130 and 152 mm artillery barrages that landed up to 1500 rounds/day into the base. Enemy trenches fingered up to the camp's defensive wire. Rats infested the bunkers. The hulks of downed supply planes lined the runway. Day and night, B-52's dropped more than 100,000 tons of explosives outside the perimeter, about one-sixth of the total during all of the Korean War. The "normal" citizen–soldier may find factors such as these to be highly traumatic when he experiences them.

But what of the career soldier, the military specialist whose personality and whose personal needs are egosyntonic to the military life? Will he decompensate, and if so, under what kind of pressure and under what amount of stress? Does his identification with the service, the introjection of its values, and the stability of a technical military specialty facilitate adjustment to combat stresses? Do many years of active peacetime service, coupled with the stability of a married life, affect his adaptation to a combat environment? How does the professional soldier–citizen view himself, and how does he respond to the ever-present stresses in a hostile environment—in a war zone? This study was designed to provide the answers to such questions.

II. Related Clinical Studies

Clinical observations of psychiatric casualties in Viet Nam made by Morriss (1967) indicated that although many of the patients were young army draftees and airmen, there appeared to be a significant proportion of men in their 20's, 30's, and 40's, many of whom were noncommissioned officers. About one-half of the patients were reported to have had eight or more years of active duty. Some of these men had over 14 years of active duty and others had more than 16 years.

A second observation was that at approximately the fourth month, there was a high incidence of individuals, who, having effected a satisfactory adjustment at first, seemed to enter a period of despair at the prospect of fulfilling the remainder of their 1-year tour. This depressive reaction which occurred in one-half of all depressed cases, appeared to be related not only to the length of the tour, but to a concurrent depression in the wife who was situated in the continental United States. It appeared that many of the wives saw the temporary loss of the husband as being more of a permanent one in terms of time distortion and prepared for it by writing letters alluding to divorce or separation. At approximately the sixth month, both partners seemed to have the end in sight, with divorce talk terminating and the depressive features disappearing.

It was also observed that many of the patients viewed their central problem as being their family's desperate need for them to be home with them when in reality it was a projection of the patient's own profound need to be with the family.

Perhaps the most striking feature of the psychiatric patient population was that most of the cases were either career airmen or noncommissioned officers who possessed outstanding records and high levels of skill, a group that had never before faced the trauma of family separation and personal danger.

Schramel (1966) in his study of US Air Force nonpsychotic psychiatric casualties evacuated from Viet Nam to Clark Air Base in the Philippine Islands from 1964 to 1966, reported that most of the psychiatric patients were married and 73% had families. The median age was reported as being 29.1. Most of the casualties (65%) had 8 or more years of service. The greatest percentage of casualties were those with 14–19 years of service. The majority of the patients had never seen "combat" before and over 86% gave some indication that their assignment had come as a "surprise." As a group, the patients offered no concerted, positive attitude toward their being in Southeast Asia, and had no favorable feelings toward their Air Force mission.

The study as conceived originally was concerned with the psychological identification of the pathological emotional signs and traits, in terms of incidence and types to be found among military psychiatric casualties in the war zone. The primary objective was to obtain data relative to facilitating the establishment of a prophylactic mental hygiene program in the war zone area that would serve the needs of the psychiatric population in the most effective manner.

The author found the USAF Hospital at Clark Air Base to be almost totally devoid of psychiatric patients from Southeast Asia. Accordingly, it was therefore decided that since the bulk of the patients were being sent to the USAF Hospital Tachikawa in Japan for further evaluation, treatment, and disposition, that the study should be focused at this casualty staging location.

III. Research Methodology

The basic research methodology of this study involved the development of two instruments, a background questionnaire and a Q sort. An intelligence test, the Otis Self-Administering Test of Mental Ability (Adult Form A) was also employed. A sample of 30 subjects, all of whom were classed as psychiatric patients from Southeast Asia during the period November 1, 1966, through May 1, 1967, were administered these instruments.

A. General Purpose

Briefly restated, the general purposes of this study were as follows: (1) To identify those personality traits and characteristics which are the most prevalent in USAF psychiatric casualties evacuated from the Southeast Asia theater of operations; (2) to quantify and correlate the levels of congruence of the self-perceptions and the self-concepts of USAF psychiatric patients as measures of personal and social adjustment; (3) to examine morale and attitudes, *ex post facto*, of the psychiatric casualties toward their assignment, AFS, peer, and supervisory relationships, and toward the Air Force in general; and (4) to recommend on the basis of objective test findings and statistical data a number of methods for the prevention, detection, and treatment of psychiatric disorders indigenous to USAF personnel stationed in Southeast Asia.

B. Research Assumptions

The following assumptions were also made: (1) It was assumed that all of the test data was quantifiable and could be treated statistically by means of small sample correlation formulas and tests of significance; (2) it was recognized that the personality qualities observed might also conceivably be the effect or result of experience rather than the predisposing qualities leading to the difficulties in adjustment and in emotional breakdown.

C. Research Tools

A background questionnaire and an attitude scale were developed. On the questionnaire, the following vital information was recorded for each patient: (1) Age, (2) rank, (3) length of service, (4) marital status, (5) Air Force occupational specialty, (6) years in Air Force occupational specialty, (7) total months in the war zone, (8) highest formal school grade completed, and (9) IQ (Table I)

IV. Research Considerations

Two basic research considerations were (1) the selection of a conceptual scheme based upon a modern theory of personality, and (2) the development of a satisfactory assessment tool anchored to a specific theory.

A. The Self-Concept

The personality theory which was selected was that of Carl Rogers, employing the self-concept as it has evolved from experiences in client-centered therapy. The theory is based on the formulation that each individual's perception of himself is of ultimate psychological significance in the organized behavior of the person and that behavior is to a large extent regulated and organized by how one perceives himself and what a person believes about himself.

Recent studies of therapeutic changes in client-centered therapy have indicated that a basic element of change in the measured acceptance of and respect for the self from the beginning to the end of therapy is reflected in the direction of greater congruence between the individual's actual self-concept (the way the person perceives himself as he thinks he is) and the ideal self-concept (the way he perceives himself as he thinks he would like to be). Specifically, as patients approach better psychological adjustment and better personality integration and as the discrepancy between the

TABLE I
Background Characteristics of the Patient Sample

Case No.	Age	Marital status[a]	Total years service	No. years in AFS	Months in SEA	Highest grade completed	IQ
1	37	M	19	12	4	12	92
2	39	S	16	15	6	8	83
3	21	S	2.5	2	10	12	92
4	23	M	5.8	5	6	11	93
5	29	M	11	11	11	11	109
6	21	S	1.3	1.3	1	12	88
7	24	M	7	7	1	9	103
8	38	M	19	19	3	8	83
9	34	M	17	17	4	10	107
10	20	S	2	2	3	12	109
11	27	M	8.5	8	0	12	96
12	28	M	5	4.7	1	12	101
13	20	S	2	2	4	12	105
14	36	M	13	13	5	11	93
15	23	S	3.8	3	7	12	93
16	26	S	3.3	3	3	12	127
17	37	M	22	9	2	9	85
18	32	M	15	14.5	4	12	110
19	33	M	14	14	9	11	81
20	34	M	10	10	4	10	92
21	30	M	12	12	4	12	93
22	36	M	17.5	17.5	2	10	87
23	29	M	11.5	2.5	4	10	93
24	23	M	5.5	5.5	5	12	98
25	26	S	4	4	3.5	12	81
26	23	M	5	5	5	10	109
27	28	S	8.5	8.5	12	12	91
28	25	M	7	7	6.5	12	86
29	21	S	3.7	3.7	8.5	10	108
30	27	M	11	11	8	11	114
	847		282.90	249.2		329	2902
Mean	28.23		9.41	8.30	4.88	10.97	96.73

[a]M, married; S, single.

actual self-concept and ideal self-concept is reduced as the self becomes better accepted and more realistic, there is a definite change in the direction of greater congruence. The resultant formulations are that (1) a low level of congruence between the actual self-concept and ideal self-concept reflects a high degree of self-dissatisfaction, and conversely (2) a high level of congruence between the actual self-concept and the ideal self-concept reflects a high degree of self-satisfaction, good personality adjustment, and good integration.

In addition, other studies have indicated that persons react to reality as they perceive it, that a definite relationship exists between the way an individual feels about himself and the way he feels about other persons. Specifically, an individual who holds negative feelings toward himself tends to hold negative feelings toward other people in general. His behavior tends to be characterized by the way he feels about other persons and by the way he feels others perceive him. As the negative feelings change during treatment to objective or positive, the person's feelings about others change in a similar direction.

B. The *Q* Technique

The *Q* technique, which was employed in this study, is a method for the intercorrelation of persons. The method was developed in England and brought to this country by Stephenson. Essentially, this technique is a method which systematically studies the notions of a person about himself. The person is given a packet of statements and is asked to sort them into a prearranged quasinormal distribution along a continuum from those most characteristic of the person doing the sorting to those least characteristic of him. The distribution of statements approximates a normal distribution and is exactly the same for all of the subjects in a given experiment. This constant feature facilitates the statistical handling of the results since all of the sortings are forced into a distribution whose mean and standard deviation are the same. The items for a *Q* sort deck may be made up in various ways. They may be made up to conform to a particular theory of personality or they may be selected from a population of items obtained from a population of items obtained from therapeutic protocols, self-descriptions, personality inventories, statements that a person may make about himself, and the like.

The *Q* sorts have several psychometric advantages which have been summarized by Cronbach (1952). Notable are the statistical advantages of the forced-choice quasinormal distribution for all subjects which provides a more meaningful correlation since all of the distributions which have a different content nevertheless have the same shape. The majority of the statements which the subject places in the middle piles frees him from making many difficult and rather unimportant discriminations he would have to make if he were forced to rank every statement. The fact that discrimination near the center of the scale is difficult is reduced in importance by the fact that in product–moment correlations the end cells receive the greatest weight.

In summary, the forced-choice technique in Q sort methodology, geared to the conceptual framework of the self-concept in client-centered therapy, provides a scientifically sound and useful means of personality measurement and assessment. It provided the major psychological tool for this study.

V. Theoretical Considerations

A. Level of Congruence

Prior to proceeding further, several terms should be made more explicit. The first of these, the term *level of congruence*, is defined as the relative cohesiveness of all of the selves which an individual may conceptualize. Although it may not be possible to measure the relationships between all of the possible conceptual entities, an approximation of cohesiveness may be obtained by determining a relationship between two of the conceptual selves or self-concepts. The term *mean level of congruence*, as used in this study, refers to the fact that since approximations of levels of congruence of the same self-concept may be found for individuals, means may be determined for groups of individuals as well.

The method, as employed in this study, involves the sampling of two conceptual selves by means of sorting into a forced-choice quasinormal distribution, a number of self-referent statements that can be meaningfully used to describe individuals. In this study the level of congruence of the self-concepts is measured by the correlation score which represents the mathematical relationship between the ideal self-sort and actual self-sort.

B. Development of the Q Sort

The theoretical rationale which appeared to be the most appropriate for this study and for the establishment of a basic evaluative instrument was that of Carl Rogers' "self-theory."

In order to develop a clinically valid and sensitive instrument it was decided that the Q sort instrument should consist of a large number of self-referent statements elicited by psychiatric patients about themselves at the US Air Force Hospital at Tachikawa Air Base, Japan. The sample of statements selected did not represent a random sample drawn from all possible items relevant to any given individual. The statements selected by the author were then scanned for content validity, logic, and meaningfulness in order to increase the validity and the reliability of the final instrument and to preclude logically meaningless choices by the patients to be examined.

Next, five senior US Air Force psychiatrists and ten senior US Air Force clinical psychologists were selected at random to serve as psychological experts for the categorization of the 76 self-referent statements into seven personality trait areas. The items which were classifiable into trait categories are contained in Table II. Items for which there was less than 61% average agreement were not placed in the specific trait categories, but were nevertheless retained in the Q sort deck.

The items which were categorized as per instructions contained in Appendixes A and B were sorted into the categories of (1) self-acceptance, (2) independence, (3) good emotional control, (4) self-rejection, (5) dependency, (6) poor emotional control, and (7) withdrawal.

The attitude questionnaire was administered to each patient. The questions were concerned with the attitude of each patient toward: (A) preparation for assignment to Southeast Asia, (B) adjustment in the Service, (C) physical health, (D) feelings about continued and further service, (E) job satisfaction, (F) pride in one's unit, (G) peer and supervisor (NCO) relationships, (H) desire to change to another military career field, and (I) attitudes toward the service in general.

A Q sort test instrument designated as the Tachikawa Q Sort was developed. It consisted of a large number of self-referent statements elicited by psychiatric patients about themselves in individual and group therapy at the USAF Hospital Tachikawa. These statements were then categorized into seven personality trait areas according to the instructions as contained in Appendix A and the criteria as contained in Appendix B, employing Carl Rogers' theory on personality and behavior.

The self-referent statements were categorized by five senior

TABLE II
Categorization of Personality Traits

Trait	Self-acceptance		Independence		Good emotional control		Self-rejection		Dependency		Poor emotional control		Withdrawal	
	Item[a]	%[b]	Item[a]	%	Item[a]	%	Item[a]	%	Item[a]	%	Item[a]	%	Item[a]	%
	1	77	5	92	3	100	24	92	19	77	7	92	6	92
	12	92	17	92	13	70	29	70	20	92	14	77	15	92
	18	70	42	100	22	92	31	70	30	100	25	77	38	100
	26	77	70	100	56	70	33	84	73	84	40	77	45	92
	36	70	74	84	58	70	54	100	75	92	51	77	65	100
	47	70	2	61	23	61	61	77	69	61	52	100		
	50	100	62	61			68	84			53	77		
	55	77					11	61			60	100		
	57	84					16	61			67	92		
	59	84									76	100		
	63	70									9	61		
	72	70									71	61		
	10	61												
Average percent agreement	78		84		77		78		84		82		95	

[a] Fifty-nine items classified into trait categories, 17 items not classified. Average of (+) items of 3 categories = 9
[b] 77.6% items classified, 22.4% items not classified. Average of (−) items of 4 categories = 8

178

USAF Medical Service Psychiatrists and ten senior USAF Clinical Psychologists, and the results were tabulated. The designated trait areas and the average percentage of agreement were as follows: (*1*) Self-acceptance, 78%; (*2*) independence, 84%; (*3*) good emotional control, 77%; (*4*) self-rejection, 78%; (*5*) dependency, 84%; (*6*) poor emotional control, 82%; and (*7*) withdrawal, 95%.

VI. Methods of Data Collection

Each of the subjects was first administered the background questionnaire followed by the Otis Test of Measurement of Mental Ability (adult form).

Each subject was then administered the Q sort instrument. The subject was asked to sort the 76 statements according to two separate sets of instructions. Each subject was handed a pack of cards and was asked to sort them according to his actual self-concept, followed by his ideal self-concept as per those instructions as contained in Appendix D.

The score obtained for each statement was the number of the space in which it had been placed. After each sort, the cards were reshuffled.

Each sorting represented a distribution as:

	Least like							Most like	
No. of cards	2	5	9	13	18	13	9	5	2
Scale value	0	1	2	3	4	5	6	7	8

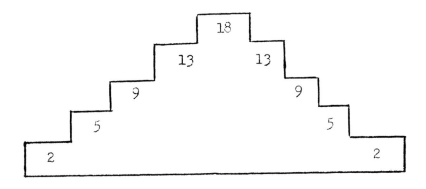

VII. Statistical Treatment of the Data

The basic data of this study consisted of two approximately normal distributions of 76 self-referent statements for each subject. Each of the self-sorts was quantified, and correlation coefficients were computed based upon an adaptation of the Pearson product–moment correlation formula

$$r = \frac{NEXY - K_1}{K_2}$$

where $K_1 = (EX)^2$ and $K_2 = NEX^2 - (EX)^2$.

This particular method of data treatment was selected since the sorts represented forced normal distributions and many of the major assumptions which are inherent in such correlations were automatically met. Also, the assumptions of linearity of regression and homoscedasticity were met. Another advantage was the fact that since in each distribution of sorts, the mean and the variance (standard deviation) are the same, the computation of r was greatly simplified.

Although r correlations were employed to represent the basic data of the study, a transformation of them prior to the application of formal statistical tests was necessary due to certain peculiarities in the sampling error of r.

Since the number of cases in this study was not large, some way of correcting for sampling errors of high values of r and relatively small numbers of subjects had to be found and applied before the correlation coefficients could be adequately treated statistically. A transformation known as Fisher's z was employed, consisting of a logarithmic transformation of r to a normalized z. The conversion of the r to z values brought about the symmetrical sampling distributions, regardless of the size of r.

Since the advantages of the z transformation are that (1) the distribution of z for successive samples is independent of the universe value, r (the sampling distribution will have the same dispersion for all values of r), and that (2) the distribution of z for successive samples is so nearly normal that it can be treated as such with very little loss of accuracy, it was decided to employ the transformation in the statistical tests to be reported.

VIII. Results

The background data was tabulated and assessed and it was found that the 30 psychiatric patients that were tested had a mean age of 28.23 years. Sixty-six percent were married. The average rank was Staff sergeant. The mean total years of service was 9.41 years. The average time in the Air Force occupational specialty was 8.3 years. The average total number of months served in Southeast Asia at the time of psychiatric breakdown was 4.88. The average number of years of formal schooling for the group was 10.97, or at the end of the junior year in high school. Average IQ as measured by the Otis Test, was 96.73 (low average).

In response to the attitude questionnaire, 63% considered that they were given adequate training or preparation for the assignment to Southeast Asia. Thirty-six percent did not. Seventy-four percent expressed a liking for the service as opposed to 27% who did not. Eighty-six percent felt that they were well-adjusted to the service as opposed to the other 14%. Eighty-three percent felt that they were in good or better physical condition, 77% wanted to remain in the service, and 73% indicated that they were interested in their Air Force occupational specialty. It was noted, however, that in this same group, 47% indicated that they would definitely change to some other job (AF specialty) if given the chance. Seventeen percent were undecided and 37% said "no." In addition, it was noted that 63% would prefer, if given the chance, an assignment to another job in another career field, 20% were undecided, and 17% said they would not consider it.

Ninety-seven percent thought it was important "to make good" in the service, as opposed to 3% who did not.

Eighty percent were proud of their unit, 80% liked their immediate NCO's and 80% thought that their organization was run pretty well or better most of the time.

Forty-three percent felt that they had "gotten a square deal" from the service, 7% said "no," and 50% were undecided.

A. Normal Subject Sample

In order to establish more meaningful results and in order to increase the validity of this study, a small sample of USAF permanent party career service personnel stationed at a USAF hospital in the continental United States was also administered the Q sort and the results were tabulated. Table III represents the background characteristics of this normal subject sample.

A comparison of a number of background characteristics of the patient and the normal subject samples are contained in Table IV.

The sample of normal subjects was also administered the Q sort and the results were tabulated.

B. Recapitulation of the Hypotheses

In recapitulation, the major hypotheses to be tested were that (1) the sample of patients tested would show evidence of acutely disturbed self-images and self-perceptions as manifested in their low levels of congruence between their perceived "selves" and that (2) they would exhibit significant differences in specific personality trait areas as compared with normal subjects.

Specifically, the hypotheses as stated in testable form, were as follows: (1) The mean correlation score between the actual-self sort and the ideal-self sort of a group of USAF psychiatric casualties

TABLE III
Background Characteristics of the Normal Subject Sample

Case no.	Age (years)	Marital status[a]	Total years service	No. years in AFS	Highest grade completed
1	33	M	14	11	12
2	37	D	20	11	8
3	42	M	19	17	10
4	30	M	10	6	12
5	44	M	22	18	10
6	38	M	17	2	10
7	26	S	8	8	12
8	38	M	18	18	11
9	41	M	19	15	8
10	37	M	19	19	12
11	37	M	17	17	8
12	30	S	11	11	12
13	33	M	14	9	12
14	26	M	7	7	11
15	24	M	6	6	12
	516		221	175	160
Mean	34.40		14.73	11.66	10.66

[a]M, married; S, single; D, divorced.

TABLE IV

Comparison of the Background Characteristics of the Patient
and Normal Subject Groups

	Age (years)	Married	Total years service	Number of years in AFS	Highest grade completed
Patients	28.23	66%	9.41	8.30	10.97
Normal subjects	34.40	80%	14.73	11.66	10.66

will be low reflecting self-dissatisfaction between their perceived "selves." (2) The mean correlation score between the actual-self sort and the ideal-self sort of a group of USAF psychiatric casualties will be significantly much lower compared with the mean correlation score of a group of USAF normal subjects. (3) The mean correlation scores of the personality trait categories of self-acceptance, independence, good emotional control, self-rejection, dependence, poor emotional control, and withdrawal will be significantly different between the patients and the normal subjects, reflecting less self-acceptance, greater self-rejection, less independence, greater dependence, poor emotional control, and a greater tendency towards withdrawal in the patient sample.

C. Tests of the Hypotheses

In examining the mean level of congruence between the Q sort arrays it was found that the patient group demonstrated a low level of congruence. The correlation coefficients obtained for the patients' $r_{A:I}$ relationship ranged from -0.42 to $+0.87$. The mean correlation value was $+0.355$. The coefficient values transformed into Fisher's z equivalents ranged from -0.44 to $+01.33$, with a mean value of $+0.427$. The conversion of the mean z value to r yielded a value of $+0.40$.

In examining the mean level of congruence between the Q sort arrays it was found that the normal subject sample demonstrated a high level of congruence. The correlation coefficients obtained for the normal subject sample $r_{A:I}$ relationship ranged from $+0.44$ to $+0.91$. The mean correlation was $+0.688$. The coefficient values transformed into Fisher's z equivalents ranged from $+0.47$ to $+1.52$, with a mean value of $+0.883$. The conversion of the mean z value to r yielded a value of $+0.71$.

It was found that the patients' mean level of congruence between the actual and ideal self-sorts was statistically significant and very much lower than that of the normal subject group. The results are tabulated in Table V.

TABLE V

Results of the Tests of Significance for the Mean r's of the Self-Sort Relationships of the Patient and Normal Subject Samples

r Relationship	Patients			Normal subjects		
	r	S.E.	t	r	S.E.	t
$r_{A:I}$	.40	.15	2.66[a]	.71	.13	5.46[b]

[a]Rejection of null hypothesis at .05 level of confidence.
[b]Rejection of null hypothesis at .01 level of confidence.

The result of the test of significance for the mean *r* after the conversion from Fisher's z indicated that the mean correlation coefficient for the patients' actual–ideal self relationship differed significantly from zero with 29 degrees of freedom.

The result of the test of significance for the mean *r* for the normal subjects' actual–ideal self relationship differed significantly from zero with 14 degrees of freedom.

The results of the tabulation of the mean trait scores for the patient and the normal subject samples were examined. The mean personality trait category scores for the patient and normal subject groups are shown in Table VI.

TABLE VI

Personality Trait Mean Scores for the Patients and Normal Subjects

Personality traits	Patients	Normal subjects
Self-acceptance	60.56	70.13
Independence	35.30	36.40
Good emotional control	22.76	27.30
Self-rejection	26.90	19.07
Dependence	23.36	21.00
Poor emotional control	45.26	37.20
Withdrawal	17.06	16.07

The *t* test of significance applied to the mean scores of the trait category of self-acceptance yielded a *t* of 3.76, which is significant at a value much higher than the 0.01 level of confidence, with 14 degrees of freedom.

The *t* test of significance applied to the mean scores of the trait category of independence yielded a *t* of 0.785, which is not significant at the 0.05 level of confidence, hence it must be accepted that there is no significant difference between the two mean scores.

The *t* test of significance applied to the mean scores of the trait category of good emotional control yielded a *t* of 2.85, which is significant at a value higher than the 0.01 level of confidence.

The *t* test of significance applied to the mean scores of the trait category of self-rejection yielded a *t* of 3.61, which is significant at a value much higher than the 0.01 level of confidence.

The *t* test of significance applied to the mean scores of the trait category of dependence yielded a *t* of 2.29, which is significant at a value higher than the 0.05 level of confidence.

The *t* test of significance applied to the mean socres of the trait category of poor emotional control yielded a *t* of 3.47, which is significant at a value much higher than the 0.01 level of confidence.

The *t* test of significance applied to the mean scores of the trait category of withdrawal yielded a *t* of 0.90, which is not significant at the 0.05 level of confidence, hence it must be accepted that there is no significant difference between the two mean scores.

IX. Discussion of Results

Based upon the results of this study, it would appear that the typical or "average" US Air Force psychiatric casualty from Southeast Asia, as evaluated at the USAF Hospital at Tachikawa Air Base, Japan, is a 28-year-old, married Staff Sergeant, with 9 years total service, eight of which have been in his primary military occupational specialty. He has served a little more than 4 months of his Southeast Asia tour. He is not a high school graduate, having left school at or near the end of his junior year. His intelligence as reflected by a standardized adult IQ test is low average (96.73).

The background data and the attitude questionnaire both indicate that the psychiatric patient sees himself as a career airman with a strong desire to continue on active duty in the service.

His self-concepts as measured by the actual and ideal selves indicate that either prior to his breakdown or, *ex post facto*, as a result of his breakdown, he has a high degree of self-dissatisfaction, limitations in personality adjustment, and limited inner personality strengths. He is less objective and significantly unrealistic in meeting basic crucial life demands. Compared with other service personnel, he tends to view himself as dissatisfied, self-rejecting, dependent, and experiencing poor control over his emotions.

He may conceivably have been a good airman with an excellent or an exceptional record. He has, however, become a psychiatric casualty, a liability, rather than an asset to his overseas field unit or organization. He appears to be a person less resilient to quick effective adaptation and to danger, perhaps lacking in the biologic strength associated with youth. His emotional ties to his family are great and the "separation anxiety" that he experiences overseas is not dealt with adequately. He is apt to be a person with a strong approach toward retirement as a basic goal. Although he espouses a strong desire to remain in the service, his focus is toward a "noncombat" milieu and an early retirement. In short, his motivation for the service is largely extrinsic rather than intrinsic.

In summary, the sample of psychiatric subjects as examined in this study appear to be career airmen who reflect a high level of conscious motivation for retention and continuance in their careers. While strong in stated interest, they appear to be weak intrinsically and carry the dormant weaknesses wherever they go. They may function adequately in many assignments either stateside or overseas when accompanied by the family. However, they experience great difficulty in having to function alone.

X. Conclusions

The airman in the US Air Force is one of the most intelligent, best trained and best equipped soldiers of the world today. He is born into a democratic society which imposes the fewest limitations for intellectual, personal, and social development of any society, past or present. He is optimistic towards the future. He is able to accept authority under conditions of wartime and is able to accept its personal and social restrictions. He is able to meet sacrifices as required, to forego his creative energies, and to direct behavior into the destructive homicidal activities that may be demanded of him. There are some who cannot effect this change. This study has indicated that such demands are too great and impose too strong a personal burden on some individuals. This is the psychiatric casualty. He may function well within the requirements of a peacetime military setting. He cannot function effectively when he is emotionally alone for long periods in a war zone. Fears, imagined or real, depression brought about by separation from friends and from family, and the deadly and continuous threat of the enemy in a land that is climatically and culturally harsh and foreign to him may eventually precipitate severe emotional disturbance leading to psychiatric breakdown.

One of the conclusions of this study which may be drawn is that the psychiatric casualty, the noncombatant serviceman who breaks down in a combat zone, can be a highly dedicated and well-motivated career serviceman, but these factors are not in themselves sufficient to maintain the individual's emotional balance under periods of long stress or duress in an anxiety situation. Other intrinsic resources would appear to be vital if he is to maintain his psychologic balance.

Another conclusion which may be drawn is that an older airman or NCO approaching retirement and beset with the usual concerns of a maturing family would appear to be a poor risk for an assignment to a war zone or to a remote or isolated area.

Conversely, it may also be concluded that the resiliency of youth, psychologic as well as biologic, is a salient factor for effective adaptation and adjustment under stress in a combat zone.

Perhaps a final and vital conclusion is that a prolonged peacetime service is not necessarily conducive for the preparation of military personnel for war.

XI. Implications for Future Research

This study, as an investigation of the personality traits, background characteristics, and self-concepts of US Air Force psychiatric casualties in Southeast Asia was limited in several ways.

First, this author was not able to obtain authority to enter the war zone to conduct this study or to observe the physical reality of the environmental conditions as they existed.

Ideally, the patients to be studied should have been selected in the war zone to insure a random sample. Further, a matched control sample of service personnel should have been studied. This attempt was made at the USAF Hospital Tachikawa, where a "normal" control sample of subjects, nonpsychiatric patients from Southeast Asia were tested. It was quickly observed that many of the nonpsychiatric patients who were hospitalized in medical wards, such as orthopedics and internal medicine, could be classed on the basis of psychological tests as the Rorschach and the MMPI as having significant psychiatric disturbances. It was found that many patients flown in by aeromedical squadrons from Southeast Asia and hospitalized for evaluation and treatment of "right knee" pain, suspected duodenal ulcers, diabetes, migratory arthritis and hypothyroidism (weight loss) showed test protocols of acute emotional turmoil, instability, emotional insecurity, and psychogenic conversion. It appeared, in effect, that a significant number of nonpsychiatric patients were denying and suppressing the trauma of their anxieties and conflicts and were channeling their emotional difficulties into psychosomatic symptoms and complaints and were being treated for their overt symptoms. Perhaps it is these patients whose psychiatric problems are not recognized, that account in part for the so-called low incidence of psychiatric disorders among military personnel in Southeast Asia.

Perhaps the most ideal approach for a study of this nature would have been to select a very large sample of subjects to be tested prior to their movement overseas to a combat theater and to test the group again after the completion of the tour of duty with the assumption that a given percentage of them would become psychiatric casualties. From such a clearly defined group, direct evidence could be obtained on the specific personality traits and personality characteristics which would be the most prevalent and the most conducive to emotional stress and breakdown among military personnel in a combat zone. Although such a research design would be highly desirable, it would not be considered to be either practical or feasible from a military standpoint.

In recapitulation, it would appear that this study whose basic hypotheses have been tested and proven on the basis of valid psychological test instruments and applied statistical methods also confirms the previous clinical investigation findings of the very few investigators of psychiatric breakdown among Air Force personnel in Southeast Asia.

It is hoped that the results of this study and the conclusions drawn from it will stimulate the development of additional hypotheses and additional scientific psychological research. It is further hoped that this study will serve to raise many questions relating to human reliability, personnel selection techniques, career development and particularly to the selection and the assignment of career service personnel to isolated, remote, and war zone areas.

Appendix A: Instructions for Judgments of Personality Traits (Characteristics)

The statements contained below are self-referent verbalizations elicited by persons undergoing psychotherapy. I would like you to categorize each statement into one of the listed personality trait areas (characteristics), according to the definitions of the traits which lie within the theoretical frame of reference contained below.

The judgments are to be based upon Carl Rogers' theory of personality and behavior. This theory is basically phenomenological in character, and relies heavily upon the concept of the self as an explanatory construct. It pictures the endpoint of personality development as being a basic congruence between the phenomenal field of experience and the conceptual structure of the self.

Rogers postulates that every individual exists in a continually changing world of experience of which he is the center and that the only person who fully knows his field of experience is the individual himself. According to this proposition, the person is the best source of information about himself and the best vantage point for understanding the behavior of the person is from the "internal frame of reference" of the individual himself.

The major portion of the personality trait areas listed below are derived from the postulations of Rogers' theory of personality. The balance of the trait areas are those selected by this writer on the basis of homogeneous characteristics of the item population.

Please read the definitions of the personality traits contained on the attached page. After you have completed this step, briefly peruse the list of PSYCHOTHERAPY PATIENTS' SELF-REFERENT STATEMENTS.

You are now ready to categorize the statements. Read each statement, then decide into which category or categories you think it should be placed. Place the category designation that you have selected in the space provided immediately to the left of the item. For the purpose of brevity each trait category may be designated according to its numerical placement on the list of DEFINITIONS OF TRAITS, as

Self-acceptance = 1
Independence = 2
Self-rejection = 4

Examples:

Statement

1 1. I am a generous person.
2 2. I do not depend on others for advice.
4 3. Things are always wrong with me.

Appendix B: Definitions of Traits

Favorable Adaptations to Life Situations

1. *Self-Acceptance*

Viewing oneself and reacting to the field of experience as a person of worth, worthy of respect rather than condemnation. The perceiving of one's own feelings, motives, social, and personal experiences without distortion of the basic sensory data and being comfortable in acting in terms of these perceptions.

2. *Independence*

Viewing oneself and reacting to the field of experience as being self-governing, self-regulatory, and autonomous and away from control by external forces. The perception of one's own standards as being based upon his or her own experience, rather than upon the attitudes or desires of others. The behavior of the organism is more spontaneous, the expression of attitudes are less guarded. The individual feels he or she is his or her "real" self.

3. *Good Emotional Self-Control*

Viewing oneself and reacting to the field of experience as being competent to cope with the affective aspects of life. Most of the relevant sensory experience is present in awareness. Sensory impulses are accepted and channeled by the self-structure without undue strain or anxiety.

Unfavorable Adaptations to Life Situations

4. *Self-Rejection*

Viewing oneself and reacting to the field of experience as an unworthy person, dissatisfied with oneself, worthy of condemnation or disrespect and characterized by feelings of unpleasantness and dejection, concomitant with a lowering of the vitality and functional activity of the organism.

5. *Dependence*

Viewing oneself and reacting to the field of experience as being influenced, sustained or subjected by external forces for regulation and support. The behavior reflects a lack in autonomy and spontaneity.

6. *Poor Emotional Self-Control*

Viewing oneself and reacting to the field of experience as lacking in competence to cope with the affective aspects of life. Much of the relevant sensory experience is not present in awareness. Reactions to sensory impulses and external forces are characterized by tension, strain, or anxiety.

Other Adaptations to Life Situations

7. *Withdrawal*

The retreat or moving away of the organism from what is perceived as a threatening or anxiety-provoking object, force, or experience. Also the gratification of the organism's needs and the reduction of tension by vicarious experience, as substituting fantasy for reality.

Appendix C
Categorization of Traits

Category (trait)	Self-referent statement
_____	1. I enjoy sports.
_____	2. I like responsibility.
_____	3. I hardly ever get upset.
_____	4. I look forward to new places and to meeting new persons.
_____	5. I like to be independent.
_____	6. I daydream a lot.
_____	7. I blush easily.
_____	8. I worry about catching diseases.
_____	9. I am more sensitive than others.
_____	10. I enjoy parties.
_____	11. I am not like other people.
_____	12. I think that I am just as good as any airman.
_____	13. My feelings are not easily hurt.
_____	14. I worry a lot.
_____	15. I prefer to be left alone.
_____	16. Life is a chore for me much of the time.
_____	17. I believe that a man should fight for his rights.
_____	18. I usually feel that life is worthwhile.
_____	19. I feel lonely and homesick when I am in a strange place.
_____	20. I depend on others.
_____	21. I have thought of suicide.
_____	22. I am calm and undisturbed most of the time.
_____	23. I am happy most of the time.
_____	24. I feel inferior to others.
_____	25. I sweat very often.
_____	26. I am a good mixer.
_____	27. I like being an airman.
_____	28. I like to talk with others.
_____	29. At times I have felt that life was not worth living.
_____	30. I like to ask the advice of others.
_____	31. I feel weak much of the time.

Appendix C (*continued*)

Category (trait)	Self-referent statement
_____	32. Life is usually exciting.
_____	33. Many times I feel alone and unimportant.
_____	34. I feel lonely a good deal of the time.
_____	35. I have trouble making friends.
_____	36. I like to meet people.
_____	37. I feel at ease in most social situations.
_____	38. I tend to withdraw from others.
_____	39. At times I feel superior to other persons.
_____	40. I do not sleep well.
_____	41. I usually try to hide my feelings.
_____	42. I can usually solve my own problems.
_____	43. I am a friendly person.
_____	44. I adjust quickly to new situations.
_____	45. I like to daydream.
_____	46. I usually find it hard to get started on a new task.
_____	47. I make friends easily.
_____	48. I like to join in many different activities.
_____	49. I can adjust to just about anything.
_____	50. I feel equal to my friends in intelligence and emotion.
_____	51. At times I feel like breaking things.
_____	52. I sometimes feel that I am about to go to pieces.
_____	53. I am a high-strung person.
_____	54. Things are always wrong with me.
_____	55. My judgment is as good as it ever was.
_____	56. In the morning I usually wake up feeling fresh and rested.
_____	57. I think that I am a well-adjusted person.
_____	58. I hardly ever worry about my health.
_____	59. I am confident of my abilities.
_____	60. I cry easily.
_____	61. Deep down I feel unsure of myself.
_____	62. I can be depended upon.
_____	63. I am self-confident most of the time.
_____	64. I feel uneasy most of the time.
_____	65. I prefer to be alone.
_____	66. I do things slowly and without worry.
_____	67. Some days I'm nervous all the time.
_____	68. Life is a mistake for me.
_____	69. I feel that other people do not understand me.
_____	70. I think that I am quite independent.
_____	71. I am a nervous person.
_____	72. I have no real problems.
_____	73. I need friendship and understanding.
_____	74. I like to be the leader in sports and other activities.
_____	75. I like to tell others about my problems.
_____	76. Many times I feel weak and dizzy.

Appendix D:
Q Sort Administration Instructions

Here is a pack of cards. You will notice that each card has a statement typed on it. I would like you to look through the pack at least once and then after examining the pack I would like you to read each statement and decide which statements describe you the most AS YOU SEE YOURSELF, which statements describe you the least or not at all and which statements are IN BETWEEN.

I would like you to sort the cards into three piles. Place the cards in the right hand pile that you think describe you the most, place these in the left hand pile that you think describe you the least or not at all, and place those cards in the center pile that you think are IN BETWEEN.

Now pick up all of the cards in the right hand pile. Decide which of the two cards describe you the most. Place them at the right hand side, in front of the card marked number 8. Look through the same pile again and select the next five that describe you the most, and place them in front of card number 7. Look through the same pile again and select the 9 statements that describe you the most and place them in front of card number 6.

Put the pile down and now pick up the left hand pile and look at the statements. Read each one, comparing them, and then choose the two statements that you think describe you the least or not at all. Place these two cards in front of card number 0. Look at the cards again and choose the five statements that you think describe you the least and put them in front of card number 1. Look at the pile again and then select nine cards that you think describe you the least and place them in front of card number 2. Put the pile down.

Now take the middle pile. Read the statements, then decide which of the thirteen statements describe you the most. Place them in front of card number 5. Read the statements again, and now decide which thirteen statements describe you the least. Place them in front of card number 3. Place the remaining eighteen cards in front of card number 4.

Instructions for the ideal-sort are essentially the same with minor substitutions.

Appendix E: Actual-Self–Ideal-Self Correlation Coefficients and Fisher's *z* Equivalents for the Psychiatric Patient Sample

Case No.	$r_{A:I}$	$z_{A:I}$
1	.65	.77
2	.51	.56
3	.52	.58
4	.01	.01
5	−.06	−.06
6	.46	.49
7	.45	.48
8	.46	.49
9	.83	1.18
10	.10	.10

Appendix E (*continued*)

Case No.	$r_{A:I}$	$z_{A:I}$
11	−.42	−.44
12	−.20	−.20
13	.87	1.33
14	.23	.23
15	.69	.84
16	.56	.63
17	.63	.74
18	.41	.43
19	.28	.28
20	.81	1.12
21	.12	.12
22	.05	.05
23	.59	.67
24	.19	.19
25	.67	.81
26	.42	.44
27	.66	.79
28	.07	.07
29	.37	.38
30	−.27	−.27
Mean z		.42
Corresponding r		.40

Appendix F: Actual-Self-Ideal-Self Correlation Coefficients and Fisher's z Equivalents for the Normal Subjects

Case No.	$r_{A:I}$	$z_{A:I}$
1	.44	.47
2	.63	.74
3	.64	.76
4	.81	1.12
5	.76	.99
6	.75	.97
7	.79	1.07
8	.60	.69
9	.62	.72
10	.71	.88
11	.48	.52
12	.78	1.04
13	.76	.99
14	.65	.77
15	.91	1.52
Mean	.68	.88
Corresponding r		.71

REFERENCES

Anderson, R. S., editor-in-chief (1966). "Neuropsychiatry in World War II," Vol. I. U.S. Army Med. Dept., Washington, D. C.

Bennett, J. R. (1957). Modification of the Self-Concept in Electroshock Therapy. Ph.D. Thesis, Boston Univ., Boston, Massachusetts.

Brill, N. Q., and Beebe, G. W. (1961). Age and resistance to military stress. *Am. J. Psychiat.* **108**, 417–425.

Brownfain, J. (1952). Stability of the self-concept as a dimension of personality. *J. Abnormal Social Psychol.* **47**, 597–606.

Burt, C. (1937). Correlations between persons. *Brit. J. Psychol.* **28**, 59–96.

Chambers, R. E. (1952). Discussion of survival factors. *Am. J. Psychiat.* **108**, 247–348.

Chase, P. H. (1957). Self-concepts in adjusted and maladjusted hospital patients. *J. Consulting Psychol.* **21**, 495–497.

Coates, C. H., and Pellegrin, R. J. (1965). "Military Sociology: A Study of American Military Institutions and Military Life." Social Sci. Press, University Park, Maryland.

Cole, C. W., Oetting, E. R., and Hinkle, J. E. (1967). Non-linearity of self-concept discrepancy. *Psychol. Rept.* **21**, 58–60.

Cronbach, L. J. (1952). Correlations between persons as a research tool. *In* "Psychotherapy: Theory and Research" (O. H. Mowrer, ed.), Chapt. XIV. Ronald Press, New York.

Dymond, R. F. (1953). An adjustment score for Q-sorts. *J. Consulting Psychol.* **17**, 339–343.

Glass, A. J. (1954). Psychotherapy in the combat zone. *Am. J. Psychiat.* **110**, 725–731.

Grinker, R. R., and Spiegel, J. P. (1945). "Men Under Stress." McGraw-Hill (Blakiston), New York.

Guilford, J. P. (1965). "Fundamental Statistics in Psychology and Education." McGraw-Hill, New York.

Hall, C. S., and Lindzey, G. (1957). "Theories of Personality." Wiley, New York.

Hanlon, T. E., Hofstaetter, P. R., and O'Connor, J. P. (1954). Congruence of self and ideal self in relation to personality adjustment. *J. Consulting Psychol.* **18**, 215–218.

Hartley, M. W. (1951). A Q-Technique Study of Changes in the Self-Concept during Psychotherapy. Ph.D. Thesis, Univ. of Chicago, Chicago, Illinois.

Hillson, J. S., and Worchel, P. (1957). Self-concept and defensive behavior in the maladjusted. *J. Consulting Psychol.* **21**, 83–88.

Holt, R. R. (1951). The accuracy of self-evaluations: Its measurement and some of its personological correlates. *J. Consulting Psychol.* **15**, 95–101.

Kogan, W. S., Quinn, R., Ax, A. P., and Ripley, H. S. (1957). Some methodological problems in the quantification of clinical assessment by Q-array. *J. Consulting Psychol.* **21**, 47–62.

McNemar, Q. (1962). "Psychological Statistics." Wiley, New York.

Merenda, P. F., and Clarke, W. V. (1967). Differences in results of inferential self measurement in self-concept analysis. *Perceptual Motor Skills* **25**, 317–322.

Morriss, L. (1967). Air Force psychiatry in Viet Nam. *Proc. 14th Ann. Conf. Air Force Behavioral Scientists, San Antonio, Texas* pp. 149–162.

Mowrer, O. H. (1952). Q-technique—description, history, and critique. "Psychotherapy: Theory and Research," Chapter XIII. Ronald Press, New York.

Pathak, N. S. (1967). Self-ideal congruence and adjustment. *Educ. Psychol. Rev.* 7, 26–31.

Raimy, V. C. (1958). Self-reference in counseling interviews. *J. Consulting Psychol.* 12, 153–163.

Richardson, M. W. (1949). An experimental study of the forced-choice performance report. *Am. Psychologist* 4, 278–279.

Richardson, M. W. (1951). Note on Travers' "Critical Review of the Forced-Choice Technique." *Psychol. Bull.* 48, 435–437.

Rogers, C. R. (1951). "Client-Centered Therapy: Its Current Practice, Implications, and Theory." Houghton Mifflin, Boston, Massachusetts.

Rogers, C. R., and Dymond, R. F. (1954). "Psychotherapy and Personality Change." Univ. of Chicago Press, Chicago, Illinois.

Schramel, D. J. (1966). U.S. military psychiatric patients Southeast Asia. *Proc. 13th Ann. Conf. Air Force Behavioral Scientists, San Antonio, Texas* pp. 343–357.

Stephenson, W. (1935). Correlating persons instead of tests. *Character Personality* 6, 17–24.

Stephenson, W. (1950). A statistical approach to typology: The study of trait universes. *J. Clin. Psychol.* 6, 26–38.

Stephenson, W. (1952). Some observations on Q-technique. *Psychol. Bull.* 49, 483–498.

Stephenson, W. (1953). "The Study of Behavior: Q-Technique and its Methodology." Univ. of Chicago Press, Chicago, Illinois.

Stock, D. (1949). An investigation into the interrelations between the self-concept and feelings directed toward other persons and groups. *J. Consulting Psychol.* 13, 176–180.

Travers, R. M. W. (1951). A critical review of the validity and rationale of the forced-choice technique. *Psychol. Bull.* 48, 62–70.

Wallen, V. (1967a). A research design for an objective study of the personality traits, characteristics, and self-concepts of U.S. Air Force psychiatric casualties in Southeast Asia. *Proc. 14th Ann. Conf. USAF Behavioral Scientists, San Antonio, Texas* pp. 136–148.

Wallen, V. (1967b). Culture shock and the problem of adjustment to a new overseas environment. *Military Med.* 132, 722–725.

Weybrew, B. B. (1953). "Methodology in Criterion Research," Med. Res. Lab. Rept. No. 239. Bureau of Medicine and Surgery, Navy Department.

White, R. (1964). The integration of personality. "The Abnormal Personality," 3rd Ed. Ronald Press, New York.

9// A Review of Stress and Fatigue Monitoring of Naval Aviators during Aircraft Carrier Combat Operations: Blood and Urine Biochemical Studies*

Frank H. Austin, Jr.

I. Introduction

During October and November of 1966, an Aeromedical Biodata Team was deployed aboard a US Navy attack aircraft carrier which was conducting combat operations in the Gulf of Tonkin against heavily defended targets in North Viet Nam. An experimental project was conducted with the aim of developing reliable stress monitoring indices for personnel in operational environments, including combat aviation. One phase of the study was the investigation of various biochemical constituents of the blood and the urine of aviators flying high-risk combat missions (Austin *et al.*, 1967).

*The project described in this chapter was conducted by the author and his co-workers while he was attached to the Navy Bureau of Medicine and Surgery and to the Office of the Chief of Naval Operations as Assistant for Aerospace Medical Flight Safety. The opinions expressed are those of the author and do not represent official endorsement by the Department of the Navy.

The experiment was designed to collect a first sample of blood from pilots in a rested state relative to acute stress or fatigue. However, these pilots were in an unknown state relative to cumulative stress effects, since in the past 5 months they each had conducted an average of 1.3 combat flights per 24 hr during the 79 accumulated days of combat operations by the ship. A second blood sample, collected near the end of the 22-day combat line period, would presume to contain biochemical indicators of the result of acute and cumulative psychophysiological stress of combat flying by this group.

No opportunity for predeployment control studies of these same aviators had been available. An attempt to obtain an approximation of control levels of the biochemical parameters was made by collecting samples from the pilots while ashore in the US during January and February of 1967, following the shipboard deployment and after the pilots had returned from leave and had resumed routine operational flying.

In a previous report concerning this project, the authors indicated that analysis for blood plasma levels of designated phospholipid compounds showed significant changes in the combat pilots in contrast to the levels previously found in other stress states and in normal control subjects (Austin *et al.*, 1967). It is the purpose of this chapter to review these studies, to report heretofore unpublished details of these blood and urine biochemical analyses of combat pilots, and to outline further studies which are being conducted and which are planned for attempting to develop valid biochemical monitoring indices of stress and fatigue in aviation operational and combat environments.

II. Method

A. Shipboard and Airfield

The population from which the sample group was chosen consisted of 123 naval aviators assigned to various squadrons of the air wing aboard a large attack aircraft carrier. Most of the 27 subjects were from two A-4 squadrons; others were pilots of F-4 or A-6 aircraft. The ship and each of the pilots selected had been deployed in the combat zone for about 5 months prior to this study. During this period they had conducted combat operations on 79 individual days, divided into three "line" periods of 28, 30, and 21 days. Between line periods, the ship was in transit or in port for maintenance, crew rest, and recreation for 10–20 days at a time. The 22-day line period during which the study was conducted was the fourth and last one scheduled for this cruise, and began 48 hr after the ship departed a liberty port. The aviators had not flown during the previous 18 days.

Twenty-seven jet aviators flying combat attack missions were randomly selected, and samples of blood were drawn following a flight early in the combat "line" period and again after about 18–22 days of almost daily flying. Concurrently, a single (individual) urine sample was collected prior to and immediately following the same flight. A single urine sample was also collected on a pilot's nonflying day at the same time as the postflight sample, in an attempt to obtain approximate baseline measures. The pilots were also monitored in flight for ECG and respiratory rates during the first 10 days of the line period. Results of these latter findings have been previously reported (Lewis *et al.*, 1967).

The blood samples consisted of 25–30 cm^3 of venous blood taken from the pilots within 30 min of carrier landing following the selected combat missions. Samples were collected in vacutainer tubes containing 25 mg of potassium oxalate and were immediately centrifuged, the plasma decanted into plastic bottles, then rapidly frozen. Samples were stored, shipped, and kept frozen until readied for analysis in the biochemical laboratory of the Aerospace Medical Research Department, Naval Air Development Center, Johnsville, Pennsylvania.

The emotional stress imposed upon the pilots by the operation was considerable. The ship was one of two Forrestal-class attack carriers operating well into the Tonkin Gulf and conducting intensive air strikes against lines of communication, roads, bridges, and military storage depots throughout North Viet Nam. At the time of this study the majority of strikes were into the area around Haiphong Harbor near Hanoi, where antiaircraft defenses were extensive. Each strike group was exposed to intensive radar guided antiaircraft weapons fire and to numerous launches of surface-to-air missiles (SAM). The threat of fighter interception was ever present, but no encounters developed during the observed period. One of the pilots being monitored was shot down and declared killed in action early in the line period. The air group itself had lost six pilots during the cruise.

Morale among the pilots was high. They were anxious to get this "last line period" over with and go home. The ship operated for 16 hr each day, generally launching strikes for a 12-hr period in alternation with the sister carrier. A typical pilot's day would involve him in a 2-hr briefing, a 2-hr flight, and a 1-hr debriefing. During the strike flight he would be exposed to high risk for about 20 or 30 min. On many days, a second mission would be flown, but these were usually less demanding support or armed reconnaissance type. Many flights were made at night, and all culminated in a carrier landing.

The pilots were at the peak of their flying proficiency. The preoccupation with carrier operations found often in the routine Navy operational environment was almost completely overshadowed by the combat environment. During this operation, the carrier itself was not under threat of attack, although the possibility was always to be considered.

The pilots ate well and regularly except for shifting of meals due to scheduled flights. All reported sleeping well but often for shorter periods than usual. Their individual adaptations to the high risk of death or capture was universally successful and was strengthened by group support and strong leadership. The most prevalent psychological mechanism of denial by the junior pilots appeared to be the decision to "not make the Navy a career." With this in mind they performed superbly, having a strong sense of salvation in sight. Many of the pilots expressed, but not vehemently, some of the general dissatisfaction with the political restraints and frustrations of the conflict, a reflection of home town feelings which rapid communication brought easily to the combat zone. But all pilots displayed a strong sense of duty and patriotism.

In the experience of this author, the 22-day line period was just short of the time when obvious fatigue sets in and emotions often erupt. However, the pilots of the sample group were all obviously stressed by the exposure, emotionally and physically drained, and greatly relieved when the last plane landed. This stress has been reflected in the biochemical alterations of their blood and urine as the data herein presented will show.

B. Laboratory

The plasma samples were analyzed for phospholipids utilizing the two-dimensional paper chromatography technique described by Schwartz *et al.* (1965) and Polis *et al.* (1968). With this technique, a paper chromatogram was obtained which yielded quantitative and qualitative information on 17 individual phospholipid fractions. The phospholipids were extracted from the plasma with mixtures of chloroform and methanol (2:1). Distribution on a paper chromatogram was obtained by separation in one axis with phenol saturated with water–acetic acid–ethanol (50:5:6) and on the second axis by ionophoresis at 2000 V for 70 min. Results were calculated in micromoles of phospholipid phosphorus per liter of plasma.

Besides the total phospholipid levels, the following fractions were obtained: phosphatidylglycerol, phosphatidic acid, cardiolipin, P-ethanolamine, P-serine; P-inositide, sphingomyelin, lecithin, cyclic glycerophosphoric acid, choline plasmalogen, ethanolamine plasmalogen, serine plasmalogen, alkyl ethers, four unknowns (X_2, X-alkali labile, X-plasmalogen, and X-acid labile), and inorganic phosphorus. The technique yielded high percentages of recovery and reproducible results upon individual reanalysis of samples. In addition to the phospholipids, levels of plasma cortisol and corticosterone were measured by Drs. Noval and Post of the New Jersey Psychiatric Institute (Polis *et al.*, 1968).

C. Graphic and Tabular Presentation

The aim of the graphic and tabular presentation for this study is to depict how the biochemical findings during the two periods of combat flying and the one period of operational flying for this group of naval aviators related to each other and to the biochemical findings in samples of plasma from normal subjects and persons undergoing other stress states. Comparisons are made with data previously obtained by Polis *et al.* on humans exposed to the stress of centrifuge acceleration (G_z) and sleep deprivation, and with data from normal laboratory subjects and institutionalized schizophrenics (Polis *et al.*, 1966, 1968). Inspection of the raw data indicated that, as in the early studies, three-dimensional plots of the levels of phosphatidyl glycerol, cardiolipin, and phosphatidic acid would probably demonstrate a distinctive correlation for stress origin. Means and standard deviations of the aviator groups were calculated by the biochemistry group at Johnsville and are presented herein.

In order to explore statistically as many correlations as possible, the data on seven plasma phospholipid fractions and the plasma cortisol levels were subjected to an extensive computer analysis utilizing discriminant functions classification. In this way, differences among normal individuals and two groups under stress are projected, "to make it possible to 'see' differences among clusters of points in a space of more than two dimensions" (Polis *et al.*, 1968). It will be noted that, "the original eight dimensional space of measurements has been projected into a plane in such a way that the 'distances' among the centroids of the clusters are maximized. . . . The Z indices, Z_1 and Z_2, are computed for each subject by taking two weighted sums of the logarithms of the individual compounds. The weighting factors are determined in such a way that the distance among clusters of points in the Z_1 and Z_2 plane is maximized while keeping the distance within clusters fixed. When this maximal separation has been achieved, the weights are standardized to the same scale so that the importance of each compound in separating the three groups can be judged" (Polis *et al.*, 1968).

According to Polis and de Cani (1968), the general method used was to combine eight measurements into a smaller set of indices in such a way that the extent of overlap in the probability distribution of the indices is minimized.

III. Results

As was observed in previous stress studies by Polis *et al.*, (1966), the phosphatidylglycerol was also the phospholipid fraction most responsive to stress of aircraft carrier combat flights. From Tables I and II and Fig. 1, it can be seen that the mean level for the groups increased approximately twofold from the relatively "rested" state early in the combat line period to the period following combat flying for about 18 days (mean 17.6, median 18.3, mode 20 days). The "control" level had not returned to the "rested" level after ending combat flying and following leave and return to operational flying. Each individual pilot was not represented in each group sampled. The subjects included in each group can be noted from Tables I, II, and III. Seven individuals had all three samples taken. Although there were marked individual variations, this pilot group could be considered somewhat homogeneous since they had all been similarly exposed to the extended cruise and the

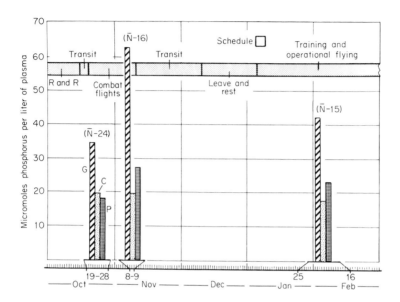

FIG. 1.   *Mean levels of phospholipid fractions for a group of Navy carrier pilots during stressful combat flights early and late in a "line period," and after return to operational flying in the United States. Phosphatidylglycerol (G), cardiolipin (C), and phosphatidic acid (P).*

combat flying. The presentation of the data as grouped is thus considered valid for the purpose of this exploratory investigation.

From comparison of Figs. 2 and 3, it may be noted how the three fractions, phosphatidyl glycerol (G), cardiolipin (C), and phosphatidic acid (P), for the three flying periods related to normal laboratory controls and to the other stress states. Figure 3 was prepared by Polis early in his studies and represents small samples and preliminary data. Figure 4 is a more recently developed three dimensional plot for the various stress states and utilizes phosphatidylethanolamine vice cardiolipin as the third variable (Polis *et al.*, 1968). A biochemical pattern for Navy attack aviation combat stress is implied from these figures. This pattern is similar to that of schizophrenia but as previously noted the individuals and groups can be differentiated by statistical analysis. In schizophrenia, the phospholipid pattern is fixed, but the combat pilots' values returned toward normal when leaving the stressful environment.

TABLE I
Data on Navy Combat Pilots Early in Combat Line Period 1966[a]

No.	Date	Time	Plasma						Pulse rates				Urine 17-OHCS			A/C	Age	Rank	Dep
			Tp	G	C	P	Cs	ADH	Ta	B	La	LSO	Pre	Post	Non-Fly				
1	10/19	1200	3467	55	47	22	12	4.3	120	105	102	3.6	—	—	—	A-4	26	2	1
2	10/19	1215	3434	9	28	7	16	0.7	123	139	133	2.6	152	392	470	A-4	38	5	7
*3	10/19	1215	2975	14	23	7	24	3.9	108	125	107	2.5	178	422	289	A-4	28	2	0
4	10/19	1600	2830	35	41	18	—	1.9	105	100	91	3.4	293	385	243	A-4	28	3	3
*5	10/19	1730	3548	41	39	6	—	4.4	109	113	108	2.4	243	173	217	A-4	39	4	4
6	10/19	1700	3079	44	47	22	18	2.4	108	117	107	2.5	—	—	—	A-4	28	2	3
7	10/20	1200	2329	31	22	21	13	8.0	120	114	113	3.2	—	—	—	A-4	27	3	3
8	10/20	1630	2916	31	53	29	14	2.7	77	87	90	3.7	—	—	—	A-4	24	2	3
9	10/20	1630	3186	27	37	19	—	4.7	110	117	108	4.0	642	230	1200	A-4	30	3	2
*10	10/20	2030	2788	31	30	23	13	1.5	107	149	103	2.4	262	205	177	A-4	35	4	2
*11	10/21	1300	3162	47	29	10	14	2.0	—	92	85	3.8	601	344	383	A-4	25	2	1
12	10/21	1530	3138	7	26	12	19	2.7	116	133	104	3.3	—	—	—	A-4	24	2	0
*13	10/21	1900	2403	24	30	14	18	6.2	100	118	101	1.0	—	—	—	A-4	26	2	2

No.	Date	Time	Tp	G	P	C	Cs	17-OHCS	ADH	Pulse Ta	Pulse B	LSO	La₁	La₂	La₃	A/C	Age	Rank	DEP
14	10/21	1830	2608	44	50	14	11	9.3	103	120	—	1.3	229	50	208	A-4	26	3	0
15	10/22	1600	2917	44	43	14	14	0.7	125	144	147	1.5	416	372	227	A-4	26	3	1
16	10/22	1330	2390	46	34	19	13	4.4	95	92	101	2.5	—	—	—	A-4	28	3	0
17	10/22	1630	3672	29	71	19	16	6.3	126	128	104	3.6	—	—	—	A-4	27	2	0
18	10/25	2315	3098	25	49	23	14	6.3	117	123	110	3.3	—	—	—	F-4	28	3	1
*19	10/25	1915	2896	66	37	38	21	—	103	98	100	3.6	358	492	—	A-6	39	5	5
20	10/26	2300	3292	27	46	15	15	5.7	118	107	119	—	—	—	—	F-4	35	3	9
21	10/28	2115	3573	18	51	17	26	5.5	150	—	—	—	—	—	—	F-4	35	4	2
22	10/28	2330	2906	28	32	26	16	2.0	107	165	86	3.5	217	400	—	A-6	31	4	3
*23	10/28	0015	2556	72	33	22	10	3.5	93	108	96	3.4	172	1031	—	A-6	24	2	0
24	10/28	1530	2754	31	39	19	15	3.7	95	115	108	3.5	—	—	—	A-6	34	4	3
MEAN			2997	34	39	18	16	4.0	110	118	106	2.9	314	375	379				
S.D.			383	16	11	7	4	2.3	15	19	14	0.8	163	242	321				
S.E.			78	3.3	2.3	1.5	0.9	0.5	—	—	—	—	—	—	—				

[a](Tp) Plasma total phospholipid (μmoles P/liter plasma); (G) Phosphatidyl glycerol (μmoles P/liter plasma); (P) Phosphatidic acid (μmoles P/liter plasma); (C) Cardiolipin (μmoles P/liter plasma); (Cs) Plasma cortisol, micrograms/100 ml plasma; (ADH) Plasma antidiuretic hormone (μU/ml); Pulse rate: (Ta) Prior to takeoff; (B) During combat bombing; (La) Landing approach; (LSO) Landing Signal Officer score of landing performance (4.0 scale); (17-OHCS) Urine hydroxycorticosteroid/creatine ratio, micrograms per 100 milligrams; (A/C) A-4—Single seat light attack jet; F-4—dual seat fighter bomber; A-6—dual seat all weather light attack; Rank: (5) CDR (and squadron CO), (4) LCDR, (3) LT, (2) LTJG, (1) Ens; (DEP) Dependents: Wife plus children.

TABLE II

Data on Navy Combat Pilots Late in Combat Line Period 1966[a,b]

No.	Date	Time	Plasma						Urine 17-OHCS			LSO	A/C	Age	Rank	Dep
			Tp	G	C	P	Cs	ADH	Pre	Post	Non-Fly					
1	11/8	2000	3817	92	64	31	25	27.7	–	–	–	2.7	A-4	26	2	1
*3	11/8	1515	2981	25	37	21	24	6.0	–	–	–	2.5	A-4	28	2	0
*5	11/8	1515	3589	49	34	19	–	3.9	–	–	–	2.0	A-4	39	4	4
6	11/8	1330	2778	55	35	31	17	3.1	–	–	–	2.7	A-4	28	2	3
7	11/8	1200	2775	86	43	38	12	3.5	–	–	–	2.0	A-4	27	3	3
*10	11/8	2130	2760	64	47	36	22	–	–	–	–	2.6	A-4	35	4	2
*11	11/8	1330	3025	44	30	22	21	3.5	–	–	–	3.5	A-4	25	2	1
12	11/8	1730	2793	63	15	14	12	4.7	–	–	–	2.3	A-4	24	2	0
*13	11/8	1700	2400	53	31	36	11	8.5	–	–	–	2.5	A-4	26	2	2
16	11/8	2215	2410	51	27	31	8	3.2	–	–	–	3.2	A-4	28	3	0
*19	11/9	0915	2776	83	30	34	12	3.9	–	–	–	3.5	A-4	39	5	5
*23	11/9	0915	2690	71	27	27	14	1.6	–	–	–	3.2	A-4	24	2	0
24	11/9	0915	2586	50	43	20	25	–	–	–	–	3.5	A-6	34	4	3
25	11/8	1215	2567	98	47	32	13	2.8	356	260	243	2.7	A-4	23	1	0
26	11/8	1530	4251	62	62	20	17	9.9	480	262	655	3.0	A-4	37	5	8
27	11/8	1930	2782	56	55	21	18	22.4	–	–	–	2.4	A-4	32	4	6
MEAN			2936	63	39	27	17	7.5	–	–	–	2.8				
S.D.			515	19	13	7	6	7.8	–	–	–	0.5				
S.E.			129	4.8	3.4	1.9	1.4	2.7	–	–	–	–				

[a] Subject Nos. 25, 26, and 27 were from the randomly selected group but no samples were drawn early in the period. No in-flight heart rate data were collected.

[b] Heading abbreviations as in Table I.

Polis and his associates (1968) had the following comments to make concerning these comparisons:

> One intriguing aspect of the stress studies is the similarity of the phospholipid pattern in chronic schizophrenia and in severe combat stress. Combat stressed subjects and schizophrenics do not differ significantly in the concentrations of the six phospholipids which distinguish schizophrenic subjects from normal. Statistical differentiation between schizophrenia and combat stress is achieved primarily on the differences in sphingomyelin and cortisol. Also, schizophrenics *do not* differ from normal subjects and combat stressed subjects *do* differ from normal in the concentrations of these two compounds. A comparison of the plasma phospholipid composition in schizophrenia and in combat fatigue is more marked by similarities than by differences. It is intuitively sensed, and experience confirms, that long exposure to combat can cause extreme psychological disturbance. Yet, from a more objective plane, it would be premature to ascribe the plasma phospholipid variations in a selected, hospitalized, small group of patients as characteristic of the complex behavioral aberrations termed schizophrenia. We interpret these findings to mean not that the combat pilot necessarily is becoming schizophrenic, but that the chronic schizophrenic patient is stressed, and that the schizophrenic brain, like the combat pilot's brain, is interpreting its environment as a threat to survival and is reacting biochemically to meet this threat.

Dr. Walter H. Moran of West Virginia University Medical Center determined the antidiuretic hormone levels on some of the frozen plasma samples. These levels are noted in Tables I and II. No significant correlations are evident.

A graph of the discriminant functions, Fig. 5, provided by Polis and de Cani (1968) indicates that the three groups (i.e., normal, combat, and schizophrenic) can be statistically described by examination of data for eight biochemical fractions of the blood plasma (seven phospholipid fractions and the plasma cortisol).

In Tables I, II, and III, other measured parameters and some biographic data are recorded to enable comparison with the biochemical measures. Trends may be noted, but no attempt at analysis will be offered at this time. Pilot age, rank, and number of dependents are all indirect indicators of "responsibility." Trends toward greater stress and biochemical response in pilots having greater responsibilities may be gleaned from the tabulations. The full scope of physical and personality variables could not be determined by the limited observation afforded the team during the combat period. The team was not able to develop any suitable

TABLE III

*Data on Navy Pilots following Combat Cruise and Return to Operational Flying
in the United States[a]*

No.	Date	Time	Plasma					Urine		A/C	Age	Rank	Dep
			Tp	G	C	P	Cs	Pre	Post				
2	1/26	1515	3098	51	44	37	11	391	221	A-4	38	5	7
*3	1/26	1100	2458	30	25	21	15	339	432	A-4	28	2	0
4	1/26	1545	2734	46	39	22	12	374	500	A-4	28	3	3
*5	1/26	1145	3562	44	48	19	21	437	171	A-4	39	4	4
9	1/31	1540	3523	21	29	29	11	—	185	A-4	30	3	2
*10	1/31	1615	2744	32	15	16	19	280	510	A-4	35	4	2
*11	2/16	1600	2502	46	23	15	16	410	737	A-4	25	2	1
*13	2/16	1230	2564	35	31	3	17	—	—	A-4	26	2	2
14	1/26	1530	2636	57	33	33	12	700	940	A-4	26	3	0
15	1/27	1200	2221	30	30	17	24	178	248	A-4	26	3	1
*19	2/16	1200	3553	46	45	33	11	307	517	A-6	39	5	5
22	2/16	1215	4263	44	47	25	10	364	363	A-6	31	4	3
*23	2/16	1100	2966	34	29	6	10	169	486	A-6	24	2	0
25	2/16	1430	2584	67	23	18	12	543	409	A-4	23	1	0
26	1/25	1930	4432	52	60	52	12	437	408	A-4	37	5	8
Mean			3056	42	35	23	14	379	438				
S.D.			670	12	12	12	4	141	212				
S.E.			173	3.1	3.1	3.2	1.1	—	—				

[a]Blood samples were collected following a simulated combat mission and airfield
landing. Urine samples were collected immediately prior to and following flight
(pre and post). Subject Nos. marked with * had samples collected during all three
periods. Heading abbreviations as in Table I.

measure of performance against which individual biochemical
responses might be correlated. An approximation of performance
as seen on individual landings aboard ship was made by scoring
of the landings by the Landing Signal Officer (LSO). These scores
(Tables I and II) are purely subjective and their validity is low due
to the small number of observations. Pilot shipboard landing performance of the group was also measured objectively by radar
tracking, but individual pilot performance data are not available
(Austin *et al.*, 1967). It should be pointed out that all of these pilots
were successful and performing satisfactorily under the combat
stress. None of the group studied developed any sign of true
"combat fatigue" or in any way failed emotionally or physically
under the stress during the period of observation.

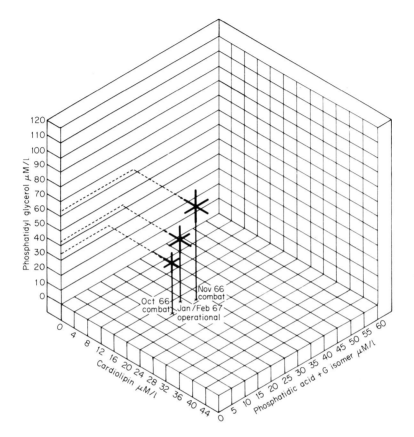

FIG. 2.   *Three-dimensional plot of mean levels of three phospholipid fractions for Navy attack carrier pilots during combat flying, early and late in the line period and after return to operational flying in the US (after Polis* et al., *1968).*

IV. Discussion

The analysis of the data presented in this study suggests the hypothesis that individuals facing various stresses will respond with similar phospholipid fraction changes, a suggestion previously made by Polis *et al.* (1966, 1968). The data tend to support the hypothesis that, by study of the phospholipid fraction levels, the type and degree of stress (and the subject's perception and response to it) can be distinguished.

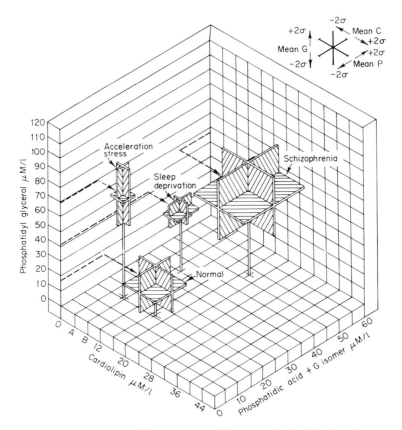

FIG. 3.   *Three-axis plot of the mean level of three phospholipid fractions for normal fasting subjects and other groups under stress. Intersecting planes depict two standard deviations of the group mean. Courtesy of Polis et al. (1966).*

Problems of aviator stress and fatigue in Viet Nam combat and the possible effects upon operations and safety were first investigated by the Navy Aeromedical Team in 1965 (Luehrs *et al.*, 1966). It became quite evident to this team that, notwithstanding major advances in biological sciences in recent years, the operational commander and his flight surgeon are still forced to rely almost exclusively upon subjective evaluation and professional judgment in evaluating physical and psychological limitations of groups or individuals undergoing combat stress. Limits for operations were, and still are, determined empirically (or perhaps arbitrarily) based on operational requirements and delimited more by material and logistic factors than by the physical or psychic capacity of the men to meet the schedule. After some three years of Navy attack aviation operations in the North Viet Nam conflict, the method used to avoid excessive fatigue remains essentially the same, modified only by the introduction of educated hindsight, experience, and precedent. The scheduled number of days on the line, rest periods, and rotations are operationally set and defined for the average aviator. Those who might "break" early are hopefully identified on an individual basis through close contact with the flight surgeon and supervision by the Command. As yet, no quantitative, objective monitoring technique is available to the flight surgeon and his commanding officer.

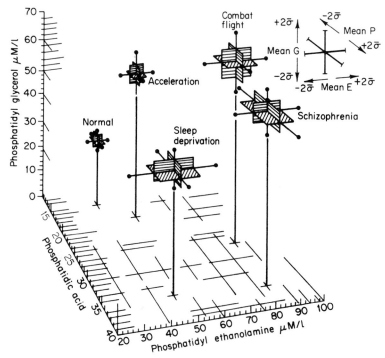

FIG. 4.   *Three-dimensional plot for means of three phospholipid fractions showing differentiation of normal and stressed populations. Note that third axis of the plot is phosphatidyl ethanolamine vice cardiolipin as used in Figs. 2 and 3. Courtesy of Polis* et al. *(1968).*

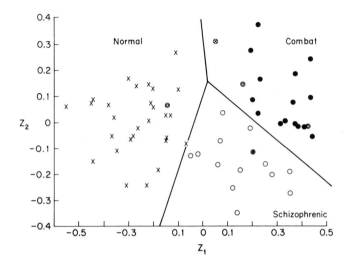

FIG. 5.   *Plots of the Z indices — adjusted log, for seven plasma phospholipid fractions and the plasma cortisol levels for normal subjects, individuals under combat stress, and the stress of schizophrenia. Individual points which are misclassified are encircled. Courtesy of Polis and de Cani (1968).*

As indicated in a previous report (Austin *et al.*, 1967), the Aeromedical Team expanded the scope of its studies and during 1966 and 1967 commenced a multidisciplinary attack on the problem. Inflight physiological monitoring utilizing the NASA Flight Research Center instrumentation techniques yielded some information on cardiorespiratory response (Lewis *et al.*, 1967). Concurrently, the aviators were interviewed to ascertain their experience level and, in a general way, their modes of response to combat stress. Their landing performance (a precise tracking task) was critically evaluated, and their blood and urine were collected for subsequent biochemical analysis. The team strived to cross-correlate group and individual subject data for these various parameters, hoping to define some indices of merit and a correlation with performance. This ultimate goal has not been fully attained; however, there is a strong suggestion that biochemical measures of the blood phospholipid fractions offer at this time the most fertile field for further intensive study.

As indicated by Fraser *et al.* (1967) and Cumming *et al.* (1967) the monitoring of physiological parameters (cardiorespiratory rates) can be expected to provide only an estimate of pilot workload during flight. Thus, inflight physiological monitoring alone should not be expected to identify a pilot's overall psychophysiological state or to diagnose unsafe levels of fatigue, impending collapse, or his adaptive and reserve resources. Nor can biochemical indices alone be expected to be conclusive, for they must, at least as indicated by the presently available data, be correlated with performance measures and possibly other indices.

The ultimate goal of the Aeromedical Biodata Team project was to develop methods to: (1) Identify those individuals who will not tolerate combat stress; (2) monitor pilots during extended operations to detect depreciated tolerance (reduced psychophysiological reserve) and to identify cumulative and acute fatigue (so as to advise rest); and (3) objectively determine when rest has been sufficient and the individual is again in an "up" status.

Tissue phospholipids were first utilized by Schwarz and Polis to elucidate mechanisms of protein metabolism as modified in rats by X-ray irradiation (Schwarz *et al.*, 1965). It was suggested that examination of the plasma for phospholipid changes in human subjects undergoing acceleration stress might yield significant information. Upon further investigation of humans under stress, Polis identified a series of biochemical phospholipid "patterns" for various stress states including acceleration, sleep deprivation, and schizophrenia. These stresses were all shown to yield different phospholipid fraction responses and to differ significantly from normal. Polis suggested "that the phospholipid composition of the human blood plasma reflects the action of cerebral metabolic control factors" (Polis *et al.*, 1968). Thus, as Polis has stated, from a "fundamental probe into the chemistry of biological energy control and utilization at a cellular level (*has come* ed.) a biochemical definition of stress in humans . . . for some physiological and pathological aberrations." Some "practical solutions for the tolerance of stress" (Polis *et al.*, 1966) and methods for monitoring it may evolve.

Since only single samples were taken for each monitored flight in the present study, the variation of phospholipid fraction levels during the day and in relation to stressful flight cannot be determined from the available data. Polis *et al.* (1966) found that subjects exposed to acceleration showed return of levels to normal in 24 hr, and sleep deprived subjects were normal following sleep. Schizophrenics, however, maintained their levels. "In schizophrenia, the distribution is again unique, but (unlike other stresses) it is maintained, which suggests that mechanisms for chemical recovery from stress is in some way lost or changed, so that stress-induced changes in schizophrenic patients persist. Considering the small schizophrenic population studied (20 subjects), these chemical changes can be considered neither as diagnostic of the disease, nor as a characteristic of its mechanism. They do, however, suggest that the schizophrenic patient is interpreting his environment as a threat to survival, and lives in a continuous state of biochemical stress." It should be noted that, although the biochemical pattern observed in combat pilots moves toward that of schizophrenia, no suggestion is intended that combat per se may produce schizophrenia. Rather, the two conditions are alike in regard to the individual "interpreting his environment as a threat to survival." Polis has elaborated more fully some suggested hypotheses concerning basic mechanisms (Polis *et al.*, 1968).

Following the suggestion of these studies by York and Polis in the laboratory, the Aeromedical Team set about to collect samples under combat operational conditions and to return them to the laboratory for similar biochemical analysis. As the results herein show, and as Polis and his co-workers indicate in their comprehensive paper, the phospholipids may indeed offer the operational flight surgeon one element of a valid index for fatigue and other stress response.

In the present study, urine samples were also collected, and some data have been obtained from these, as shown in Tables I, II, and III. Studies of individual samples, even when the 17-OHCS/creatinine ratios as described by Hale and Shannon (1967) were considered, do not yield results which can be validly correlated with the other data. The steroid response to stress of flight as studied for years by numerous investigators (Schreuder 1966) and more recently in the Viet Nam conflict (Bourne *et al.*, 1967) has yielded no specific indication of how this data might be used as a stress monitoring index. Bourne *et al.* (1967) noted that the 24-hr urine 17-OHCS levels of seven helicopter ambulance medics flying combat missions were lower than predicted upon body weight, varied little on a daily basis from overall means, and bore no direct relationship to flying combat missions. In other studies he has found indications that any combat personnel having greater responsibility (higher rank, leadership, etc.) showed higher levels of steroid excretion. The Navy combat pilots of this study appear to demonstrate similar phenomena. Subjects 2 and 26 were squadron commanding officers. Their 17-OHCS excretion was higher on a nonflying day, which may indicate the leader is stressed more by performing nonflying chores than by flying (even in combat), an empirical conclusion drawn often by senior aviators.

From an operational standpoint, it should be noted that single blood samples were less difficult to collect and handle and more certain of being valid than were 24-hr urine samples. This was a surprise, but the aviators proved exceptionally cooperative in allowing blood to be drawn, even though flying daily combat. Perhaps the reason is that only two samples were requested, and the squadrons were thoroughly briefed on the ultimate goals and possible benefits of the project. The "stress" of venipuncture itself did not appear to alter the results. This author is convinced that use of individual urine samples or some other readily obtainable fluid in pilot monitoring would be a relative panacea, if a suitable constituent therein can be identified to serve as a valid fatigue–stress indicator. Further studies should be undertaken to find such an indicator, if not for diagnosis, at least for screening purposes.

The restraints imposed on experiments conducted under the realities of combat operations are significant. Thus, in this study the flights which were monitored were those which the randomly chosen pilots were scheduled for by chance. Time of day was uncontrolled, as was the relation of sample collection to food intake. To limit the blood sampling, primarily in deference to the pilots, the team chose to draw only two samples from each pilot, one "early" in the line period and one "late." Both followed a combat flight and carrier landing. As was indicated above, there was no opportunity for classic "control" samples on these subjects (i.e., prior to combat); and each individual is not represented in each of the groups (early, late cruise, and postcruise "controls"). In spite of these deficiencies, which were essentially uncontrollable, the data appear to indicate the convincing trends discussed above. Certainly further studies are warranted, and these are presently being undertaken. Samples have been recently collected from pilots on two additional aircraft carriers, early and late in the combat cruise, with emphasis on morning flights. In one group, the samples were taken both before and after the same combat flight. These data should support the hypothesis that the evening rise in phospholipids which Polis *et al.* (1968) have noted in laboratory studies and the influence of acceleration during the attack mission have relatively minimal effect on the levels attained due to combat stress alone.

During the summer of 1967, samples were collected from Marine helicopter pilots flying under combat conditions in South Viet Nam, but who were facing a different type of enemy ground fire. Samples have also been collected on a matched group of attack carrier pilots prior to combat deployment. All of these data and future collections from pilots in training should serve as a basis for the longitudinal study envisioned by the authors in the previous report (Austin *et al.*, 1967).

An additional effort must be expended to obtain blood samples and pertinent case histories to enable the development of a Fatigue Monitoring Index. Whether the phosphatidyl glycerol rises to even higher levels, or precipitiously drops with fatigue, collapse, and failure, or whether in response to a measured stress test the phosphatidyl glycerol level will not become elevated (to provide physiological protection against the stress) are questions yet to be answered by further study.

If the biochemical measures are to be useful in operational and combat environments, analyses which can be performed in the field must be developed. From the results of these biochemical studies, it would appear that adequate justification exists for attempting to develop techniques for use by field and shipboard laboratories. If not definitive or diagnostic tests, at least a screening test would offer the flight surgeon a much better index by which to judge operational fatigue. He will thus have a quantitative adjunct to the subjective and empirical evaluations already at his disposal. By utilizing current techniques for collecting, freezing, and air shipping plasma samples, results of analysis at a continental laboratory could now be provided to the field in 6–8 days. Designation and equipping of laboratories closer to the scene of operations could easily reduce such a time lag to 4 days or less.

If further studies of the phospholipid fractions and the development of a stress and fatigue monitoring index prove valid and fruitful, efforts should be made to provide the necessary laboratory support to field and shipboard units at the earliest opportunity. The Aeromedical Biodata Team and the research laboratories should continue these studies and remain alert for the identification of any biochemical, physiological, or psychological parameter, the measure of which will contribute to the better identification of operational fatigue and/or stress.

V. Conclusions

A study of blood plasma phospholipid fractions in a group of 27 Navy attack carrier pilots flying highly stressful combat flights over North Viet Nam during 1966 revealed an apparently distinctive pattern of response when results were compared to normal and other stress states. The phosphatidylglycerol responded to this type of stress more markedly and consistently than the other fractions. A discriminant functions formula has been developed which may facilitate identification of the stress type and degree of subject response up to and including psychophysiological exhaustion and collapse.

Further investigation of biochemical parameters is necessary to define a reliable index of stress and fatigue to support the hypotheses developed in this study and to correlate with other measures of stress and performance.

ACKNOWLEDGMENTS

The project and data discussed in this chapter are literally the accumulated efforts of scores of individuals. The author hastens to assure the reader that he has acted only as the coordinator and instigator to encourage the application of basic laboratory research to a special problem in combat and operational aviation medicine.

Without the help and encouragement of B. D. Polis, Ph.D., and his associates at Naval Air Development Center, Johnsville, no results could have been reported. All of the scientific work is theirs. I am indebted to Dr. Polis for supplying most of the data in Tables I, II, and III and for permission to reprint Figs. 2, 4, and 5. Drs. Noval and Post of Princeton, N. J., performed analyses on 24-hr urine samples, but the results have not been reported herein. The urine data in Tables I, II, and III was provided by Lt. Don Furry of the Naval Medical Research Institute, who was a team member. Dr. C. E. Lewis and co-workers from the NASA Flight Research Center collected and analyzed the cardiac rate data for Table I which was reported by him in 1967 (Lewis *et al.*, 1967). LCDR Thomas Gallagher, MSC, USN, was a team member and collected the biographical information and provided invaluable assistance in sample collection and data handling.

The project would not have been possible without the cooperation of all the dauntless combat pilots and their flight surgeons, and the support of numerous Navy commands.

Finally, but most significantly, the travel and the scientific studies all required funding, a great deal of which was supplied through the efforts of Dr. Walton Jones of NASA HQ, Washington, D.C., and Dr. Harry Older of Software Systems, Inc., Washington, D.C. Additional funding support was supplied by the Navy Department through the Bureau of Medicine and Surgery and the Naval Air Systems Command. Project task assignments are cited where applicable in the reference.

To all these co-workers and supporters, and countless others unnamed, goes this author's heartiest appreciation and sincerest thanks.

REFERENCES

Austin, F. H., Gallagher, T. J., Brictson, C. A., Polis, B. D., Furry, D. E., and Lewis, C. E. (1967). Aeromedical monitoring of naval aviators during aircraft carrier combat operation. *Aerospace Med.* 38, 593–596.

Bourne, P. G., Rose, R. M., and Mason, J. W. (1967). Urinary 17-OHCS levels, data on seven helicopter ambulance medics in combat. *Arch. Gen. Psychiat.* 17, 104–109.

Cumming, F. G., and Corkindale, K. G. (1967). Physiological and psychological measurements of pilot workload. Royal Aircraft Establishment Technical Memo HFG 101, Inst. AvMed, Farnborough, Hampshire, England.

Fraser, A. M. H., Rolfe, J. M., and Smith, E. M. B. (1967). Pilot response under ground simulation conditions and in flight. AGARD Conf. Proc. CP 25, 3366, NASA, Langley Field, Virginia.

Hale, H. B., and Shannon, I. L. (1967). Validity of the human 17-hydroxicortico-steroid/creatinine ratio. *Aerospace Med.* 38, 1095–1098.

Lewis, C. E., Jones, W. L., Austin, F. H., and Roman, J. (1967). Flight research program: IX. Medical monitoring of carrier pilots in combat-II. *Aerospace Med.* 38, 581–592.

Luehrs, R. E., Austin, F. H., and Ireland, R. G. (1966). Fatigue in aircraft carrier combat operations. Panel Session on Problems in Combat Operational Aviation Medicine, Aerospace Medical Association Meeting, Las Vegas, Nevada (unpublished).

Polis, B. D., and de Cani, J. (1968). Personal communication.

Polis, B. D., Martorano, J. J., and Schwarz, H. P. (1966). Plasma phospholipid composition as a biochemical index to stress. AGARD Conf. Proc. CP 14, 2985, NASA, Langley Field, Virginia.

Polis, B. D., Polis, E., de Cani, J., Schwartz, H. P., and Dreisbach, L. (1968). "Effect of Physical and Psychic Stress on Phosphatidyl Glycerol and Related Phospholipids," NADC-MR-6805. Aerospace Med. Res. Dept., Naval Air Development Center, Johnsville, Pennsylvania.

Schreuder, O. B. (1966). Medical aspects of pilot fatigue with special reference to the commercial pilot. *Aerospace Med.* 37, 4–Section II.

Schwarz, H. P., Deisbach, L., Polis, E., Polis, B. D., and Soffer, E. (1965). Effect of whole-body X-ray irradiation on phospholipids of rat liver particulate fractions. *Arch. Biochem. Biophys.* 11, 422–430.

10// Military Psychiatry and the Viet Nam War in Perspective

Peter G. Bourne

I. Introduction

In the gradual acquisition of knowledge, significant advances have come in one of two ways: Either through the progressive accumulation of incremental fragments of knowledge the weight of information leads eventually and inevitably to a conceptual breakthrough or, due to some sudden and often chance discovery of major proportions, a field will be dramatically moved to a new and previously unexpected level of understanding. In this latter case, many years of subsequent work may then be necessary to consolidate that position and to fill out a theoretical base upon which that revelation can comfortably rest. Sudden spectacular discoveries, particularly in the areas of technology and medicine, have often been the result of chance occurrences in the environment or a response to an overwhelming need in society.

Through the course of history, one social institution that despite its negative aspects has consistently stimulated and precipitated technological, scientific, and medical advance has been warfare. Not withstanding the obvious horrors of war and the maladaptive aspects of man's unrelenting urge to visit violence and death with

increasing effectiveness upon his fellow men, much of the knowledge that has been gained through military expediency has resulted in the long run in peacetime benefits for mankind which
frequently have transcended the immediate destructive consequences of the initial discovery.

In few fields has war produced so many startling advances with
ultimate benefits for the welfare of man than in the area of medicine. Most readily apparent has been the progress in surgery, and
particularly the treatment of traumatic injuries. Not only have specific technical advances been developed from battlefield improvi-
sation, but many generations of surgeons have acquired levels of
technical proficiency through wartime service that subsequently
benefited their civilian patients. Less well appreciated but at least
as significant has been the military contribution to preventive
medicine and particularly the control of infectious diseases such
as tetanus and yellow fever. In both of these instances discoveries
prompted by the urgency of military considerations have resulted
in the saving of thousands of civilian lives which might otherwise
have been lost.

While the contribution of military medicine to the saving of civilian lives is quickly recognized, few outside the field are aware
of the debt which civilian psychiatry owes to the military. The
experiences in two world wars and in Korea altered the basic concepts that were held concerning the etiology of mental illness by
bringing to the awareness of practicing psychiatrists the immense
importance of immediate environmental stress in the development of psychological illness. This challenged in a dramatic manner the belief that mental illness grew solely out of inherent constitutional factors or experiences suffered by the individual many
years before the onset of symptoms. Based on this new understanding, highly effective treatment regimens were developed
which permitted the recovery and satisfactory return to duty of
many severely disturbed individuals whose prognosis previously
would have been considered hopeless. Awareness of the importance of environmental stress factors which many psychiatrists
gained through their military experience was carried back into
civilian life. The result was that they became cognizant of the sub-
tler manifestations of comparable stressful events in the lives of
their patients in peacetime. At the same time, there was a significant conceptual shift in their understanding of the etiology of
mental illness.

While the primary contribution of the military to civilian psychiatry has unquestionably been in the clinical sphere, resulting from the need to treat the large numbers of individuals who succumbed to the often overwhelming circumstances of combat, a secondary function has also been served. In providing a fortuitous stress laboratory, the combat situation has offered some answers to basic questions about man's reaction to extreme situations. In addition, more recently the military has also been able, by virtue of its organizational structure, to contribute to our understanding of man's behavior in various social groupings. The contribution of military psychiatrists in focusing in this area has directly influenced the development and interest in civilian social psychiatry.

II. Historical Background

Over the years, combat psychiatry has evolved from a barely recognized entity to a sophisticated science with ramifications in every area of military planning. Beginning with the Civil War, each subsequent conflict has led to a refinement of treatment techniques and has added progressively to our understanding and conceptualization of man's ability to deal with the stresses of combat. To fully appreciate what has been learned in Viet Nam and how it contributes to the overall body of knowledge as it now exists, a brief review of the evolution of combat psychiatry is perhaps warranted.

During the Civil War, William Hammond (1883), who was Surgeon General of the Union Army, described a condition which he termed "nostalgia" which afflicted the minds of soldiers, making them incapable of performing their duties although there was no evidence of physical injury. His treatment proposal contains the essential elements that we still recognize today. He wrote:

> The best means of preventing nostalgia is to provide occupation for the mind and the body . . . Soldiers placed in hospitals near their homes are always more liable to nostalgia than those who are inmates of hospitals situated in the midst of or in the vicinity of the Army to which they belong.

The Union Army reported 5213 cases of nostalgia during the first year of the Civil War — 2.34 cases per 1000 troops. The rate rose to 3.3 per 1000 in the second year of the war. In addition, 20.8 men per 1000 troops were discharged with paralysis and 6 men per 1000 were discharged for "insanity" (Hausman and Rioch, 1967).

The first time in any army that mental illness in military personnel was treated by specialists in psychiatry was in the Russo–Japanese War of 1904–1905. However the Russian psychiatric casualties were so numerous that the service was soon overwhelmed and it became necessary to turn over large numbers of patients to the Red Cross for treatment and disposition (Anderson, 1966).

It was not until World War I that the planning for psychiatric casualties became an integral part of the overall medical organization. For the first time also, systematic observations were made on the phenomenon of psychic disintegration in combat, and copious if often inaccurate speculations were generated as to the possible etiology of the condition. In a war characterized by relentless and heavy artillery bombardment of both sides, the reasonable assumption was made that a soldier's brain became chronically concussed by his constant proximity to exploding shells, with multiple petechial hemorrhages occurring in the cerebrum. For this reason the term "shell shock" was coined to describe such cases. The French, however, distinguished between "*emotionee*," the less severe cases that were felt to occur on an emotional basis, and "*commotionee*," a term generally reserved for those exhibiting psychotic symptoms and considered to have an organic etiology to their condition (Hausman and Rioch, 1967).

One of the most detailed accounts of the psychological aspects of combat in World War I was made by Lord Moran, in his book "The Anatomy of Courage" (1945). While not a psychiatrist, he was sensitive to the suffering of those in the trenches with him, and his astute sense of observation made his work a classic in the field. However, even Moran's humanitarian nature did not prevent him from occasionally lapsing into the moralistic stance characteristic of most physicians of his day towards combat psychiatric casualties. He wrote:

> There were others who were plainly worthless fellows. One without moral sense had taken a commission under the shadow of compulsion . . . Sitting there with his head in his hands at the bottom of the trench, he could do no good to the men of 1916. He showed none of the extreme signs of fear, he was just a worthless chap, without shame, the worst product of the towns.

Interestingly it is cases of this type — now more generously classified as character and behavior disorders — which make up the bulk of psychiatric casualties in Viet Nam.

Many other distinguished psychiatrists of the period including Southard, Jones, Kardiner, Ferenczi, and Freud drew upon the military experience of World War I to formulate their explanations of man's response to the stresses of combat and extrapolated from it to explain how comparable traumatic events are dealt with in a civilian setting.

By the time the United States entered the war, the psychological aspects of combat stress were better understood, and Thomas W. Salmon, assigned to direct the psychiatric program in support of the American Expeditionary Force (AEF), was able to benefit from the past experience and failures of both the French and British. The French and British had made the acknowledged mistake of evacuating their psychiatric casualties out of the combat zone. In 1917 Salmon assigned a psychiatrist to each American division with instructions to treat all but the most severe or persistent psychiatric casualties at forward medical facilities, maintaining the expectation that these men would return to combat. So effective was his approach that in the few remaining months prior to the armistice, 65% of the casualties were returned to duty after an average stay of only 7 days (Salmon, 1919).

At the start of World War II, military psychiatry in the United States was in marked disarray and poorly prepared to provide organization and staffing of a psychiatric support program for combat operations. There seemed to be little awareness of the hard lessons of the previous war, and the treatment program of proven efficacy established by Salmon was apparently forgotten. Between January 1943 and December 1945, there were 409,887 neuropsychiatric patients admitted to army hospitals overseas, and 127,660 of these patients were evacuated to the United States (Anderson, 1966). At one point early in 1943, psychiatric casualties were occurring faster than recruits were being drafted into the service (Tiffany and Allerton, 1967). The highest rate of neuropsychiatric casualties — 101 per 1000 troops per year — occurred in the First United States Army in Europe, and compared with 37 per 1000 per year in Korea and 12 per 1000 per year in Viet Nam. Much of this attrition might have been avoided had the military been better prepared, and had it not been necessary to relearn with considerable anguish the lessons of 20 years earlier.

Many distinguished psychiatrists served the military during World War II, and several utilized their talents to apply scientific research methodology to the data they obtained on psychiatric casualties (*Bulletin US Army*, 1949; Glass, 1947). Particularly, the work of Grinker and Spiegel, described in their book "Men Under Stress" (1963), represented a major advance in the systematic evaluation of man's psychological response to combat. These data assumed particular significance after the war when it became apparent that observations on the adaptation of the individual to the extreme stress of war had significant application to our understanding of civilian stress situations.

Aside from the observations made upon the individual's psychological adaptation to combat, sociologists examined the social organization in which the soldier functioned. They identified the "primary group" as the critical social unit in providing emotional support for the individual (Shils, 1950). Solidarity and intimacy with fellow soldiers on a small group level as well as an intense desire to preserve the group as a social entity was seen as characterizing the social organization in that war.

In Korea, after an initial period of hesitancy, an effective program for the treatment of neuropsychiatric casualties was established under the direction of Albert Glass (1954). Salmon's principles of proximity, immediacy, and expectancy, rediscovered in World War II, were further refined. Between 15 and 75% of those diagnosed as having "combat exhaustion" at the division level or foreward were returned to duty. Colonel Donald B. Peterson, who replaced Glass as Far East Command Consultant in October 1951, demonstrated a drop in the ratio of neurotic to psychotic evacuees from the theater between the last quarter of 1950 and the first half of 1951 of from 19.4:1 to 3.6:1. This ratio further dropped as the psychiatric services developed, to 1.5:4 in 1952 and 1:9.3 in 1953 (Peterson, 1955).

For the first time in Korea, investigators entered the war zone expressly to study the effects of combat stress on man. Under the direction of Dr. David Rioch of Walter Reed Army Institute of Research, a systematic assessment was made of the soldier's response to combat both as an individual and as a member of an organizational unit.The field study team headed by Major F. Gentry Harris concerned itself not only with men who became casualties, but also with the methods by which the overwhelming majority of soldiers coped with the stress of the environment without psychological disintegration (Harris *et al.*, 1955). Harris and his colleagues and Little (1964) found that whereas in World War II the "primary group" provided critical emotional support for the soldier, in Korea the diadic relationship of the "buddy system" performed this function.

In addition to psychological responses to stress, for the first time an attempt was made to measure the physiological correlates of psychic adaptation to combat. Hampered to some extent by logistical problems and the limited assay methods of that era, a multidisciplinary team collected blood and urine samples from men in combat to measure altered excretion of 17-ketosteroids (Elmadjian, 1955).

With the advent of the Viet Nam war, the military was well prepared to handle large numbers of psychiatric casualties with all the experience and expertise gained from three previous wars. There was every reason to believe that the number of psychiatric casualties would be high. The physically demanding conditions of jungle warfare, the ubiquitous enemy, and the absence of established battle lines, plus political controversy surrounding the war, all suggested that the stress on the individual GI would be considerable. However the effects of these factors, if any, have not been reflected in the number of psychiatric casualties.

The incidence of psychiatric problems requiring hospitalization has remained about the same as that for a comparable stateside force. Many of those seen by psychiatrists in Viet Nam have problems unrelated to the direct stresses of war, and indeed the bulk of cases come from support units rather than those actually engaged in combat. In World War II psychiatric casualties were common occurrences in fighter and bomber pilots (Hastings, Wright and Glueck, 1944), while in Viet Nam the problem has been virtually nonexistent. Six percent of all medical evacuations from Viet Nam are for psychiatric reasons as compared with 23% in World War II. Only approximately 5% of psychiatric admissions have been diagnosed as having "combat fatigue," while 40% or higher are classified as character and behavior disorders (Bourne and San, 1967).

III. Current Concepts and the Contribution of the Viet Nam War

In considering the status of combat psychiatry as a result of the experience gained in the Viet Nam war, a convenient division may be made between the advances in clinical treatment and our progress in the research sphere. While this is clearly an artificial distinction, it has considerable heuristic value in providing clearer historical continuity with the advances made in this field in previous wars. It also perhaps more clearly delineates those basic areas of knowledge which are most widely applicable to our general understanding of man's response to extreme circumstances.

A. Clinical Advances

The most important development for military psychiatry to come out of the war in Viet Nam is the relatively low incidence of psychiatric casualties and an appreciation of the factors contributing to this fortunate state. As Allerton stated in Chapter 1, the reasons are multiple, although either directly or indirectly most of the ameliorating influences can be attributed to the significant increase in psychological awareness of the military command. A new level of sophistication exists in this area among military planners which was not present even during the Korean conflict but which has made itself felt in Viet Nam (Westmoreland, 1963).

In Chapter 2, Tischler has reviewed the previously identified factors which are acknowledged as contributing to psychiatric attrition in combat. In summary, these are, first, factors related directly to combat. Those exposed to actual combat are more likely to become casualties than those who are not, and a significant relationship has been shown to exist between actual danger and the incidence of combat neurosis. Also, when the number of wounded in action was utilized as an indirect measure, psychiatric attrition was shown to correlate with the intensity of combat. Second, nonbattle factors have been demonstrated to contribute significantly to the incidence of psychiatric casualties. Isolation, boredom, inadequate diet, chronic physical discomfort, exhaustion, and physical illness have all been significantly implicated as contributing to psychiatric casualties even in relatively low hazard situations. The effects of both privation and exposure to combat increase with time.

All other factors being equal, it has been demonstrated that the incidence of psychiatric casualties varies considerably from one unit to another. This is attributable to an aggregate of forces which are collectively described as morale. While morale remains difficult to define in specific terms, it may be considered to refer to the general sense of wellbeing enjoyed by the group, and to be a reflection of confidence in their ability to successfully survive environmental stresses, faith in the quality of their leadership, and an overall sense of cooperation and cohesiveness among the members. Morale is further enhanced for the individual by factors such as the quality of his training, the reliability and vintage of his weapons, and the quality and availability of medical care should he be wounded. There is ample evidence to substantiate the belief that morale serves as an important emotional force in a unit providing group support and mutual reinforcement which reduces the vulnerability to psychological breakdown.

A third area with direct bearing on the incidence of psychiatric casualties involves the nature of the combat itself. Neuropsychiatric casualties in combat occur predominantly when the lines of battle are static and diminish sharply when the troops are on the move, even though they may be in full retreat. It is also accepted that artillery or other bombardment without any effective method of retaliation is more likely to produce psychiatric casualties than any other combat circumstance.

Command planning for the war in Viet Nam has taken into consideration many of these factors. It is fortuitous that the style of combat in this war has been characterized by brief battles and an emphasis on mobility, with only rare instances where United States troops were subjected to prolonged bombardment in fixed defensive positions. These are all circumstances which predispose to a lower incidence of psychiatric casualties. However, the command has enhanced these favorable factors by emphasizing the need for adequate training, equipment, leadership, and medical evacuation. At a very practical level, attempts have frequently been made to provide hot meals by helicopter to men in the field, and immediate withdrawal to secure areas for rest and physical recuperation for those engaged in episodes of unusually prolonged and intensive combat.

Of all the administrative decisions that have been made concerning conduct of the Viet Nam war, the one with the most far-reaching implications for combat psychiatry is the 1 year tour.* The GI in Viet Nam knows that if he can merely survive for 12 months his removal from combat is assured. There is not the sense of hopelessness that prevailed in previous conflicts where death, injury, or peace became the only possible ways in which the sol-

*Thirteen months for the Marines.

dier could find himself extricated from combat. A related factor is the rest and recuperation program which provides the soldier with 1 week of vacation during his tour in one of the surrounding countries in Southeast Asia. These policies clearly exert a profound although unmeasured effect in reducing the incidence of psychiatric casualties.

Despite careful attention to the well-identified preventive measures and their diligent implimentation as a matter of command policy, psychiatric casualties have occurred in Viet Nam in significant if not impressive or alarming numbers. This then suggests the importance of other less well-identified factors, particularly those related to the level of psychological vulnerability that the individual brings with him to the combat zone.

In Chapter 2, Tischler has pointed out that conflicting data exist as to whether preexisting psychological conditions are a contributing factor to psychiatric attrition in a combat zone. Hastings *et al.* (1944) reported that in a series of fliers who failed under minimal stress there was no evidence of predisposing neurotic illness. On the other hand, Brill and Beebe (1955) found that men with preexisting neuroses had 7–8 times the probability of developing overt symptomatology and behavioral disorders as compared with previously well-integrated individuals. In studying a series of 150 men who successfully completed their tours in the combat zone, Grinker and Spiegel (1963) found that one-half had a previous life pattern of emotional instability.

With the advent of the Viet Nam war, this question still remained unanswered. However with the careful control of the more grossly predisposing factors and the isolation of a more select and smaller group that became casualties, we are now in a position to provide a definitive answer. Tischler (Chapter 2), Strange (Chapter 4), and Wallen (Chapter 8) have all identified specific personality factors that certain individuals who became psychiatric casualties brought with them to the combat zone making them particularly vulnerable to the stresses to which they were exposed. These traits had not necessarily jeopardized the successful functioning of these individuals in civilian life, but did prevent them from utilizing the adaptive ploys in coping with the stresses of combat or merely the war environment that were employed by the majority of men. Some of these individuals did have histories of debilitating psychopathology in civilian life. Strange (Chapter 4) points out in his discussion of "pseudocombat fatigue" that many of his patients had past histories of difficulty in impulse control, social, family, and school relationships, all of which had significantly impaired their functioning. In the light of this data, the answer now seems clear that certain identifiable personality attributes do predispose individuals to greater vulnerability to psychiatric attrition in the combat zone.

During World War I, combat exhaustion was considered largely a time-determined phenomenon, and it was assumed that once a man "broke" he was lost for good from the battlefield. As a result, the belief existed among line officers that the men should be pushed hard in order to obtain a maximal performance from them before they were irretrievably lost as psychiatric casualties. We now know that combat exhaustion is not necessarily a progressive phenomenon but more a dynamic state, influenced by a variety of external and constitutional forces, and is potentially reversible at any point in its development. It was also true in previous conflicts that great attention was paid to nosology and considerable energy was expended in an attempt to classify adequately the wide variety of symptoms with which patients presented. A slowly shifting emphasis, culminating in the Viet Nam experience, has led to a conceptualization of the psychiatric casualty as an adaptive failure of a basically temporary nature rather than as a disease entity. This approach has proven particularly valuable in this war where, diagnostically, the majority of patients have fallen into the category of character and behavior disorders, while a relatively small percentage have exhibited the picture of "classical" combat fatigue which was more prevalent in earlier conflicts.

To a certain extent, the actual presenting symptoms become irrelevant as the critical issue is the fact that the man has ceased to cope with and function in the environment of the combat zone. Whether he presents with a hysterical paralysis or a self inflicted gunshot wound may be largely socially or culturally determined, as San's material in Chapter 3 would suggest.

The basic approach to treatment of psychiatric casualties in Viet Nam differs little from that of previous wars and in essence dates back to the original concepts laid down by Salmon (1919) in World War I. What distinguishes the psychiatric services in this war is that optimal care, drawing fully upon the accumulated knowledge of the past, was implemented from the start of the conflict. The success of military psychiatry in Viet Nam has served to underscore the efficacy of treatment methods which were refined in Korea but were put into practice only as that conflict was terminating.

A major improvement in the quality of psychiatric care in Viet Nam over Korea has resulted from the significant increase in psychiatric knowledge and sophistication among general medical officers that has taken place in the last 15 years. These young physicians serving as batallion surgeons, many of whom entered the military immediately following internship, are well educated and competent in treating basic psychiatric illness. In addition, there is a higher level of interest in mental illness among these men than in their predecessors during World War II and Korea. As a result they are capable of recognizing and treating minor psychological disturbances at the batallion level. This diminishes the number of individuals who become labeled as psychiatric casualties, and yet they are treated at an optimal point in the medical evacuation chain, at which they have the greatest chance of successfully returning to duty.

The advent of the phenothiazines and other tranquilizing drugs came too late in the Korean War to permit an adequate assessment of their potential in the treatment of combat casualties. At the start of the conflict in Viet Nam, there was some speculation as to how effective these drugs would prove in enabling men to return to duty, and even perform in combat when previously they would have required evacuation. While these drugs have been effectively used in Viet Nam with psychotic casualties (Strange, 1967), their impact overall has been relatively slight, and the use of drugs has had little bearing on the return to duty rate. Rest, emotional support, the opportunity to ventilate, and time to reintegrate adaptive abilities that were temporarily overwhelmed have proven infinitely more significant than any specific pharmacologic agent in enabling the basically healthy individual to return to duty. The milder tranquilizers have been used widely with outpatients in noncombat jobs, but the pattern of use is essentially the same as in a civilian context.

The Viet Nam experience has enhanced in many respects our ability to provide psychiatric service in time of war. It has been shown that we have now successfully identified most of the major correlates of psychiatric attrition in the combat zone and that we have been able to incorporate into our conduct of the war many measures based on this knowledge that have significantly reduced the psychological vulnerability of the average fighting man to combat stress. It is also now demonstrated that when attention is paid to providing the support that enhances the adaptive capacity of the soldier he is able to make a highly successful adaptation to combat at both psychological and physiological levels. It is then only under very unusual circumstances, when combat is extremely heavy or when he becomes excessively tired, that a healthy man will become a psychiatric casualty, and when he does, prompt appropriate treatment will rapidly reestablish his capacity to cope with his environment so that he can return to duty. Significant psychiatric attrition has been in Viet Nam, and presumably will be in the future, largely confined to those who bring some psychological liability with them to the combat zone. However, even with this group diligent attention to the proven preventive measures that enhance successful adaptation will minimize the incidence of psychiatric casualties. Our level of knowledge of combat psychology has now reached a point where with adequate vigilence psychiatric casualties need never again become a major cause of attrition in the United States military in a combat zone.

B. Research

Combat is a uniquely life-threatening experience. However, with the advent of space travel, undersea exploration, and the exposure of man to other extreme situations, knowledge gained about his performance in battle is having increasingly wider application. It has become of extreme importance to identify those factors which will maximize an individual's ability to tolerate high levels of stress in his environment as well as to know what physiological changes can be anticipated when he is subjected to such conditions. Casualties both physical and psychological are an accepted aspect of combat, whereas the prevention of casualties in any form is mandatory in the deliberate exposure to stress involved, for instance, in space exploration. It has, therefore, become particularly important to utilize the information which is inevitably available in combat and apply it to peaceful uses.

Combat research was largely confined during both world wars to observations made by social scientists incidentally to their assigned military occupations. In addition, a certain amount of retrospective analysis was made on the basis of available data after the hostilities were ended. In Korea, for the first time a planned attempt was made to exploit the combat situation in order to obtain specific psychological and physiological data on man's response to this life-endangering experience. This initial work had its inevitable sequel in the research that has been done in Viet Nam, although for many reasons, largely political, there has not been as concerted an emphasis on pursuing research in this war as there might have been.

Research of a psychological nature in earlier wars focused either upon the individual psychiatric casualty which has been largely covered in the previous section, or upon the socialization of the soldier with his peers and with his organization. As mentioned briefly above, social scientists studying troops in World War II identified the "primary group" as the basic and critical unit in the maintenance of morale and social support. The intimacy in small units, often squad size or smaller, was stressed where commitments were to personal relationships and the individual member counted on the group for emotional support. Allegiance to their own group as a social entity was seen as overriding, in importance, identification with the larger organization. Preservation of the group often took precedence over the individual's own sense of self-concern. In Korea, while the face-to-face contact of the "primary group" remained significant, a diadic relationship as expressed in the "buddy system" was additionally perceived as a critical source of support for the individual.

In Viet Nam, many of these social phenomena described by investigators in earlier wars appear to be of minimal significance or even absent. The question may then be raised whether this represents a true difference in social behavior or is merely a reflection of the changing conceptual framework into which social scientists are attempting to fit their observations. Moskos (1969), who to the present has made the only definitive attempt to assess social behavior and its relationship to motivation in Viet Nam, believes the former to be true. There are certain aspects of the Viet Nam conflict that are common to all wars, and also features which are quite unique.

In his studies of social behavior in Viet Nam, Moskos has shown that the rotation system with its staggered arrivals and departures has broken down the traditional solidarity of the small unit. The deemphasis of the "primary group" as a source for dependence and emotional support is further facilitated by the possibility of phone calls to the United States and the relative excellence of the mail service. The feasibility of maintaining continuity with preexisting emotional ties in the United States and the knowledge that they can be reintensified at a predictable point within the next 12 months greatly reduces the need to seek gratification from sentimental attachments to those in the immediate and temporary environment. With each soldier concerned primarily with his own personal survival until his rotation date, at which point his own involvement in the war will be over, the conflict has taken on a uniquely individualized character. The man feels no continuity with those who precede or follow him; he even feels apart from those who are with him but rotating on a different schedule. The result as Moskos found in his interviews has been that the "primary group" and the "buddy system" have become of very minor significance in this war.

The military system has informally recognized and reinforced this shift from the unit to the individual by frequently permitting "short timers"—men within a few weeks of returning to the United States—to be excused from the hazards of patrolling. In this and other ways, the system has acknowledged the new combat ethos which distinguishes Viet Nam from Korea and World War II; namely the intensely personalized struggle of each individual to survive emotionally and physically until his own day to return to the United States.

During the Korean conflict, an attempt was first made to investigate physiological changes occurring in soldiers in combat (Elmadjian, 1955). However, logistical problems and the relative lack of sophisticated methodology at that time restricted the meaningfulness of that work. Viet Nam is the first war in which a significant amount of data has been collected in this area. In Chapters 5, 6, 7, and 9 of this volume, this work has been detailed.

The presumption had long existed that the life-threatening experience of combat would represent a stress of such magnitude that profound physiological changes would occur in the individual. While the studies in Viet Nam have demonstrated that somatic changes in response to the combat environment do occur, they have not been of the magnitude or in some instances even in the direction that might have been anticipated. It would appear that accurate and objective intellectual assessment of the environment is sacrificed by the utilization of various psychological mechanisms in order that the individual can maintain his physiological functions within a certain limited range. This is perhaps less true when the stress is acute and of brief duration. However, with prolonged exposure to stressful circumstances, no matter how great the objective danger, there appears to be a strong need to maintain physiological homeostasis at the expense of psychological function.

In two separate studies presented in Chapters 5 and 9, it would seem that there is evidence to support the belief that interpersonal stress in the form of social demand or assigned role exerts a more powerful effect upon certain physiological parameters than does an objectively life threatening situation. The latter circumstance can presumably be more easily and effectively dealt with at a psychological level.

While our knowledge and understanding of the psychological aspects of combat has reached a high level of sophistication, our recognition of the corresponding physiological changes remains in its infancy. It is perhaps primarily in this area that the most significant research advances will occur in any future studies of combat stress.

IV. Conclusions

The obvious success of the psychiatric treatment and prevention program in Viet Nam has created the impression that the specialty has largely conquered the disease. To a certain extent this is true, for with adequate application of the available knowledge on combat psychiatry we now have the tools to keep casualties and particularly evacuations at a nearly negligible level. Particularly if the personality factors predisposing certain individuals to increased psychological vulnerability in a war zone could be adequately systematized to permit selection for duty on this basis, attrition could theoretically be eliminated. Unfortunately, attempts in the past by the military to predict performance on the basis of psychiatric screening have been singularly unsuccessful. This may have been because the criteria for selection were not adequately refined, or because our techniques of evaluation are not yet good enough to permit us to gather sufficient relevant information on an individual in a reasonable period of time to be practical. It does seem, however, that on the basis of the findings in Viet Nam, a certain percentage of individuals could be identified as being unusually vulnerable long before they are sent overseas.

While the incidence of psychiatric casualties in Viet Nam has remained gratifyingly low, we should not lose sight of the fact that the quality of warfare has differed significantly from previous conflicts. While we have continued to carefully refine our identification of factors contributing to psychiatric attrition in combat, we still do not know the relative weight each may wield in inducing the condition. It may well be that in a different type of war, despite every precaution, psychiatric casualties could again assume major proportions. Although this would seem improbable, it should serve as a reminder not to allow complacency to undermine our future planning.

As an extreme human circumstance, combat continues to offer an unusual and rewarding source of information concerning man's response to stress. By accentuating adaptive maneuvers to deal with ultimately life-endangering circumstances, combat can throw light on areas of human behavior that pass unnoticed in a less demanding civilian existence. The lessons of war may thus serve to provide a fuller and more enduring enjoyment of the peace.

REFERENCES

Anderson, R. S. (1966). Neuropsychiatry in World War II, Vol. I. Office of the Surgeon General, Washington, D. C.

Bourne, P. G., and San, N. D. (1967). A comparative study of neuropsychiatric casualties in the United States Army and the Army of the Republic of Viet Nam. *Military Med.* 132, 904.

Brill, N. Q., and Beebe, B. W. (1955). A Follow Up Study of War Neuroses, Veterans Administration Medical Monograph, U.S. Government Printing Office, Washington, D. C.

Bulletin US Army Medical Department. (1949). Combat Psychiatry. (Suppl.).

Elmadjian, F. (1955). *In* G. W. Wolstenholme, Ed., "Adrenocortical Function of Combat Infantry Men in Korea," *Ciba Colloquium — Endocrinology.* Vol. VIII., p. 627.

Glass, A. J. (1947). Effectiveness of forward neuropsychiatric treatment. *Bulletin US Army Medical Department* 7, 1034.

Glass, A. J. (1954). Psychiatry in the Korean campaign, parts I and II. *United States Armed Forces Med. J.* 4, pp. 1387–1401 and 1563–1583.

Grinker, R. R., and Spiegel, J. P. (1963). "Men Under Stress." McGraw-Hill, New York.

Hammond, W. A. (1883). "A Treatise on Insanity in its Medical Relations." H. K. Lewis, London.

Harris, F. G., Mayer, J., and Becker, H. A. (1955). Experiences in the study of combat in the Korean theater. I. Report on psychiatric and psychological data. Walter Reed Army Institute of Research, Washington, D. C.

Hastings, D. W., Wright, D. G., and Glueck, B. C. (1944). "Psychiatric Experience of the Eighth Air Force, First Year of Combat, (July 4, 1942–July 4, 1943)." New York, Josiah Macy Jr. Foundation.

Hausman, W., and Rioch, D. (1967). Military psychiatry. *Arch. Gen. Psychiat.* **16**, 727.

Little, R. W. (1964). Buddy relations and combat performance. *In* "The New Military" (M. Janowitz, ed.). New York, Russell Sage.

Moran, Lord C. M. (1945). "The Anatomy of Courage." London, Constable.

Moskos, C. C. (1969). "The American Enlisted Man." New York, Russell Sage. (In press.)

Peterson, D. B. (1955). The psychiatric operation Armed Forces Far East, 1950–1953. *Am. J. Psychiat.* **112**, 23.

Salmon, T. W. (1919). The war neuroses and their lesson. *N. Y. J. Med.* **109**, 993.

Shils, E. A. (1950). Primary groups in the American Army. *In* "Continuities in Social Research: Studies in the Scope and Method of the American Soldier" (P. F. Lazarfeld, ed.). Free Press, Glencoe, Illinois.

Strange, R. E., and Arthur, R. J. (1967). Hospital ship psychiatry in a war zone. *Am. J. Psychiat.* **124**, 37.

Tiffany, W. J., and Allerton, W. S. (1967). Army psychiatry in the mid-60s. *Am. J. Psychiat.* **123**, 810.

Westmoreland, W. C. (1963). Mental health — An aspect of command. *Military Med.* **128**, 209.

Subject Index